the information store

SAM S/u/i~

01 DEC 2014

23 FEB 2015

31 OCT 2017

07 JAN 2019

03 JUN 2019

26 SEP 2019

A fine will be charged for overdue items

CHALLENGING MINDS, INSPIRING SUCCESS. CITY COLLEGE NORWICH

2 0 891

Understanding Children's Social Care

Politics, Policy and Practice

Nick Frost and Nigel Parton

Los Angeles | London | New Delhi
Singapore | Washington DC

SAGE Publications Ltd
1 Oliver's Yard
55 City Road
London EC1Y 1SP

SAGE Publications Inc.
2455 Teller Road
Thousand Oaks, California 91320

SAGE Publications India Pvt Ltd
B 1/I 1 Mohan Cooperative Industrial Area
Mathura Road
New Delhi 110 044

SAGE Publications Asia-Pacific Pte Ltd
33 Pekin Street #02-01
Far East Square
Singapore 048763

Library of Congress Control Number: 2008934325

British Library Cataloguing in Publication data

A catalogue record for this book is available from the British
Library.

ISBN 978-1-4129-2349-1
ISBN 978-1-4129-2350-7 (pbk)

Typeset by Cepha Imaging Pvt Ltd
Printed in Great Britain by CPI Antony Rowe,
Chippenham, Wiltshire
Printed on paper from sustainable resources

Mixed Sources

Product group from well-managed
forests and other controlled sources
www.fsc.org Cert no. SGS-COC-2953
© 1996 Forest Stewardship Council

Contents

Acknowledgements

This book has been in the planning and the writing for over two years. Over this period we have benefited from discussions with a whole variety of colleagues, both in Leeds and Huddersfield, and also with practitioners, policy makers, managers and researchers all over the country. In particular we would like to acknowledge the contributions from the candidates who have studied for the West Yorkshire Post Qualifying Child Care Award and the MA Child Welfare and Safeguarding at the University of Huddersfield. Their experiences and insights have been invaluable. Finally, we would like to thank Sue Hanson and Pam Irwin for making sure it all came together at the end. We are, of course, completely responsible for what follows.

Introduction

The aim of this book is to describe and analyse the nature and development of children's social care. In doing this we will explicitly locate our discussion in a framework informed by both political and policy contexts and their implications for practice. While our analyses will be of a wider international interest, it is important to state at the outset that our focus is England.

In many respects, 'children's social care' is a term that is used mainly in England and to a lesser extent in other parts of the United Kingdom. It is a term very much of the twenty-first century and one closely associated with the major changes introduced in England as part of the *Every Child Matters: Change for Children* programme (Department for Education and Skills [DfES], 2004a).

At its simplest, the term is primarily referring to those services and responsibilities previously carried out by local authority social services departments and which have been taken over by the newly created departments of children's services. Whereas previously the term might have been 'child care' (Packman, 1981), or 'child welfare' (Frost and Stein, 1989), the term in official use now is 'children's social care'.

More generally, 'social care' began to be used from the late 1980s onwards as an all-embracing term for what up until that time had usually been called 'personal social services'. While the term 'social care' might include social work, it was introduced in explicit recognition that many people who worked in the services were not qualified social workers and worked in a variety of settings including residential, day-care and community settings. However, the use of the term 'social care' has been used primarily to describe the provision of services for adults who require assistance with aspects of daily living as a result of disability, illness or ageing, and the interface with health care is seen as being of particular importance. So that when Dame Denise Platt produced her report on the status of social care (Platt, 2007) and defined it as:

> the group of services that provide personal care and support to people in a social situation – such as family; the community; a communal setting; to help them achieve independence and to promote their positive contribution as citizens (Platt, 2007: 4)

it was very much services for adults she had in mind. As we will demonstrate, the remit of children's social care is almost exclusively with 'children in need', as defined by the 1989 Children Act, including those in need of protection, those who are looked after and disabled children with complex needs. It provides a range of targeted and specialist services for the most vulnerable children in society, and in many respects this very particular focus has been reinforced by developments in policy and practice in recent years.

A report by the *Children's Workforce Development Council* (CWDC, 2008) on the state of the children's social care workforce provides a good basis for understanding some of the key components of children's social care. It estimated that in 2006, the local authority social care workforce working specifically with children totalled around 55,000 headcount and 46,700 full-time equivalent (FTE), of which around 67 per cent were employed in fieldwork, 12 per cent in day care, and 21 per cent in residential care/special needs establishments. Total FTE employment in local authorities grew by 15 per cent between 1997 and 2006, mainly due to a 58 per cent rise in 'area' employment, whilst day care and residential care fell by 29 per cent and 19 per cent respectively. In addition 5,500 FTE agency staff were engaged, equating to around 13 per cent of the total local authority children's social care workforce.

Sixty-eight per cent of the workforce were full-time, 80 per cent were female, 11 per cent of minority ethnic origin, and around 70 per cent aged between 25 and 49 years, with a slowly ageing profile.

In addition, there were over 5,000 education welfare officers employed by local authorities and around 2,950 staff working in children's social care elsewhere in the statutory sector, including 1,850 workers in the Children and Family Court Advisory and Support Service (CAFCASS) and 1,050 lead inspectors at OFSTED (for the whole of social care).

The CWDC report estimated there were 25,340 staff working in private and voluntary children's residential homes. In addition, 7,180 staff worked in fostering and adoption agencies and there were 37,000 foster families in 2006.

In total, it was therefore estimated that there were 168,340 working in the children's social care sector, broken down as follows:

Table 0.1 The children's social care workforce

Sector	Headcount
Local authority	60,085
Other statutory sector	2,955
Voluntary sector	32,300
Private sector	36,000
Other (foster care)	37,000
Total	168,340

Source: CWDC, 2008.
[Crown Copyright, reprinted with permission. License # C02W000670.]

The children's social care sector can thus be seen to be growing and changing in important ways.

The book is structured into three parts. In Part I we locate children's social care in its historical and political contexts. In Chapter 1 we look in particular at the changes and developments up until New Labour came to power in 1997. Chapter 2 analyses in some detail the New Labour approach to children and families and to social policy and welfare more generally. We then, in Chapter 3, set out the thinking behind and key elements of the *Every Child Matters: Change for Children* programme.

Part II provides a more detailed analysis of a series of key areas of children's social care. We look at: safeguarding, child protection and children in need; youth offending; looked-after children and care leavers; disabled children with complex needs; unaccompanied asylum-seeking children; and Sure Start and Children's Centres.

Part III provides something of an overview of the current state of children's social care in England. Chapter 10 identifies a number of key tensions and challenges which can be seen to characterize the area, while the final chapter looks at the possible future for children's social care in an increasingly integrated professional and service world.

Part I

From Children's Departments to Departments of Children's Services

1

Local Authority Children's Services in the Post-war Period

The purpose of this introductory chapter is to outline the changing role and nature of what is now called children's social care in the post-war period. While it might appear that the current changes, which have seen the establishment of departments of children's services, give the impression that we may be witnessing a 'return to the future', nothing could be further from the truth. Rather than simply be concerned with children who are in the care of the local authority, as was originally the case with children's departments, the new arrangements aim to prevent poor outcomes for *all* children and young people and to ensure they fulfil their potential. *Every Child Matters: Change for Children*

> sets out the national framework for local change programmes to build services around the needs of children and young people so that we maximise opportunity and minimise risk. The services that reach every child and young person have a crucial role to play in shifting the focus from dealing with the consequences of difficulties in children's lives to preventing things from going wrong in the first place. The transformation that we need can only be delivered through local leaders working together in strong partnership with local communities on a programme of change. (DfES, 2004b: 2)

The vision is of integrated services meeting the needs of all children and being available as soon as problems and/or extra needs are identified. It aims to transform the way universal, selective and targeted services work together and it is the 'well-being' of all children which is the focus. However, this has not always been the case. In this chapter we outline how the focus and responsibilities of local authority children's services developed in the post-war period prior to the election of New Labour in 1997.

The Children Act 1948 and Post-war Changes

The blueprint for the Children Act 1948 was provided by the report of the Curtis Committee, which was established at the end of the Second World War. In particular it attempted to provide a simplified and unified administrative framework at both central and local government levels for all children who, for whatever reason, were deprived of a 'normal' home life. The focus was very specific – those who were living in care, often in large institutions, and where the dominating philosophy continued to be the Poor Law. While the children came into care via a number of routes and for different reasons, the largest group was those in the care of local authority public assistance committees as 'poor persons in need of relief', and were either orphans or had been deserted by their parents, or had mentally or physically ill parents who were unable or unwilling to care for them. The total number of children and young people in care at the time was 124,900 (Curtis Report, 1946: 8).

The main purposes of the Children Act 1948 were: the establishment of local authority children's departments which would take over responsibilities from other local departments for children in care, while, at central government level, the Home Office would take overall national responsibility; a new emphasis on boarding out (fostering) in preference to residential homes; the restoration of children in care to their natural parents whenever possible; and a greater emphasis on adoption.

Beyond this, however, the new departments tried to lay to rest the Poor Law and embodied the revolutionary principle that they should seek the *best* development of the children they were responsible for. Under Section 15 of the Poor Law Act 1930 it was the duty of the local authority to: 'set to work and put out as apprentices all children whose parents are not, in the opinion of the council, able to keep and maintain their children'. Until 1948 the influence of the 1601 and 1834 Poor Law Acts was explicit and there was no reference to any duties to educate, compensate or care for the children involved. However, the responsibilities in Section 12 of the Children Act 1948 were much more generous and stated that:

(1) Where a child is in the care of the local authority, it shall be the duty of that authority to exercise their powers with respect to him so as to further his best interests and to afford him opportunity for the proper development of his character and abilities.

(2) In providing for a child in care, a local authority shall make such use of facilities and services available for children in the care of their own parents, as appears to the local authority reasonable in his care.

As Jean Packman (1981) has argued, children in care were in future to be treated as individuals and not as an undifferentiated category of youngsters, and should have access to the same range of facilities as other children. The new departments were to be staffed by a new kind of personnel who were professionally trained in the psycho-social sciences and who had a thorough understanding of human relationships and the importance of the family and parental attachments, particularly in relation to mothers, for a child's development.

However, while the changes were significant, the focus of children's departments was circumscribed and specific to children in care. The new service played a residual and particular role in the overall context of welfare services.

The post-war welfare state was based on a particular model of the economy and the family. Not only did it assume full male employment, it also assumed a traditional role for the patriarchal nuclear family (Pascall, 1986; Williams, 1989). The idea of the 'family wage' was central, linking the labour market to the distribution of social roles and dependency by age and gender within the family. Within the family, women were to trade housework, childbirth, child rearing and physical and emotional caring in return for economic support from a male 'breadwinner' (Finch and Groves, 1983). It was assumed that most 'welfare work' was carried out within the family, either by using the family wage to buy goods and services or by women caring for children. The provision of state welfare was intended to support, not replace, this arrangement. Such an approach was key to the work of the newly established children's departments which were explicitly designed to provide a residual service for children deprived of a 'normal family life'.

Clearly, however, the work and rationale of the departments would be subject to a whole series of tensions and difficulties if any of the underlying assumptions were to be seriously questioned or if there were to be significant changes in the key institutions that provided the key pillars for its work – particularly the labour market, the patriarchal nuclear family or the other universal state welfare services – health, education, and social security. Beyond this, further stresses and challenges would be created if the political consensus which underpinned the post-war welfare changes was itself to be put under strain. These were to become important issues from the mid-1980s onwards; however, between 1948 and the early 1970s, the focus and rationale of the work was to broaden and develop in significant ways.

The Establishment of 'the Family Service'

During the 1950s children's departments were increasingly finding their role far too narrow and restrictive and they began to expand their operations and reframe their responses (Packman, 1981; 1993). Increasingly it was felt that waiting until children came into care was doing too little too late. There was a need to intervene with families earlier in their own homes and thereby prevent children coming into care. Such thinking was given a major boost when influential members of the Fabian Society, prominent academics and senior civil servants, made explicit the links between child neglect, deprivation and delinquency such that providing help to families earlier would not only help prevent admissions into care but would also prevent future delinquency. The statutory power to provide services to families in the community in order to prevent children being received into care was provided in Section 1 of the Children and Young Persons Act 1963. It provided the legislative backing for what a number of children's departments were already doing in practice.

Moves to expand the remit and rationale of the work developed further in the 1960s. There was an increasing conviction that better services could be provided by means of reorganizing all local authority children's and welfare services and bringing them together in an enlarged *family service*. This led to the establishment of local authority social services departments in 1971 following the Seebohm Report of 1968 and the Local Authority Social Services Act of 1970 (Hall, 1976; Clarke, 1980; Cooper, 1983). The new department would be generic in nature with a focus upon the family and the community, and the new profession of social work would lie at its core. While the emphasis on genericism reflected a number of issues and was interpreted in a variety of ways, crucially it was premised on the view that the work drew on certain common values, knowledge and skills and was embodied most clearly in the role of the professional social worker. There were key similarities in, for example, assessment, support and counselling tasks regardless of whether the client was a child, an adult or an older person.

The role of the new social services departments was not just to provide a range of services and professional help but to coordinate aspects of other state services, such as health, education, housing and social security, and thereby make them more responsive to need, particularly with regard to the functioning of a small number of families who were seen as causing a disproportionate number of problems and were often referred to as 'problem families' (Philp and Timms, 1962). Social service departments, while clearly residual and small scale compared to the other state welfare services, were established as the 'fifth social service' (Townsend, 1970). They would provide the personalized, humanistic dimension of the welfare state, the primary tool being the professional worker's personality and understanding of human relationships. The early 1970s marked the high point of optimism and confidence in social work, which had been fostered by the approaches developed in the children's departments and its key political and academic advocates. However, during the 1970s not only were the assumptions on which it operated found wanting, but the social, political and economic contexts began to change significantly.

The Growing Crisis in Child Protection

The consensus that had been established in the post-war period, based on the family as the primary mechanism for ensuring the welfare of children, with social workers entrusted with the key responsibility for state child welfare, began to collapse during the 1970s. What became evident from the mid-1980s onwards was that the problems had become considerably more complex and high profile and were not amenable to easy resolution. Up until this point social work was seen as having the key role to play in mediating and resolving the difficult and sometimes ambiguous relationship between the *privacy* of the family and the *public* responsibilities of the state, so that children could be protected and the privacy of the family was not undermined. However, the tragic death of Maria Colwell and the subsequent public inquiry (Secretary of State for Social Services, 1974) were to change all that (Parton, 1985; Butler and Drakeford, 2005, Chapter 5).

Maria had been in the care of the local authority in Brighton, East Sussex, and at the time of her death at the hands of her stepfather was subject to a supervision order. Although the authorities received numerous calls expressing concerns about her treatment and the home was visited by a number of professionals, she died a tragic and brutal death. The case received considerable media, political and public attention.

> The Public Inquiry into the death of Maria Colwell can be seen as a watershed in the contemporary history of social work, particularly in social service departments. Prior to this, social work practice was seen primarily as a private activity carried out between clients and professionals, the latter optimistically feeling their skills and techniques could tackle, even solve, many social problems. The case of Maria Colwell and the numerous subsequent inquiries into cases of child abuse have quite changed all that. (Parton and Thomas, 1983: 56–7).

Between the publication of the Colwell Inquiry report in 1974 and 1985 there were 29 further inquiries into the deaths of children as a result of abuse (Corby et al., 1998). There was considerable similarity between the findings (DHSS, 1982). Most identified: a lack of interdisciplinary communication; a lack of properly trained and experienced front-line workers; inadequate supervision; and too little focus on the needs of the child as distinct from those of the parents. The overriding concern was the lack of coordination between the different agencies. The intensity of political and media concern increased further in the mid-1980s with the public inquiries into three other child deaths in different London boroughs – Jasmine Beckford (London Borough of Brent, 1985), Tyra Henry (London Borough of Lambeth, 1987) and Kimberley Carlile (London Borough of Greenwich, 1987). Until this point, all the public inquiries had been concerned with the deaths of children at the hands of their parents or carers. The child welfare professionals were seen as having failed to protect the children and did too little, too late.

However, the Cleveland 'affair' which broke in the summer of 1987 was very different. This time over 100 children were kept in hospital against the wishes of their parents, on 'place of safety orders', on suspicions of sexual abuse (Secretary of State for Social Services, 1988; Parton, 1991). Not only was it the first scandal and public inquiry into possible over-reaction by professionals, it was also the first when the actions of paediatricians and other doctors, as well as social workers, were put under the microscope and subjected to criticism.

The issues that were articulated through the inquiries into child deaths and the Cleveland 'affair' resonated with a number of developments in the wider political environment, and contributed to the increasing questioning of the welfare consensus around the family. From the 1960s onwards, with the growth of the women's movement and the increasing recognition of violence in the family, it was argued that the family may not be the 'haven in a heartless world' (Lasch, 1977) it had previously been assumed to be. While campaigning was initially concerned with improving the position of women, from the mid-1970s, particularly with the growing attention to sexual abuse, energy was also directed at the position of children (Rush, 1980; Nelson, 1987). Such critiques helped disaggregate the interests of individual family members and supported the sometimes contradictory development during the period of the emerging children's rights movement (Freeman, 1983; Franklin, 1986, 1995).

The period also witnessed the emergence of a more obviously civil liberties critique which concentrated on the apparent growth of intervention into people's lives in the name of welfare (Morris et al., 1980; Taylor et al., 1980; Geach and Szwed, 1983). Increasingly, lawyers drew attention to the way the administration of justice was unjustly applied to various areas of child welfare and the need for a greater emphasis on individual rights. During the mid-1980s, the parents' lobby gained its most coherent voice with the establishment of Parents Against INjustice (PAIN). Thus, while quite different in their social location and focus of concern, there was a growing range of constituencies that were critical of the post-war consensus in child welfare. These were most forcefully articulated in and through the various child abuse inquiries.

These developments need to be located in the context of the more wide-ranging changes that had been taking place in the political environment. From the mid-1970s there was an increasing disillusionment about the ability of the post-war welfare state to both manage the economy effectively in the context of rising unemployment and inflation, and overcome a range of social problems, such as the growth in violence and crime more generally, via the use of wide-ranging welfare programmes. The growth of the New Right (Levitas, 1986) and the election of the Conservative government under Margaret Thatcher in 1979 proved particularly significant in shifting the political discourse in the 1980s. For the New Right, the problems in the economic and social spheres were closely interrelated and the approach stressed the importance of individual responsibility, choice and freedom and supported the disciplines of the market against the interference of the state. It had its roots in an individualized concept of social relations whereby the market was seen as the key institution for the economic sphere, while the family was the key institution for the social sphere.

The family was seen as essentially a private domain from which the state should be excluded but which should be encouraged to take on its 'natural' caring responsibilities, particularly for children. The role of the state should be confined to ensuring that the family fulfilled these responsibilities, while making sure that no one suffered at the hands of the violent and abusive. Clearly, however, a fine balance had to be struck between protecting the innocent and weak and protection from state interference. By 1987/8 it seemed that the state was falling down on both counts. For while the state, in the guise of local authority social workers, was failing to protect children in the family (as in the Beckford, Henry and Carlile inquiries), it was, at the same time, invading the privacy of the family, as exemplified by events in Cleveland.

The Children Act 1989

It is in this context that we need to understand the significance of the Children Act 1989. As David Mellor, the Minister of State at the Department of Health, said when introducing the Bill for its second reading into the House of Commons:

> We hope and believe that it will bring order, integration, relevance and a better balance to the law – a better balance not just between the rights and responsibilities of individuals and agencies, but most vitally, between the need to protect children and the need to enable parents to challenge intervention in the upbringing of their children. (Hansard, vol. 151, no. 94, col. 1107)

While the legislation was an explicit attempt to address the wide-ranging disquiet about the practices of health and welfare professionals in the area of child protection, it was not simply responding to the recommendations of child abuse inquiries. It was also informed by research and a series of respected official reports during the 1980s which aimed to update and rationalize child care legislation, particularly the Short Report (Social Services Committee, 1984) and the *Review of Child Care Law* (DHSS, 1985).

The central principles of the Act encouraged an approach to child welfare based on *negotiation* with families and involving parents and children in agreed plans. The accompanying guidance and regulations encouraged professionals to work *in partnership* with parents and young people. In an attempt to keep the use of care proceedings and emergency interventions to a minimum, the legislation strongly encouraged an approach which emphasized *support* for families with 'children in need'. In the process the concept of prevention was elevated and broadened from simply the duty to prevent children coming into care to a much broader power to provide services to *promote* the care and upbringing of children within their families. The aim was to establish a new balance in policy and practice between 'family support' and 'child protection', with a much greater emphasis on the former.

Section 17 of the Act was key to bringing this change about.

Under s17(1) of the Children Act 1989:

> It shall be the general duty of every local authority (in addition to the other duties imposed on them by this Part) –
> (a) to safeguard and promote the welfare of children within their area who are in need; and
> (b) so far as is consistent with that duty, to promote the upbringing of such children by their families,
> by providing a range and level of services appropriate to those children's needs.

while in s17(10) a child is deemed to be 'in need' if:

> (a) he is unlikely to achieve or maintain, or to have the opportunity of achieving or maintaining, a reasonable standard of health or development without the provision for him of services by a local authority under this Part;
> (b) his health or development is likely to be significantly impaired, or further impaired, without the provision for him of such services; or
> (c) he is disabled.

The definition of a 'child in need' was further expanded by reference to the concepts of health, development and disability in s17(11). Thus, 'development' meant physical, intellectual, emotional, social or behavioural development; 'health' meant physical or mental health; and a child was described as 'disabled' where she/he was blind, deaf or dumb or suffered from a mental disorder of any kind or was substantially and permanently handicapped by illness, injury or congenital deformity or such other disability as may be described.

The Act also introduced a new threshold criterion which had to be satisfied before compulsory state intervention into the family, via court proceedings, could be warranted. The criterion was: 'that the child concerned is suffering or is likely to suffer significant harm' (s31(2)(a)) where harm was defined in s31(9) as 'ill-treatment or the impairment of health or development'. For the first time the criterion for state intervention included a prediction of what 'is likely' to occur *in the future*. The harm should be *significant* and, where this was concerned with issues of health and development, these should be compared with that 'which could be reasonably expected of a similar child' (s31(10)).

Thus, while it was not intended that minor shortcomings in health or development should give rise to compulsory intervention (unless they were likely to have serious and lasting effects on the child), it was clear that, in theory, the role of local authorities was broadened, not only because of the much wider notion of prevention but also because of the need to try and anticipate what might happen to a child in the future. The overall duty for local authorities was to *safeguard and promote the welfare of the children* who were 'in need'.

Section 47(1) laid a specific duty upon local authorities, that where they:

> have reasonable cause to suspect that a child who lives, or is found, in their area is suffering or is likely to suffer, significant harm, the authority should make, or cause to be made such enquiries as they consider necessary to enable them to decide whether they should take any action to *safeguard or promote the child's welfare* (emphasis added).

Section 47(3) continued:

> the enquiries shall, in particular, be directed towards establishing:
> (a) whether the authority should make any application to the court or exercise any of their other powers under this Act, with respect to the child.

The balance that local authorities struck between its new 'preventive' duties under Section 17 and its responsibilities in terms of a narrower focus on investigating cases of child abuse, under Section 47, was to prove an important issue.

Overall, the Children Act 1989 was welcomed on all sides as a progressive piece of legislation, although it was recognized that it was being introduced in a 'hostile climate', out of step with the philosophy and aims of most of the other social and economic policies of the Conservative government at the time, and that its success would be dependent on whether resources were going to be made available for the more extended family support provisions (Frost, 1992).

Developments in the 1990s

By the mid-1990s it was becoming increasingly evident that the approach envisaged by the Children Act 1989 was being only partially implemented. A number of developments and debates took place which not only illustrated the nature of the difficulties but also suggested how things might change in the future. In the process they provided key foundations for the way the New Labour government might take policy and practice forward following its election in May 1997. We will focus on three areas in particular:

- the 'refocusing' of the children's services debate;
- the development of the 'Looking After Children' (LAC) project; and
- the growing emphasis on the importance of early childhood prevention.

The 'refocusing' of the children's services debate

A number of reports demonstrated that local authorities were struggling to implement the key principles and aims of the Children Act 1989. The *Children Act Report 1993* argued that:

> A broadly consistent and somewhat worrying picture is emerging. In general, progress towards full implementation of Section 17 of the Children Act has been slow. Further work is still needed to provide across the country a range of family services aimed at preventing families reaching the point of breakdown. Some authorities are still finding it difficult to move from a reactive social policy role to a more proactive partnership role with families (Department of Health, 1994, para. 239).

At the same time, the Audit Commission (1994) argued that the aspirations of the Children Act were not being achieved because local authority and community health services were poorly planned and coordinated, resulting in a large part of the £2 billion expenditure being wasted on families who did not need support. The focus should be on assessing need, with a much greater emphasis being placed on prevention and less on reactive interventions.

However, it was the publication of *Child Protection: Messages from Research* (Department of Health, 1995a), which summarized the key findings from a major government research programme on child protection practices, which was to prove crucial in opening up a major debate about the future shape of child protection policy and practice and children's services more generally (Parton, 1997). It demonstrated that only around one in seven of those referred to as children at risk of abuse were ever placed on a child protection register and less than one in 25 was ever removed from home as a result. Thresholds for registration on the child protection register varied between authorities, but in all there was a tendency to concentrate on investigating whether there was any risk of abuse rather than to assess whether the child was 'in need'. Even those children who were registered were provided with little treatment, and many children who were not registered still often had considerable difficulties but received little help.

The report argued that any '*incident* [of abuse] had to be seen in *context* before the extent of its harm can be assessed and appropriate intervention can be agreed' (DH, 1995a: 53, original emphasis). The research demonstrated that 'with the exception of a few severe assaults and some sexual maltreatment' (p. 53) long-term difficulties for children seldom followed from a single abusive incident – rather, they were more likely to be a consequence of living in an unfavourable environment, particularly one which was *low in warmth and high in criticism*. Only in a small proportion of cases in the research was abuse seen as extreme and warranting immediate child protection interventions.

The report argued that 'if we put to one side the severe cases' (p. 19), the most deleterious situations in terms of longer-term outcomes for children were those of *emotional neglect* and a prime concern should be the *parenting style* that failed to compensate for the inevitable deficiencies that become manifest in the course of the 20 years or so that it takes to bring up a child. Unfortunately, the research suggested that these were just the situations where the child protection system was least successful. Many children and parents felt alienated and angry and there was an overemphasis on forensic concerns, with far too much time and resources being spent on child protection investigations with a failure to develop longer-term coordinated preventive strategies. The significance of the 'refocusing' debate was that it had the effect of relocating concerns about child protection in a much wider context of providing services to children 'in need', particularly where there were concerns about emotional neglect and parenting style, and thereby arguing for the greater integration of children's services more generally.

Subsequent government research, carried out in the mid-1990s, which reviewed the progress in implementing the Children Act, painted a similar picture. While the overview on the 'messages from research' was not available until 2001 (Department of Health, 2001), most of the projects had been completed and submitted to government some years earlier. Crucially, the research reinforced the message that while there was some progress, local authority social service departments had found it very difficult to 'refocus' their services in the way suggested. Recommendations from the overview called for: improvements in inter-agency work, particularly between social services, health and education; the development of a wide range of accessible and appropriate services; and an improvement in the ability of social workers to work with families to use these resources appropriately. The difficulty of different agencies working together was not helped by the lack of a common language for describing 'need', together with a tendency for agencies to defend themselves against demand and 'pass the buck'. Particular problems were identified with the assessment of children and their families for the purposes of identifying 'need' and thereby allocating appropriate resources.

The essential message was to emphasize the importance of working with families in a way that would keep children in their families and improve their outcomes. These outcomes were conceived widely and included the child's education, emotional and physical well-being, their ties with their family, together with their sense of identity and preparation for the future.

The 'Looking After Children' (LAC) Project

These were all themes that were reflected in the 'Looking After Children' (LAC) project. For running alongside the 'refocusing' debate was the development of the LAC project which aimed to improve the life changes and outcomes for children who were 'looked after' by the local authority, the first stage of which was the publication of the report by the original working party (Parker et al., 1991). The project was prompted by growing political and professional concerns about the poor outcomes achieved by 'looked after' children according to a wide range of criteria and the scandals concerning the treatment and abuse of children in children's homes, which received wide media coverage from the late 1980s onwards (Corby et al., 2001). It was seen as vital that local authorities fulfilled their responsibilities as 'corporate parents' to the children and young people they 'looked after' (Jackson and Kilroe, 1996). Much of the evidence suggested that not only did 'looked after' children not succeed educationally but that their health, mental health, general well-being and integration into mainstream society was poor. Those who had been 'looked after' appeared to make up a disproportionate number of the unemployed, criminals and a variety of other problematic groups later in life. At the heart of the LAC project was an attempt to make explicit what 'good parenting means in practice' (DH, 1995b: 22) so that local authorities could fulfil their corporate parenting responsibilities.

Seven 'developmental dimensions' were identified as being key to achieving long-term well-being in adulthood:

- health
- education
- identity
- family and peer relationships
- emotional and behavioural development
- self-care and competence
- social presentation

The key components of the LAC system were a series of six age-related *Assessment and Action Records* (AARs) and within the seven developmental dimensions the AARs set specific age-related objectives for children's progress. They then posed two types of question: first, how far were children progressing towards recognized developmental objectives; and second, whether they were being given the experiences or services that were necessary for their attainment. The AARs were set within a system for gathering information and reviewing children's cases that would provide baseline information about the specific needs of individual children, the situation of their families and the purpose of providing the service. While the AARs were implemented initially as a practice tool, this was secondary to their original purpose which was to provide local authorities with a systematic means of gathering information that would enable them to assess the outcomes of 'looked after' children away from home. Information on individual children could be aggregated to assess the effectiveness of the service as a whole.

While originally introduced specifically for use with children being 'looked after', increasingly local authorities and researchers began to examine how far the LAC system could be adapted and developed for assessing outcomes in relation to a much wider population of children who came into contact with social service departments and other health and welfare agencies (Ward, 1998). The system was to provide a crucial foundation for the development of the *Framework for the Assessment of Children in Need and their Families* (Department of Health et al., 2000b), the *Integrated Children's System* (ICS) (Department of Health, 2003; Walker and Scott, 2004), and the *Common Assessment Framework* (CAF) (Department for Education and Skills, 2006e,f), all of which we will discuss in subsequent chapters.

'Early Childhood Prevention'

The third development during this period was located on the margins of debates in mainstream child welfare and protection and was much more associated with growing concerns about youth crime. Increasingly, a powerful case was made in the 1990s from a diverse set of constituencies, which included the Family Policy Studies Centre (Utting et al., 1993), the Joseph Rowntree Foundation (Utting, 1995) and the National Children's Bureau (Sinclair et al., 1997; Utting, 1998), that 'early childhood prevention' strategies should be placed at the centre of policies for children and families, and that the current approaches were unnecessarily restrictive. The case for prevention was pragmatic and rooted in the changing nature of family life but argued for a higher profile for the state:

> While believing the relationships and choice of lifestyle within families should normally be a private matter, it accepts that this cannot always be the case. The welfare and safety of children, in particular, are viewed as a collective responsibility which can be met through the public provision of preventive services and intervention where necessary. ... Indeed, the financial and social costs which fall to the community as a result of family malfunction and breakdown are reason in themselves to justify the essential contribution of public policy involvement (Utting, 1995, p. 8).

The way children grow up was seen as key to their future attitudes, behaviour and achievements and this was seen as being crucially 'conditioned by their relationships with parents and other members of their families' (Utting, 1995: 32). In a rapidly changing world, the role of parents was seen as providing the key mediator between the challenges of adult life and the way children develop. The attitudes and behaviour of parents were key to the way children develop from the moment of their conception.

The importance of prevention for pre-empting future crime was underlined. Criminological studies over many years had consistently identified a range of family-based factors linked to an increased risk of offending. David Farrington, perhaps the leading proponent of the theory and practice of youth criminality prevention, identified a number of key 'risk factors' including: poor child rearing; hyperactivity; low intelligence; harsh or erratic parental discipline; divorce; low income and poor housing, which significantly contributed to future criminality

(Farrington, 2000). Overlapping personal and environmental risk factors were identified not only in relation to drug abuse, criminal behaviour and violence but also for educational failure, unsafe sexual behaviour and poor mental health (Dryfoos, 1990; Mrazek and Haggerty, 1994; Goldblatt and Lewis, 1998).

However, the role of prevention was not only to combat the negatives or risks involved but to enhance the positives and opportunities for child development by maximizing protective factors and processes. Rutter (1990) conceived of risk and protection as processes rather than fixed states and saw protectors as the basis for opening up opportunities. The timing of interventions was crucial for, if they were to have the most impact, the 'early years' were key and success depended on recruiting parents – usually mothers – into the role of educators. The notion of protection was thus wider than simply protection from harm or abuse. Trying to maximize childhood 'strengths' and 'resilience' was thereby emphasized. Crucially, such an approach was seen as providing a major contribution to policies which aimed to tackle the causes of crime and anti-social behaviour.

Importantly, these developments were taking place shortly after the abduction and murder in February 1993 of two-year old James Bulger by two eight-year old boys, Jon Venables and Robert Thompson. Media and political responses suggested that childhood was in 'crisis' (Scruton, 1997) and was in need of serious attention, and where the relationship between the state, the child and the family was in need of realignment. It coincided with Tony Blair becoming shadow Home Secretary when he coined the phrase 'tough on crime, tough on the causes of crime' (Blair, 1993) which was to lie at the core of the emergence of New Labour in the mid-1990s. No longer could policy be based on the premise of trying to ensure the privacy of a traditional nuclear family, which had been a central assumption of the Conservative government. If crime was to be taken seriously and social disadvantage overcome, the state would have to take a much more active and interventional role in relation to children and their development.

Conclusions

Taken together, the 'refocusing' debate, the development of the LAC project and the growing arguments for the need to emphasize 'early childhood prevention' in order to tackle a number of social problems, particularly in relation to crime and anti-social behaviour, were to provide important foundations for the key developments that were to take place following the election of the New Labour government in May 1997. What is also apparent is that the nature, focus and aspirations of social work in social services departments had changed considerably from the early 1970s. The various research projects carried out in relation to child protection and child welfare more generally clearly demonstrated that social service departments defined their role narrowly and that social workers were having to set strict priorities as to what they did and were engaged in various forms of rationing of both their time and, more generally, the allocation of services. They had moved away from the much more generic, community-based vision of social work outlined in the Seebohm Report (1968) and the Barclay Report (1982). This process had been reinforced by organizational changes following the Children Act 1989 and the NHS and Community Care Act 1990, whereby all departments became much more specialist. Not only did departments separate their functions in terms of adults and children, but within each there was much greater specialization. Rather than be organized in terms of localities, teams covered much larger – often authority wide – populations and concentrated on certain specialist tasks, including: intake; long term; looked-after children; fostering; adoption; leaving care; family support; out-of-hours emergencies, etc. In addition, local authority social services had become particularly tarnished by the high profile child abuse inquiries and, as Jordan with Jordan (2000) have argued, were seen as very much associated with the 'Old Labour' approach to welfare – something which New Labour was determined to move beyond. It is the New Labour approach to social policy and welfare we turn to in the next chapter.

2

New Labour, Social Exclusion and Children

When New Labour came to power in May 1997 it presented itself as wanting to introduce a new political philosophy and strategy based on the ideas of the 'Third Way' (Blair, 1998; Giddens, 1998). The approach claimed to transcend the Thatcherite free-market model of the neoliberal state and the old-style social-ism of both the Soviet command economy and the 'Old Labour' variety of the post-war period, with its emphasis on a universal, collectivist welfare state. The globalized nature of the market economy was accepted as a given, together with the assumption that the nation state could do very little to influence it. Rather than intervene in the economy on the demand side, as with the 'Old Labour' Keynesian approach, the emphasis was to be on improving the supply side. In the context of increased economic globalization, the 'Third Way' argued that national competitiveness and prosperity were crucially dependent on the skills and knowledge of the workforce, which needed to be flexible, adaptable and educated. Instead of job security, the new aim was 'employability', which would aid both economic performance and social cohesion.

At the centre of the New Labour project was an emphasis on the need to estab-lish a new set of values. 'The Third Way is a serious reappraisal of social democ-racy, reaching deep into the values of the Left to develop radically new approaches' (Blair, 1998: 3). Along with the mantra of 'tough on crime, tough on the causes of crime', there was a commitment to the notion of 'no rights with-out responsibilities'. There was an insistence that rights implied responsibilities, and that benefits entailed contributions, for it was asserted that the social citizen-ship created by the post-war welfare state had a one-sided emphasis on rights. Collective protection in the context of 'social' security was to be replaced by a greater emphasis on individualized compulsion, training and support. Thus, while people had a right to security, job opportunities and a stable community, they also had a responsibility to act honestly, not violate the rights of other citizens and actively participate in the work-force.

In addition, the role of the state should shift its focus from *compensating* people for the 'diswelfares' they might have experienced as a consequence of the market to investing much more directly and strategically in human capital, so that individuals could compete in the market. Such a social investment perspective frames social policy expenditures as investments rather than expenditures, with the aim of increasing future dividends and improving the economic value and competitiveness of the population by, in particular, improving systems of education and providing income supplements to 'make work pay' and thereby reduce dependency (Dobrowolsky and Jenson, 2005). Social spending in the past is characterized as too passive, too present-oriented and insufficiently *focused on anticipated returns on investment.* The term 'social investment state' was coined by Anthony Giddens when he argued that:

> The guideline is investment in *human capital* wherever possible, rather than the direct provision of economic maintenance. In place of the welfare state we should put the *social investment state,* operating in the context of a positive welfare society (Giddens, 1998: 117, original emphasis).

While calling for a new partnership between families, markets and states, Giddens also challenged the state to develop an entrepreneurial approach which would encourage positive risk taking. Thus security would come from the capacity of the individual to change, which required investing in human capital and lifelong learning. The role of social investment was to encourage a level of skill and flexibility suited to the labour markets of global capitalism and an ability to withstand and positively negotiate the increasing stresses and complexities of daily life. For social spending to be effective, therefore, it should not be consumed by current needs but should focus on future benefits. The balance of welfare spending should therefore shift from social security to services that are explicitly preventive, promotional, positive and future oriented – particularly health and education.

In this context, the section of the population that would most benefit from investment for the future is children, particularly very young children. As Tony Blair argued in his Beveridge lecture, where he made a commitment to abolish child poverty within 20 years, there needed to be a refocusing of the objectives and operation of the welfare state:

> If the knowledge economy is an aim then work, skill and above all investing in children become essential aims of welfare ... we have made children our top priority because, as the Chancellor memorably said in his budget, 'they are 20 per cent of the population, but they are 100 per cent of the future' (Blair, 1999: 16).

In a context where social investment for the future in order to compete in the global market was the top priority, policies in relation to children and childhood thus lay at the heart of the New Labour project to refashion the welfare state.

New Labour and Modernization

If New Labour presented its strategy in terms of the 'Third Way', the manner in which it characterized its approach was in terms of a process of 'modernization' whereby the key elements of both the state and civil society would be renewed to make them 'fit for purpose' for the globalized economy (Cabinet Office, 1999; Department of Health, 1998a). It aimed to increase opportunity and strengthen community by combining both liberal individualism and a conservative communitarianism (Driver and Martell, 1997).

New Labour drew on a version of *communitarianism* informed by the American sociologist Amitai Etzioni (1993; 1997). Appeals to community were seen as a focus for moral renewal, asserting the need to restore to communities their moral voices and requiring a much greater sense of individual responsibility towards others. Communitarianism attempts to reactivate the institutions of civil society, particularly schools and families, into vibrant forms of social regulation and opportunity. However, New Labour's main preoccupation has not been the centrality of marriage, the unity of the couple or even the permanence of parental relationships, as clearly the nature of 'family' and 'family practices' had changed considerably during the previous generation. The focus of policy has thereby shifted from the nuclear family to an approach that is concerned with childhood vulnerability and well-being and, crucially, upholding 'parental responsibility' (Lewis, 2001).

The approach is premised on the idea that our initial moral commitments are derived from the families and communities into which we are born, and are reinforced by other forms of community membership. The community is conceptualized as a key site for both explaining and intervening in a range of social problems. Strategies should thereby be developed to link individuals to their communities, and central to these are attempts to enhance connections to the labour market and ensure that the control and discipline of children by their parents is strengthened so that they are brought up appropriately. However, while appealing to the spirit of an idealized working-class community, because the community was rediscovered in the context of moral panic about the collapse of order and the growing lawlessness of the young following the murder of Jamie Bulger, it was necessary for the state to actively take the lead in reinvigorating communities.

New Labour's emphasis on modernization has also been heavily influenced by the *new public management approach* first introduced in the mid-1980s (Horton and Farnham, 1999). Originally, under the Conservative government, the primary impetus was to rein in public expenditure and introduce some of the disciplines of the private sector, particularly via the introduction of the quasi-market and the contract culture into public services. However, the Conservative changes were not simply concerned with trying to improve 'economy, efficiency and effectiveness', but also emphasized the need to make the actions of professionals and the services they provided more 'transparent' and 'accountable' (Power, 1997). What occurred was a significant shift towards giving managers the right to manage, instituting a whole variety of systems of regulation to achieve value for money and thereby producing accountability to the taxpayer and the government on the one hand, and to the customer and the user on the other (Clarke et al., 2000).

Under New Labour, the changes became even more rapid and intensive with the promulgation of a range of new performance targets, inspection regimes and league tables, with the avowed intent to maximize 'best value' and improve effectiveness. The process of 'audit' increased inexorably (Munro, 2004a; C. McDonald, 2006). Indicators and targets have been used to both drive and measure improvement (Newman, 2001; Martin, 2005). The techniques are built upon the positivist assumption that 'performance', 'outputs' or 'outcomes' can be measured in an objective, invariable, quantified manner (Tilbury, 2004, 2005; McAnulla, 2007).

However, New Labour's 'modernization' also had a clear normative inflection in that it was used to designate ways in which the institutions of government and public services must change to respond to the social changes prompted by globalization and the demands of the individualized citizen-consumer. In doing so, the approach has emphasized the importance of rational and scientific approaches in order to get rid of the 'traditional, old-fashioned' practices of the past. In the future, practice should be based on evidence of 'what works' and best outcomes.

In the process, research and evaluation have been drawn upon to set standards and criteria whereby performance can be measured. While this is used to measure the performance of organizations and practitioners, it is also used to measure the behaviour of the people with whom they work. Such an approach became increasingly evident in the field of children's social care, which had been tested in the first instance with the 'Looking After Children' (LAC) project. For example, the *Quality Protects* (QP) programme (Department of Health, 1998b), implemented between 1998 and 2003 as a means, primarily, of improving the standards of local authority 'corporate parenting', had a set of specified child welfare outcome measures defined in terms of developmental progress and educational attainment and linked to various organizational targets and indicators. A similar process was evident in the development of *Sure Start.* The performance of managers, practitioners and parents was thereby inextricably linked and subject to continual monitoring and evaluation.

Closely associated with the growth of managerialism, and central to the process of 'modernization', has been an emphasis on *joined-up government* in order to address particularly 'wicked problems'. For 'to improve the way we provide services, we need all parts of government to work together better. We need joined-up government. We need integrated government' (Cabinet Office, 1999: 5). The idea of *partnership* has been a central theme for New Labour in that it exemplifies the drive to move beyond the old ways of organizing public services in 'silos'.

The importance of partnership and inter-agency coordination had been a key recommendation of all child abuse inquiries since 1973 and was at the centre of the Children Act 1989. However, New Labour saw such approaches as being fundamental to its whole approach to government, and a key element which made its approach politically distinctive (Glendinning et al., 2002).

> The Third Way recognizes the limits of government in the social sphere, but also the need for government within those limits, to forge new partnerships with the voluntary sector. Whether in education, health, social work, crime prevention or the care of children, 'enabling' government strengthens civil society rather than weakening it, and helps families and communities improve their own performance. ... New Labour's task is to strengthen the range and quality of such partnerships (Blair, 1998: 14).

Networks of a variety of agencies drawn from the public, private and voluntary sectors have been heralded as alternatives to approaches based on either traditional bureaucracies or markets and are seen as the bedrock of a new form of governance (Clarke and Glendinning, 2002). While partnership can be seen to exemplify an approach which aims for pragmatic solutions to practical policy problems, partnerships are also intrinsically associated with networked forms of governance, where information and communication technologies (ICTs) are seen to play a key transformational role in developing new ways of ordering the new and complex governmental systems (Rhodes, 1997). The development of *electronic government* is seen as key to the process of modernization (Hudson, 2002, 2003) where the introduction of a range of new ICTs is given high priority. This has been encouraged by a variety of mutually reinforcing features of New Labour policy.

These include the development of social intervention programmes involving a focus on extremely small neighbourhoods, groups or individuals; a shift towards holistic, multi-agency approaches to such interventions; the establishment of ambitious social policies at a time of continuing resource constraint; government's response to administrative discretion in a policy context calling for more finely-judged selectivity; and the desire to base interventions on more precise evidence (Perri et al., 2005: 112–13).

Such developments provide a particular challenge to practitioners for, aside from the technical problems involved in their implementation, there is a significant tension. For while such technologies are particularly associated with strengthening the capacities for governmental surveillance, and there is an emphasis on the importance of sharing citizens' personal information between different public services, there is also an increased expectation that citizens' rights and privacy will be respected (Bellamy et al., 2005; Surveillance Studies Network, 2006).

These issues have been sharpened by the emphasis New Labour places on the importance of *prevention* and *early intervention.* As we noted earlier, New Labour has been keen to develop a much more proactive approach in order to address problems before they occur and before they become chronic. Not only would this be better for the individuals concerned, but it would provide considerable financial savings. An emphasis on *positive welfare* (Giddens, 1994, 1998, 2000) aimed to move beyond focusing on the negative problems, identified in the Beveridge Report (1944), of 'want, disease, ignorance, squalor and idleness', and saw welfare as a crucial component in promoting both economic growth and individual well-being.

Such an approach borrows many of its concepts and technologies of calculation and intervention from the public health model, with its emphasis on primary, secondary and tertiary prevention (Freeman, 1992, 1999). In the process universal benefits which individuals previously received on the basis of their citizenship rights are reconceptualized as primary services designed to maximize their health, well-being and employment. More significantly, the approach attempts to identify 'at risk' groups or individuals in the population and engage in early intervention before the onset of problems or to prevent the problems getting worse. Simply treating everyone the same and waiting for the crisis to occur is simply not adequate; *targeting* 'at risk' populations or individuals on the basis of their extra needs or vulnerabilities via early intervention becomes a key strategy for improving individual and social health in the future.

We discussed in the previous chapter how research related to 'early childhood prevention' was increasingly being taken seriously in policy debates in the 1990s. What France and Utting (2005) call the 'risk and protection-focussed prevention paradigm' provided a key rationale and framework for developing a number of initiatives for children and parents in the first New Labour government, including the 'Sure Start' programme, 'On Track' and projects funded by the 'Children's Fund'. In its second term there was an explicit effort to make prevention a central focus for mainstream services. For example, in September 2003 the then Minister for Young People, John Denham, announced that the government was requiring local authorities to develop coordinated local plans for the implementation of preventive strategies for children and their families. He articulated his belief that early identification of risks and problems should become a core activity for children's services.

> The local preventative strategy should set a framework for services, through which effective support can be provided at the most appropriate level and point in time. At all levels of service (universal, targeted, specialist and rehabilitative) *the aim should be early intervention, in response to the assessment of risk and protective factors,* to improve the outcomes of the children they serve (Children and Young People's Unit [CYPU], 2002, para. 1.3, emphasis added).

The guidance to local authorities also said that:

> By addressing the risk factors that make children and young people vulnerable to negative outcomes, such as being excluded from school, running away from home or by becoming involved in crime, the local preventative strategy will set the direction for services to reduce *social exclusion* (CYPU, 2002, para. 1.2, emphasis added).

Finally, no discussion of New Labour would be complete without reference to issues of image and news management (Franklin, 2003) which have had a profound impact on both the nature of policies and how they are presented to the media and the wider public. A preoccupation with language has frequently distracted attention, often by design, from more constructive approaches (Fairclough, 2000). In the process there has been a continual tension between short-termism – where government is seen as responding to 'public opinion' – and the longer term 'modernization' project. As a consequence New Labour has not seemed confident in the face of high profile 'bad news' stories and has wanted to be seen as authoritative and 'tough'. Such concerns have been particularly evident in the arenas of criminal justice, immigration and asylum where New Labour has been keen to be seen as *the* political party of 'law and order'.

Combating Social Exclusion

While the overall approach of New Labour social policy emphasized the idea of 'social investment' and should therefore focus on future benefits, it also recognized it was important to address certain current needs and problems. Where the focus was on present needs, this should be targeted on those sections of the population who were marginalized and posed a threat to social cohesion, either now or in the future. A focus on addressing social exclusion was thus a necessary current expenditure and a central plank in its approach to social policy, reflecting many of the themes, principles and tensions in the New Labour approach.

One of the first acts of the New Labour government, in December 1997, was to establish the Social Exclusion Unit with a strategic relationship to all government departments and located in the Cabinet Office, thus putting it 'at the heart of government'. It produced a wide range of reports on, for example, school exclusion, deprived neighbourhoods, unemployment, drug use, teenage pregnancy and the reintegration of ex-offenders into society.

There were a number of underlying assumptions which informed the New Labour approach to exclusion from the outset. Firstly, social exclusion was seen as emerging from the major changes arising from increased globalization which led to a loss of many extraction and manufacturing jobs and which contributed to the collapse of many traditional working class communities and thereby their cultures and values:

> We came into office determined to tackle a deep social crisis. We had a poor record in this country in adapting to social and economic change. The result was sharp income inequality, a third of children growing up in poverty, a host of social problems such as homelessness and drug abuse, and divisions in society typified by deprived neighbourhoods that had become no go areas for some and no exit zones for others. All of us bore the cost of social breakdown directly, or through the costs to society and public finances. And we were never going to have a successful economy while we continued to waste the talents of the many (Blair, 2001: 1).

Secondly, social exclusion was seen as a series of linked problems. It did not simply arise because of a lack of money but referred to what happens when 'people or areas suffer from a combination of problems such as unemployment, poor skills, low income, poor housing, high crime, bad health and family break-down' (Social Exclusion Unit, 2001, p. 11); it was thus necessary to respond in a 'joined-up' way. Thirdly, social exclusion was addressed in the context of an emphasis on rights and responsibilities, whereby government makes 'help available but requires a contribution from the individual and the community' (Social Exclusion Unit, 2001, p. 3).

A particular emphasis was placed on getting people into paid work. Key policies included the introduction of the national minimum wage and alterations to taxes and benefits to increase the incentives to enter the labour market through tax credit and with support for child care through the national child care strategy. At the centre of government policy on jobs was the New Deal, with its various special programmes for distinct groups, including young people, single parents and the long-term unemployed. While opportunities were offered, a life on long-term benefit was not seen as an option for most. Much stricter tests of availability for work were introduced and 'unemployment benefit' was changed to 'jobseeker's allowance'. Budgets also contained some redistributionist measures through a series of 'stealth taxes' which tended to benefit the working poor at the expense of the middle classes.

Addressing social exclusion, however, was not only concerned with trying to get people into work, for it was also intimately concerned with improving behaviour and social functioning. A variety of factors associated with certain individuals, families and communities were seen as putting certain people 'at risk' of social exclusion: poor parenting; truancy; drug abuse; lack of facilities; homelessness; as well as unemployment and low income. In particular, an attack on social exclusion also required an attack on the causes of crime as well as crime itself. The behaviour of children and young people was seen as being in need of attention and, in particular, it was important that parents took their responsibilities seriously. As we will discuss in more detail in Chapter 5, the introduction of parental control orders, curfew orders and a general concern with 'anti-social behaviour' have all been given a high priority, together with the major reform of policy and practice in relation to youth offending.

However, rather than increase social inclusion, a number of these policies can have the effect of increasing exclusion, for there is a 'contradiction between zero tolerance and criminalizing anti-social behaviour on the one hand and the welfarist, rehabilitative philosophy underlying some of the government's youth justice and prison policies' (Hoyle and Rose, 2001: 80). In part, such tensions arose because New Labour has always had a strong populist dimension, which is particularly prevalent in the way it approaches issues associated with crime and also immigration and asylum (Morris, 2001).

What we have, therefore, is a particular model of social exclusion which sees the challenges of globalization as resulting in problems of social cohesion brought about by those who have been left behind by economic change:

> It presents 'society' as experiencing a rising standard of living by defining those who have not done so, who have become poorer, as excluded from society, as 'outside it' (Levitas, 1996: 7).

As a result, policy has been less concerned with redistribution to aid social and material equality and more concerned with integration, either by getting people into work and reattaching them to the labour market or by altering the behaviour and characteristics of the excluded themselves. Those who, for whatever reasons, are resistant are subject to increased regulation and discipline (Veit-Wilson, 1998; Byrne, 2005). The emphasis is on equality of opportunity, not outcome.

Ruth Levitas (1996, 2005) has argued that New Labour's explanation and approach to social exclusion reflects a 'new Durkheimian hegemony' which sees deprivation and inequality as peripheral phenomena occurring at the margins of society and ignores forms of domination that structure the lives of the excluded and included alike. For New Labour, poverty and disadvantage, as Durkheim argued, are symptoms not of the capitalist market economy, but of pathological deviations from what is essentially a fair and harmonious society. Such a conception of social exclusion implies minimalist reform and is concerned with 'exclusion from access to the ladders of social improvement' (Kruger, 1997: 20) and not a problem relating to 'the length of the ladder or the distance between the rungs' (Levitas, 2005: 153). Similarly, Goodwin notes that 'couching the argument in terms of "inclusion of the excluded" constitutes an argument for pushing them "just over" the line. They remain borderline' (Goodwin, 1996: 348).

Levitas argued that the New Labour approach to social exclusion was poised between the influences of two major discourses. The first, what she calls the *social integrationist discourse* (SID), stresses the importance of moral integration and social cohesion, and regards the economy in general and paid work in the labour market, in particular, as the necessary means for achieving this. What is absent is any serious recognition of the existence and value of alternative modes of social integration outside the ambit of economic relations of exchange. There is little acknowledgement of the social contribution made by unpaid workers, notably by women, and a failure to address the way paid work for many does not provide a strong source of social identity, discipline and self-esteem. This is particularly the case for many males with the collapse of the traditional manufacturing and mining industries.

The second discourse identified by Levitas, the *moral underclass discourse* (MUD), deploys cultural rather than material explanations of social exclusion and was particularly associated with the work of Charles Murray in the late 1980s and early 1990s (Murray, 1990, 1994). Murray had argued that an underclass had long existed in the United States, but was now spreading in Britain. He likened it to a 'contagious disease' which was spread by people whose values were contaminating the life of whole communities by rejecting both the work ethic and the family ethic which were central to the mainstream culture. Importantly, not all the poor were part of such an underclass and were keen to strengthen their links with the mainstream and take advantage of the opportunities available to them. According to Murray, the existence of an underclass could be diagnosed by three symptoms: illegitimacy; crime; and dropping out from the labour force.

> If illegitimate births are the leading indicator of an underclass and violent crime is a proxy measure of its development, the definitive proof that an underclass has arrived is that large numbers of young, healthy, low-income males choose not to take jobs (Murray, 1990: 17).

These three factors, Murray argued, interacted to produce pathological communities in which the socialization of children, especially boys, was inadequate. The absence of fathers meant there was a lack of role models, particularly for boys, who then felt driven to prove their masculinity in destructive ways. The benefits system encouraged a culture of idleness and welfare dependency, where family structures and socialization processes had broken down and where only a reinforcement of the work ethic, achieved by means of a continual tightening of the benefit eligibility criteria, could reintegrate the excluded into mainstream society. Such an approach has certain similarities to the communitarianism of Amitai Etzioni, and would support approaches which aimed to emphasize 'no rights without responsibilities' and being 'tough on crime and tough on the causes of crime'.

Levitas also outlines a third discourse on social exclusion, which she terms the *redistributionist discourse* (RED) and which had its roots in the critical social policy literature, particularly of Peter Townsend (1971), a number of publications from the Child Poverty Action Group (CPAG) (Golding, 1986; Lister, 1990; Walker and Walker, 1997) and other writers on the left (Jordan, 1996). Such an approach recognized

> their resources are so seriously below those commanded by the average individual or family that they are, in effect, *excluded* from ordinary living patterns, customs and activities (Townsend, 1971: 32, emphasis added).

The prime cause of social exclusion was seen as arising from the increasing inequalities of income, wealth and power. The solutions proposed were explicitly redistributive and included increasing taxation on the rich, a reduced reliance on means-tested benefits and that benefits should be paid primarily on the basis of citizenship rights. While a redistribution of resources in terms of income and wealth was important, the analysis recognized the increasing social divisions evident in housing, health and the workplace, including a range of fringe benefits received at work. Social exclusion was explicitly located in wider issues of power. While New Labour has engaged in some redistribution via the tax system, this has been minimal. Such an approach recognizes that the problem of social exclusion was as much, if not more, to do with the behaviour and life style of the rich as it was to do with that of the poor and must therefore be subject to change.

New Labour's Policy for Children and Families

While all three discourses on social exclusion identified by Levitas have played some role in informing New Labour policy towards children and families, it is the first two, the social integrationist discourse (SID) and the moral underclass discourse (MUD), which have dominated. New Labour's policies in relation to children and families are located in the priority given to emphasizing 'social investment' in order to compete in the increasingly globalized economic order, and to combat social exclusion. The latter is addressed primarily in terms of providing more opportunities and encouragements for paid work while trying to modify the life styles and behaviours of those who are not able to do so, together with ensuring they do not undermine the rights of others and in the process engage in crime and other anti-social behaviour. Policies in relation to children and families have been at the core of New Labour's social programme.

Since coming to power, New Labour has introduced a plethora of new policies and made significant changes to other long-established ones (see Millar and Ridge, 2002; Skinner, 2003; Pugh and Parton, 2003; Fawcett et al., 2004). These have included:

- *General support for all parents with children,* including increasing the value of child benefits, the introduction of children's tax to replace the married couple's tax allowance, the introduction of a national child care strategy, improving maternity and paternity leave.

- *Specific and targeted support for poor families with children,* including the introduction of the working tax credit, the child tax credit and the child care tax credit; the special services to aid welfare-to-work under the New Deal initiatives where personal advisors give practical advice and support and there is considerable encouragement and finances available to enter the labour market or take up training.
- *Initiatives specifically targeted at disadvantaged children who are 'at risk' of being socially excluded,* particularly the Sure Start programme, Connexions, and the Children's Fund.

Taking these initiatives together, we can see that New Labour has placed a high priority on supporting 'hard working families' (Williams, 2005) by: encouraging and rewarding parental involvement in employment; attacking poverty, particularly amongst lone parents and other low-income families; providing the basis for a prosperous and competitive economy; and acting as the role model that parents can provide for their children.

At the same time there is a considerable emphasis on the 'responsibilization' of parents. Not only are entitlements and support conditional on the exercise of proper individual responsibility, but adults with children carry extra responsibilities. The idea of 'parental responsibility' lies at the centre of a range of policies in the broad criminal justice, education, health and child welfare areas. 'Parental responsibility' is not only concerned with ensuring that children attend and achieve at school, but that they do not engage in criminal or anti-social behaviour, and that their health and development are fully supported. Parents are seen to play a central role in creating the 'hard working' and 'pro-social' adults of the future.

Conclusion

We can thus see New Labour as drawing on a number of diverse elements to produce a distinctive approach to social policy and its attempts at social and economic renewal more generally. Perhaps its most distinctive characteristic has been its attempt to combine an emphasis on both liberal individualism and conservative communitarianism. Some have gone as far as to suggest that such a 'liberal-communitarian' policy mix is supported by a variety of coalitions which rule a large number of the major EU member states, whichever party is dominant, while recognizing that the detail and balance of the policy mix will vary (Jordan, 2006a). The approach has brought together an emphasis on the importance of individual autonomy and the mobility of market relations with elements of a socially conservative view of the family and civil society, particularly in terms of its emphasis on 'responsibility'.

It assumes that individuals aim to maximize their utility within a set of insti-tutions – families, markets, polities – inherited from earlier generations but constantly renewed in their interactions. The approach has also sought to erode or transform the collectivist legacy of the Keynesian period. It is assumed that not only do individuals want more consumer freedoms and choices but that they will also be required to become more independent and self-reliant than they had been in the welfare state era. Instead of expecting collective solutions to issues of the life cycle, the economic cycle, change and crisis, they are required to develop personal resources and material property to cope with all eventualities.

Increasingly, New Labour has been keen to give more scope to individuals to choose among a range of alternative amenities and providers in terms of hospi-tals, schools and social care resources, and has encouraged citizens to develop strategies for finding the 'best' facilities. In particular the 'choice agenda' has been promoted as the key mechanism for improving competition and thereby driving up quality in public services (Jordan, 2005, 2006b; Clarke et al., 2006), particularly at the beginning of its third term of government following its re-election in May 2005. For example, increased freedoms for and greater differentiation between schools, particularly secondary schools, were seen as a major way of improving the performance of the schools themselves and the academic achievements of their students.

While presented as a coherent and logical mix of principles and policy devel-opments, the potential for tensions and contradictions cannot be underestimated. In particular it cannot be assumed that an emphasis on greater individualism, choice and personal responsibility in order to encourage greater innovation and competition in the global economy will not undermine attempts to increase a sense of community cohesion and national solidarity. The emphasis on the need to maximize our ability to attract foreign capital by keeping taxation low in order to ensure the UK, and London in particular, becomes a global centre of finance may increase social inequality and thereby undermine attempts to improve social inclusion. These are important issues, which we will return to in the final section of the book. What is clear is that policies towards children have been a key focus for social policy change by New Labour, and it is to these we turn in the next chapter.

3

Every Child Matters: Change for Children

From the outset, New Labour had a much wider and more proactive approach to policies towards children than the previous Conservative government. Policies towards parents, children and young people lay at the heart of New Labour attempts to refashion the welfare state in terms of its twin-track approach to tackling social exclusion and investing in a positive, wealth-creating knowledge economy. Not only were children and young people the focus of attempts to educate and improve the quality of the future work force but they were seen as particularly 'at risk' of social exclusion and were identified as in need of special attention. The numbers of children in poverty had trebled between 1979 and New Labour coming to power, to include a third of all children and young people, and children were seen as particularly vulnerable to the effects of increasing divorce, single parenthood and the growing violence and malaise in certain communities, often accounting for a high proportion of crime and anti-social behaviour. Mechanisms of enforcement as well as support were required to ensure that all parents carried out their child care responsibilities appropriately.

The policies introduced more specifically in relation to children's social care were located in this wider policy context. As the White Paper *Modernising Social Services* argued:

> Social services for children cannot be seen in isolation from the wider range of children's services delivered by local authorities and other agencies. The Government is committed to taking action through a broad range of initiatives to strengthen family life, to reduce social exclusion and anti-social behaviour among children, and to give every child the opportunity of a healthy, happy, successful life. Examples of Government action on the wider front include the 'Sure Start' programme, the Crime Reduction Programme, Early Years Development and Child Care Partnerships, and the Green Paper 'Supporting Families'. Children's social services must be seen within this wider context (DH, 1998a: 41).

A major emphasis in the White Paper was upon the need to introduce a range of new regulations, targets, monitoring and management information systems for social services departments. This was made explicit with the launch of the *Quality Protects* (QP) Programme (DH, 1998b), which invested £885 million between 1999 and 2004 on the basis of detailed annual 'management action plans' (MAPs) from each local authority. At the core of the QP programme were eight broad objectives, together with numerous performance indicators. While a central feature of QP was to improve outcomes for 'looked after' children, following the Utting Report (1997), particularly in terms of their educational achievement and support for care leavers, the programme was much wider. In particular it was framed in terms of social service departments 'improving the well-being of children in need for whom our local authority has taken on direct responsibility' (DH, 1998b: para. 5.2).

However, following its re-election in June 2001, the Government made it clear that it felt progress was slow and that further reform was warranted and that a review of services for 'children at risk' would be the subject of one of the seven initial cross-cutting reviews as part of the *2002 Spending Review* (HM Treasury, 2002a). When it was published, the *Spending Review* argued that despite extensive investment in children's services, most were not having the desired impact on the most disadvantaged children. The recommendations sought to ensure that support for children 'at risk' should be better focused on preventive services and also that the preventive elements of mainstream services should address 'the known risk factors'. The *Spending Review* took a three-pronged approach to strengthening preventive services: improving strategic coordination at a local level; delivering sustainable services; and filling gaps and improving services. It stated that achieving 'integration' required strong leadership at both national and local levels, underpinned by 'effective performance management, driving forward reform'. While reform had already begun, the government believed that it was crucial to bring about further change. In particular:

> local partners must agree to carry out new functions including: better strategic planning; systematic identification, referral and tracking regimes to ensure children don't fall through the services safety net; and allocating responsibilities for individualised packages of support for those at greatest risk. The Government believes there is a case for structural change to effect the better coordination of children's services, and will pilot Children's Trusts which will unify at the local level the various agencies involved in providing children's services (HM Treasury, 2002a: para. 28.5).

As the above quotation demonstrates, the framework for the 'transformation' of children's services, which was to take place from late 2004 onwards, was clearly outlined in the *2002 Spending Review*.

However, when the Green Paper *Every Child Matters* (Chief Secretary to the Treasury, 2003) was published in September 2003, it was presented as the government's response to the Laming Report (2003) into the death of Victoria Climbié, who had died at the hands of her 'aunt', Marie Therese Kouao, and her boyfriend, Carl Manning, on 25 February 2000. Victoria had been born in the Ivory Coast on 2 November 1991 and brought to London via France in April 1999. In the following 18 months up to Victoria's death, the family were known to four different London social services departments, two hospitals, two police child protection teams and an NSPCC family centre; however, none had been able to intervene to save her life and at no point had the seriousness of her situation been recognized. The case seemed to have many of the similarities of most of the tragic child death scandals of the previous thirty years (see Parton, 2004, for a critical discussion). The government set up a public inquiry, chaired by Lord Laming, which published its report on 28 January 2003.

Every Child Matters and the Children Act 2004

What is apparent is that, while the Green Paper was informed by the Laming Report, it was primarily concerned with taking forward the government's agenda for reforming children's services (Parton, 2006a,b), but with a much broader remit than previously envisaged. For rather than being entitled 'Children at Risk', as suggested by the *2002 Spending Review,* the consultative Green Paper was entitled 'Every Child Matters'. This was not to say the Green Paper was not centrally concerned with 'risk', as clearly it was, but this was framed in recognition that any child, at some point in their life, could be seen as vulnerable to some form of risk. The government therefore deemed it necessary that *all children* should be covered by its proposals. Universal services were seen as offering early (primary) intervention to prevent the emergence of specific risk factors. It was therefore important to ensure the *integration* of universal, targeted and specialist services. Risk was seen as a pervasive, potential threat to all children and for a variety of reasons, and it is in this context that two figures included in the Green Paper (see Figures 3.1 and 3.2) are particularly helpful in understanding how the reform of children's services was being conceptualized.

Underpinning the proposals were two basic assumptions concerning the nature of recent social change and the state of current knowledge. First, the Green Paper stated that, over the previous generation, children's lives had undergone 'profound change'. While children had more opportunities than ever before and had benefited from rising prosperity and better health, they also faced more uncertainties and risks. They faced earlier exposure to sexual activity, drugs and alcohol, and family patterns had changed significantly. There were more lone parents, more divorces and more women in paid employment, all of which made family life more complex and, potentially, made the position of children more precarious.

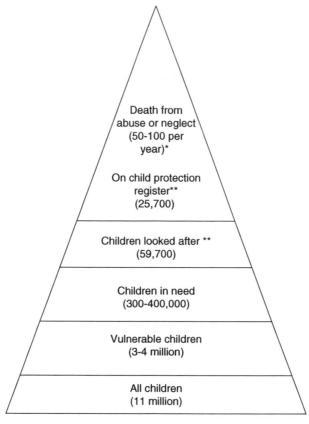

Death from
abuse or neglect
(50-100 per
year)*

On child protection
register**
(25,700)

Children looked after **
(59,700)

Children in need
(300-400,000)

Vulnerable children
(3-4 million)

All children
(11 million)

*   These children may or may not be on the child protection register, nor looked
after, nor vulnerable.

**   These children are included in the children in need figure, but not all children on
the child protection register are children looked after.

Fig. 3.1 'Every Child Matters': Categorizing children
[Crown Copyright, reprinted with permission. License # C02W000670.]

Second, however, the Green Paper asserted that these changes had come about
at a time when we now had increased knowledge and expertise and therefore were
in a better position to respond to these new uncertainties and risks. In particular,
'we better understand the importance of early influences on the development of
values and behaviour' (p. 15). It was thus important to ensure that this knowledge
was drawn upon to inform the changes being introduced. For:

> we have a good idea what factors shape children's life chances. Research
> tells us that the risk of experiencing negative outcomes is concentrated in
> children with certain characteristics (p. 17).

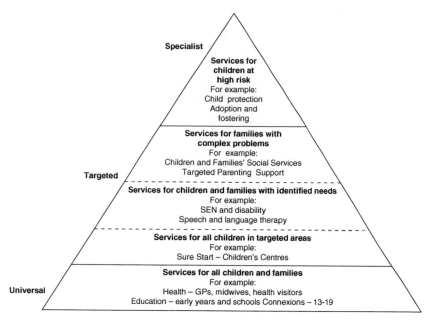

Fig. 3.2 'Every Child Matters': Targeted services within a universal context
[Crown Copyright, reprinted with permission. License # C02W000670.]

While research had not built up a detailed picture of the causal links, certain factors were said to be associated with poor outcomes. These included:

- low income and parental unemployment
- homelessness
- poor parenting
- poor schooling
- postnatal depression amongst mothers
- low birth weight
- substance misuse
- individual characteristics, such as intelligence, and community factors, such as living in a disadvantaged community.

The more risk factors a child experienced, such as being excluded from school and family breakdown, the more likely it was that they would experience negative outcomes, and the Green Paper stated that:

> research suggests that parenting appears to be the most important factor associated with educational attainment at age ten, which in turn is strongly associated with achievement later in life. *Parental involvement in education*

seems to be a more important influence than poverty, school environment and
the influence of peers (p.18, emphasis added).

Because of this increased knowledge about risk factors associated with a
child's development, it was seen as important to intervene at an earlier stage in
order to forestall problems in later life, particularly in relation to anti-social
behaviour, crime and unemployment. Early intervention in childhood thus provided a major strategy for overcoming social exclusion for children and for
avoiding problems in adulthood.

The other area where knowledge and expertise had grown and which was seen
as vital in order to take policy and practice forward, was in relation to the major
changes that had taken place in the development of systems of Information,
Communication and Technology (ICTs). The age of electronic government was
seen as having major implications for the reform and development of children's
services. Not only would this provide the potential for identifying problems and
enhancing attempts to intervene at an earlier stage but it would also allow different organizations and professionals to share information in order to ensure that
children's problems were not missed and that children did not fall through 'the
net'. The integration of different services was seen as crucially dependent on the
introduction of new ICTs.

In order to 'put children at the heart of our policies, and to organize services
around their needs' (p. 9), the Green Paper argued that radical reform was
needed not just to 'break down organizational boundaries' but also to overcome
local and national 'fragmentation'. The government's aim was that there should
be one person in charge locally and nationally and that key services for children
should be integrated within a common organizational focus at both levels,
thereby enhancing *integration* and clarifying the lines of *accountability*. At the
central government level this would be via the creation of a new minister based
in the Department for Education and Skills (DfES), the Minister for Children,
Young People and Families; and at the local authority level via the creation of
new Directors of Children's Services who would be responsible for children's
social services and education, together with the establishment of a lead council
member responsible for children. In the longer term it was planned to further
integrate all local services for children and young people via the establishment
of 'Children's Trusts'. In many respects the template for integrating services by
children's trusts was developed from the way Sure Start programmes had operated (Hawker, 2006). Apart from education and children's social care, it was
hoped that children's trusts would include most children's health services and
could include other services such as youth offending teams. It was also proposed
to create statutory 'Local Safeguarding Children's Boards' and create a new
office of a Children's Commissioner for England. In effect, the proposals would
bring to an end the organizational structures introduced in 1971 with the

establishment of a *family* service and would bring about the dissolution of social service departments.

While there were some minor changes, in the form of a relaxation in the time-frames and a greater level of flexibility that local authorities could have with the organizational structures they might develop, in the spring of 2004 the government announced it was going ahead with the changes and published *Every Child Matters: Next Steps* (DfES, 2004b), together with the Children Bill, which received royal assent on 15 November 2004. It was planned that all the changes would be in place by the end of 2008.

While the Children Act 1989 was to continue to provide the primary legislative framework for children's services, the government felt it needed strengthening in certain respects. The key theme of the Children Act 2004 was to encourage partnership and sharpen accountability between a wide range of health, welfare, education and criminal justice agencies. The key provisions were:

- placing a new duty on agencies to cooperate among themselves and with other local partners to improve the 'well-being' of children and young people so that all would work to common outcomes (Section 10);
- a tighter focus on child protection through a duty on key agencies to safeguard children and promote their welfare (Section 11), and the establishment of new statutory Local Safeguarding Children's Boards to replace Area Child Protection Committees (Sections 13–16);
- the power to establish a national database or index, via secondary legislation and guidance, that would contain basic information about all children and young people to help professionals to work together to provide early support, but in which case details were specifically ruled out (Section 12);
- a requirement that all local authorities with children's services responsibilities appoint a Director of Children's Services and a Lead Council Member to be responsible for, as a minimum, education and children's social service functions, but local authorities would have the discretion to add other relevant functions to the ones they felt were appropriate, such as leisure or housing (Sections 18 and 19);
- enabling and encouraging local authorities, Primary Care Trusts, and others to pool budgets into a Children's Trust, and share information better to support more joining up on the ground, with health, education and social care professionals working together in the same location such as schools and children's centres (Section 10);
- creating an integrated inspection framework to assess how well services work together to improve outcomes for children (Sections 20–5);
- the requirement for local authorities to produce a single Children and Young People's Plan to replace a range of current statutory planning requirements (Section 17 and Schedule 5);
- the creation of a Children's Commissioner (Sections 1–9).

Every Child Matters: Change for Children

On 1 December 2004 *Every Child Matters: Change for Children* (DfES, 2004a) was launched under the signature of 16 ministers from 13 government departments. It set out the national framework for the local 'change programme', together with the timetable for introducing the statutory changes and the publication dates of the statutory guidance.

Outcomes for all children

At the centre of the changes was an ambition to improve the *outcomes* for all children and to narrow the gap in outcomes between those who do well and those who do not. The outcomes were defined in terms of: being healthy; staying safe; enjoying and achieving; making a positive contribution; and achieving economic well-being. Together these five outcomes were seen as key to 'well-being in childhood and later life'. Such an ambition required 'whole system' change in local children's services and would be secured through more integrated frontline delivery, processes, strategy and governance. The model of 'whole system change, the children's trust in action' was represented in *Every Child Matters: Change for Children* as shown in Figures 3.4 and 3.5.

At the core were the 'outcomes for children and young people':

> The outcomes are inter-dependent. They show the important relationship between educational achievement and well-being. Children and young people learn and thrive when they are healthy, safeguarded from harm and engaged. The evidence shows that educational achievement is the most effective way to improve outcomes for poor children and break cycles of deprivation (DfES, 2004a, para. 2.2).

The final sentence of this quotation is of particular significance. Ever since the general election of 1997 with its claims that its main priorities were 'education, education, education', New Labour had given education a central role in its social programme. Not only was it a key element in its aim to prepare the future workforce to participate in a 'knowledge economy' so that Britain could compete and lead in the increasingly globalized world, but it was a key element in its policy agenda to tackle social exclusion. As a consequence, education in its broadest sense and including its younger sibling, early years services, had become the primary vehicle for trying to address a series of social issues and problems which previously may have been seen as the preserve of social work and social care. This becomes even more evident in the third term of the New Labour government, particularly with the publication of *The Children's Plan* in December 2007, to which we will return in the final section of the book.

Every Child Matters: Change for Children (DfES, 2004a) also set out in more detail what the five outcomes would mean in practice and how progress towards

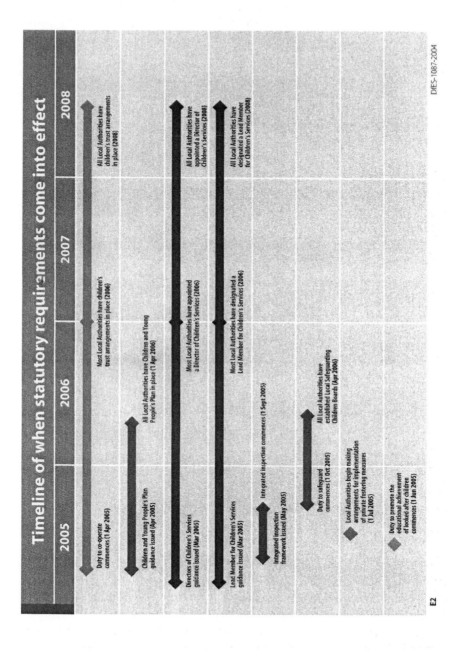

Fig. 3.3 Timeline when statutory requirements would come into effect
Source: Every Child Matters: Change for Children (DfES, 2004a, p. E2).
[Crown Copyright, reprinted with permission. License # C02W000670.]

Timeline of when statutory requirements come into effect

| 2005 | 2006 | 2007 | 2008 |

Duty to co-operate commences (1 Apr 2005)

Most Local Authorities have children's trust arrangements in place (2006)

All Local Authorities have children's trust arrangements in place (2008)

Children and Young People's Plan guidance issued (Apr 2005)

All Local Authorities have Children and Young People's Plan in place (1 Apr 2006)

Directors of Children's Services guidance issued (Mar 2005)

Most Local Authorities have appointed a Director of Children's Services (2006)

All Local Authorities have appointed a Director of Children's Services (2008)

Lead Member for Children's Services guidance issued (Mar 2005)

Most Local Authorities have designated a Lead Member for Children's Services (2006)

All Local Authorities have designated a Lead Member for Children's Services (2008)

Integrated inspection commences (1 Sept 2005)

Integrated inspection framework issued (May 2005)

Duty to safeguard commences (1 Oct 2005)

All Local Authorities have established Local Safeguarding Children Boards (Apr 2006)

Local Authorities begin making arrangements for implementation of private fostering measures (1 Jul 2005)

Duty to promote the educational achievement of looked after children commences (1 Jun 2005)

E2

Fig. 3.4 The Children's Trust in Action
Source: Every Child Matters: Change for Children (DfES, 2004a, p. 6).
[Crown Copyright, reprinted with permission. License # C02W000670.]

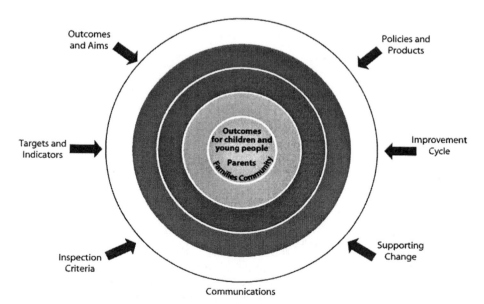

Fig. 3.5 National framework for local change
Source: Every Child Matters: Change for Children (DfES, 2004a, p. 6).
[Crown Copyright, reprinted with permission. License # C02W000670.]

them would be measured. Twenty-five specific aims for children and young people and the support needed from parents, carers and families were identified (see Table 3.1) in order to achieve the aims, which were then developed into a more detailed 'outcomes framework' to provide the basis for agreeing local priorities, planning, and local change. The 'outcomes framework' provided a detailed map of the five 'outcomes' and the 25 'aims' in relation to the 'targets'

Table 3.1 The 25 specific aims for children and young people and the support needed from parents, carers and families in order to achieve these aims

Be healthy	Physically healthy Mentally and emotionally healthy Sexually healthy Healthy lifestyles Choose not to take illegal drugs *Parents, carers and families promote healthy choices*
Stay safe	Safe from maltreatment, neglect, violence and sexual exploitation Safe from accidental injury and death Safe from bullying and discrimination Safe from crime and anti-social behaviour Have security, stability and are cared for *Parents, carers and families provide safe homes and stability*
Enjoy and achieve	Ready for school Attend and enjoy school Achieve stretching national educational standards at primary school Achieve personal and social development and enjoy recreation Achieve stretching national educational standards at secondary school *Parents, carers and families support learning*
Make a positive contribution	Engage in decision-making and support the community and environment Engage in law-abiding and positive behaviour in and out of school Develop positive relationships and choose not to bully and discriminate Develop self-confidence and successfully deal with significant life changes and challenges Develop enterprising behaviour *Parents, carers and families promote positive behaviour*
Achieve economic well-being	Engage in further education, employment or training on leaving school Ready for employment Live in decent homes and sustainable communities Access to transport and material goods Live in households free from low income *Parents, carers and families are supported to be economically active*

and 'indicators' which local services would be measured against and which would inform the 'evidence' and 'judgments' which future inspections would consider. There was thus a serious attempt to ensure that the five outcomes were the primary focus for measuring quality.

Right at the centre of the changes was an explicit performance management approach which brought a long-established way of working from the world of corporate business to the improvement and measurement of children's lives. The performance of both professionals and parents was to be managed and monitored in the interests of improving outcomes for children (Luckock, 2008). The reforms can be seen to constitute the epitome of rational decision-making with everything flowing from a top-down, outcomes-led approach (Hudson, 2005a,b,c). However, *Every Child Matters* claimed that the five outcomes that shape well-being – being healthy, staying safe, enjoying and achieving, making a positive contribution, and economic well-being – were formulated following consultations with children and young people. In the process it suggests that the needs of the service users would be at the forefront of change and provide the basis for judging progress. In practice, however, the measurement of outcomes was to be restricted to the existing standards, indicators and targets across the partner agencies. As a result, 'enjoying and achieving', for example, was to be judged primarily in terms of school attendance and performance, while 'making a positive contribution' was to be measured primarily in terms of reduction in offending, school exclusions and anti-social behaviour.

The 'whole system change' was much wider and more ambitious than the concerns that lay at the heart of the Laming Report. Being 'safe from maltreatment, neglect, violence and sexual exploitation' was just one of the 25 aims and just one of the six aims seen as important for achieving the 'staying safe' outcome, indicating just how far the changes were trying to ensure that narrowly defined child protection concerns did not dominate day-to-day policy and practice as it had done in the past. The development and outcomes of all children, particularly those who were vulnerable, were the focus, and improving educational achievement and improving behaviour were seen as the key. In this, parents, carers and families were to play the pivotal role and it was seen as important to shift from an emphasis on intervention to one premised on prevention. Beyond developing systems for integrating local governance arrangements and strategies, there was also an emphasis on integrated frontline delivery and integrated processes.

Integrated frontline delivery

The integration of children's services required the personalization and integration of universal services which would also provide easy access to effective and targeted specialist services, following the frameworks outlined in *Every Child Matters* (see Figures 3.1 and 3.2). The *Change for Children* programme was to be introduced alongside, and be consistent with, the *National Service Framework for Children, Young People and Maternity Services* (DH, 2004), the government's

10-year strategy for early years and childcare (HM Treasury et al., 2004) and the strategy in relation to young people (DfES, 2005c), thus ensuring that early years and childcare services, schools and health services were integrated into the new arrangements. The resulting ability to identify at an early stage children who might be experiencing problems and/or had extra needs was a central part of the strategy:

> High quality, more integrated universal services will work together with targeted and specialist services for children with additional needs, such as those with disabilities, those whose parents have mental health problems or those who need to be protected from harm.

These children and young people will need:

- a high quality multi-agency assessment;
- a wide range of specialist services available close to home; and
- effective case management by a lead professional working as part of a multi-disciplinary team (DfES, 2004a, paras. 3.11 and 3.12).

To bring this about, it was seen as important to develop a strategy for the 'children's workforce' (DfES, 2006b), whereby a national single qualifications framework to improve career opportunities could be established, together with identifying the 'common skills and knowledge' that everyone working with children, young people and families should be able to demonstrate (DfES, 2005a). Developing the role of the *lead professional* was seen as key. The lead professional would act as a single point of contact for the child or family, coordinating delivery and reducing the overlap and inconsistency in the services received. Lead professionals would work with children and young people with additional and complex needs, who therefore were deemed to require an integrated package of support from more than one practitioner. The lead professional could be designated from any of the professionals working with the child and did not need to come from any particular professional background – it depended on the particular circumstances and needs (DfES, 2006c,d).

Integrated processes

The development of common processes, a common language and better information sharing were all seen as important for the integration of services. The introduction of the Common Assessment Framework (CAF) and Information Sharing Index (ISI) were both to play a key role.

The CAF would be used whenever it was felt a child might have additional needs requiring extra targeted support:

> Children and families may experience a range of needs at different times in their lives. All children require access to high quality universal services.

Some children are at risk of poor outcomes. These are *children with additional needs* and they will require targeted support from education, health, social services and other services (DfES, 2006e).

Such needs may be 'cross-cutting' and, according to the guidance (DfES, 2006e,f), might include:

- disruptive or anti-social behaviour;
- overt parental conflict or lack of parental support/boundaries;
- involvement in or risk of offending;
- poor attendance or exclusion from school;
- experiencing bullying;
- special educational needs;
- disabilities;
- disengagement from education, training or employment post-16;
- poor nutrition;
- ill health;
- substance misuse;
- anxiety or depression;
- housing issues;
- pregnancy and parenthood.

The guidance suggested that a CAF should be carried out at any time when someone working with a child or young person felt that they might not progress towards the five *Every Child Matters* outcomes without additional services. It was important 'to identify these children early and help them before things reach crisis point. The CAF is an important tool for intervention' (DfES, 2006e, para. 3.5). It was designed to be an electronic assessment form to be completed by any professional when they considered a child to have 'additional needs' that required the involvement of more than one service. The idea was that it would save time as one assessment could be used thereafter. It included a wide-ranging set of data covering most aspects of a child's health and development, including details about parents and siblings. It followed the format introduced by the *Assessment Framework* in 2000 (DH et al., 2000a). On 25 July 2007 the government announced that the implementation of the CAF would be based upon a single national IT system and would, in future, be known as eCAF.

The CAF Guidance for practitioners (DfES, 2006e) and managers (DfES, 2006f) provided an important conceptual map of the way services were seen to relate to particular categories of children and the role that the new 'processes and tools to support children and families' were to play in the new arrangements. In many respects, Figures 3.6 and 3.7 demonstrate how thinking about the integration of children's services had moved on from *Every Child Matters* in 2003, represented earlier in Figures 3.1 and 3.2.

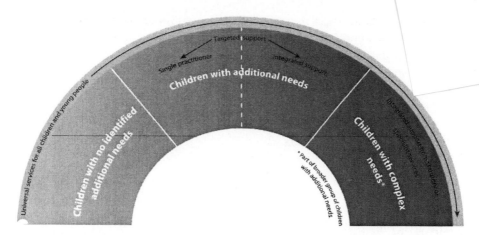

Fig. 3.6 Continuum of needs and services
Source: The Common Assessment Framework for Children and Young People: Practitioners' Guide (DfES, 2006e, p. 6).
[Crown Copyright, reprinted with permission. License # C02W000670.]

Within the group of children with additional needs, it was argued that a small proportion had *complex needs* which might meet the threshold for statutory involvement, and that these children were:

- children who were the subject of a child protection plan;
- looked-after children;
- children for whom adoption was the plan;

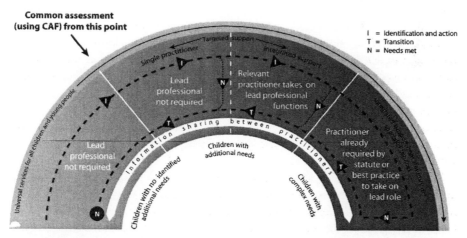

Fig. 3.7 Processes and tools to support children and families
Source: The Common Assessment Framework for Children and Young People: Practitioners' Guide (DfES, 2006e, p. 7).
[Crown Copyright, reprinted with permission. License # C02W000670.]

- children with severe and complex special educational needs;
- children with complex disabilities or complex health needs;
- children diagnosed with significant mental health problems;
- young offenders involved with youth justice services (community and custodial).

These are very much the groups of children who were likely to be the prime responsibility of children's social care.

In parallel with the CAF, children's services were expected to improve the practice of sharing information between professionals. Section 12 of the Children Act 2004 required Children's Services Authorities (local authorities) to operate a national *Information Sharing Index* (IS Index) covering all children living in the area. The government intended that the index would assist practitioners in achieving the five outcomes for all children and young people identified in the legislation, in terms of: being healthy; staying safe; enjoying and achieving; making a positive contribution; and achieving economic well-being. The index was not intended to be narrowly focused on child protection but aimed to improve the sharing of information between professionals, in order to improve the well-being of *all* children.

It would contain: the child's name, address, gender and date of birth; a number identifying the child; the name and contact details of any person with parental responsibility or who had care of him/her at any time; and the name and contact details of any educational institution, primary medical services, or any specialist or targeted service which was, or had been, provided to the person by, or on behalf of, a local authority; also, the name and contact details of a lead professional for that child (if appointed). Section 12 also allowed for the inclusion of any other information, excluding medical records or other personal records, as the Secretary of State might specify by regulation. For sensitive areas (that is, those relating to sexual health, mental health and substance abuse) information would be included on the database only with the consent of the parent or young person. The lack of consent could be overridden in certain circumstances, to be specified in regulations, but would include cases where there were genuine child protection concerns. Access to the contact details of personnel in sensitive services would be restricted to index management teams. In addition to the information about services in contact with the child, Section 12 also allowed for inclusion of 'information as to the existence of any cause for concern in relation to him [the child]'.

Both in debates on the Children Bill in the House of Lords and following its passage into law, there was considerable criticism about this element of the legislation, including a Report by the House of Commons Education and Skills Committee (2005) which had 'significant reservations' about costs and certainly did not feel the Bill was the most cost-effective way of improving outcomes for children. The Committee also had 'significant concerns' about the security, confidentiality and access arrangements. The Information Commissioner (2005) also raised concerns about children's and young people's rights to privacy and the need to justify the sharing of information, while research exploring the views of young people found they would be reluctant to share information of a sensitive nature and some said that they would prefer to forego vital services if their need for privacy was not respected (Hilton and Mills, 2007). These criticisms were developed in detail in a report for the Information Commissioner's Office by the Foundation for Information Policy Research (Anderson et al., 2006).

What was seen as particularly alarming was the broad, inclusive and ill-defined concept of 'a cause for concern' which was introduced as the key threshold to share information and which was dependent upon the subjective interpretation of practitioners (Munro, 2004b; Penna, 2005; Munro and Parton, 2007). In response, the government made a number of revisions and finally deleted any explicit reference to including information on the database in response to 'a cause for concern'. The *Explanatory Memorandum to the Children Act 2004 Information Database (England) Regulations 2007* (para.7.17), published in June 2007, replaced 'a cause for concern' by *indications,* where an indication would consist of:

- recording a universal service or the active involvement of a specialist/targeted service. A practitioner who is providing such services can be expected to hold information which could be important to another practitioner and which they may consider appropriate to share;
- recording the name of the nominated *Lead Professional* who is taking action to coordinate a response to a child's needs;
- recording when an assessment has been undertaken under the system known as the *Common Assessment Framework* (CAF) which indicates action taken and, potentially, information to share; and
- where the provision of a service has ceased and a decision is made to extend the period of retention beyond the one year minimum, this would indicate that the practitioner still, potentially, has information to share which they believe to be relevant and important to others.

Clearly, while posting an 'indication' on the database would still rely on professional judgement, the government was keen to be seen to be responding to the criticisms. As a result, the database was repackaged in May 2007 as *ContactPoint* and its *objectives* stated a little less ambitiously to:

- help practitioners identify quickly a child with whom they have contact, and whether that child is getting the universal services (education, primary health care) to which he or she is entitled;
- enable earlier identification of needs and earlier and more effective action to address these needs by providing a tool for practitioners to identify who else is involved with a particular child; and

- be an important tool to encourage and support better communication and closer working between different professionals and practitioners (DCSF, 2007c).

ContactPoint was presented as a key element of the *Every Child Matters: Change for Children* programme to transform children's services by aiming to support more effective prevention and early intervention. In particular, it would provide a tool to support better communication among authorized users across education, health, social care and youth offending. It aimed to provide a quick and cost effective way for practitioners to find out who else was working with the same child or young person, allow them to contact one another more effectively, thus making it easier to deliver more coordinated support and identify gaps in service provision, particularly of a universal nature. Because of the concerns about human rights issues and the security of the information, a complex process of managing access to and use of the system was to be established. Each local authority would need to establish a specialist team to support the ongoing migration, matching and cleansing of the data and provide technical support and advice for authorized users. Before being able to access ContactPoint all users would need security clearance (including enhanced Criminal Records Bureau clearance), a user name, PIN and security token. All ContactPoint users would complete mandatory training which would include components on the safe and secure use of ContactPoint and which would make explicit the importance of compliance with the Data Protection Act 1998 and the Human Rights Act 1998.

While it was to be a national system, the data would be partitioned into 150 parts, each relating to a local authority in England. The total set-up cost was £224m, costing £41m/annum to operate once fully established. It was estimated that £88m/annum would be saved to existing services, primarily as a result of the time saved by practitioners trying to identify and make contact with other professionals and services who knew the child concerned (Parton, 2008a).

ContactPoint was just one element of the *Every Child Matters: Change for Children* programme. However, even in its less ambitious form, it demonstrates the priority given to the importance of practitioners sharing information in order to provide a coordinated and integrated range of services to enhance prevention and early intervention. The accumulation and exchange of information about children has taken on a strategic role to ensure that children do not fall through the various 'nets' designed to protect them from harm and to ensure they receive early help and thereby fulfil their potential. In the words of Margaret Hodge, when she was Minister for Children, in her foreword to *Every Child Matters: Next Steps* (DfES, 2004b: 3), the vision was of 'a shift to prevention whilst strengthening protection'.

The role of the *lead professional, CAF* and this renewed emphasis upon *sharing information* were seen as key elements in the transformation and integration of children's services.

> Children and families are supported most effectively when CAF, the lead
> professional and information sharing procedures are planned and delivered
> in a co-ordinated way to offer integrated support across the continuum of
> needs and services (DfES, 2006d: para. 2.6).

and this was represented in Figure 3.7 above. That figure – the 'windscreen' –
demonstrates how the integration of universal, specialist and targeted services
has been conceptualized; the role that the *lead professional,* the CAF and *information sharing* will play; and how, in the process, children in the population will
be categorized into those with 'no identified needs', those with 'additional
needs' and those with 'complex needs'. Social workers and children's social care
are almost exclusively concerned with those on the far right of the 'windscreen';
however, the notion of 'a child in need' as defined by Section 17 of the Children
Act 1989 does not appear.

In addition, the electronic *Integrated Children's System* (ICS), which was
designed specifically for children's social care, would include the case records
and details of all children and families known to social workers whether they
were accommodated in care, on the child protection register, or a 'child in need'
(DH, 2003; Walker and Scott, 2004).

It is clear that the introduction of the ICS has posed major challenges for both
managers and front-line practitioners and it is unclear whether the benefits will
outweigh the major investment of time and resources it has taken to introduce
the system (Bell and Shaw, 2008; Cleaver et al., 2008; Parton, 2008b; Shaw and
Clayden, forthcoming).

All these changes were taking place at the same time as the introduction of
electronic records in all areas of social care (Information Policy Unit, 2003).
What is clear is that the gathering, storing, sharing and analysis of information,
particularly in electronic form, lay at the centre of the *ECM: Change for Children*
programme.

Conclusions

The changes introduced under the *Every Child Matters: Change for Children*
programme were clearly the most ambitious and radical since the Seebohm reor-
ganization of the early 1970s and were far more wide-ranging than anything ever
attempted in the history of children's services in England. In casting its gaze
upon all children to ensure that 'every child' achieved his or her potential and in
trying to integrate universal, targeted and specialist services there were considerable implications for everyone who worked with children and young people.
As one of us has argued elsewhere (Parton, 2006a,b), it pointed to a significant
shift in the relationships between children, parents, professionals and the state

and suggested we were witnessing the emergence of the 'preventive-surveillance state' (Parton, 2008a). The growing use of various electronic databases in relation to children has been identified as a key element in recent debates about how far England is becoming a 'surveillance society' (Surveillance Studies Network, 2006; House of Commons Home Affairs Committee, 2008).

As already indicated when discussing Figure 3.7 earlier, the role envisaged for children's social care was to work primarily with children and young people who had 'complex needs'. This was made explicit in *Every Child Matters: Change for Children in Social Care* (DfES, 2004c), published at the same time as *Every Child Matters: Change for Children:*

> Social workers and social care workers need to be at the heart of the Every Child Matters Change for Children programme. You play a central role in trying to improve outcomes for the most vulnerable through your work with children in need including those in need of protection, children who are looked after and disabled children. The aim of the programme is to achieve whole system-change to improve outcomes for all children but especially the most disadvantaged and vulnerable (DfES, 2004c: 2).

This was reinforced a little later on:

> As social workers and social care workers, you have a unique contribution to make in assessing and analysing information in order to make judgements about, for example, risks to a child's welfare or how best to promote the educational achievement of a child looked after by the Local Authority.
>
> In addition the legal responsibilities that social workers carry in relation to family law give you a distinct and vital role in safeguarding children from harm. These contributions made as part of a multi-disciplinary team whether based together, perhaps in a school-based service hub, or on a virtual basis will be central to the change programme. The changes do not mean a one size fits all approach or that we can all do each other's job (DfES, 2004c: 5).

The role for children's social work and children's social care was specific and clearly focused to the point where the aspirations that were clearly articulated in the Seebohm report had disappeared or been passed to others in the new arrangements. While social workers made up a small number of the total employed in social services departments, the Seebohm report envisaged that they would lie at the core and provide the professional face of the new departments. Beyond this, social workers would provide something of the professional glue that would pull departments together and provide the human and personalized dimension to the practice of welfare services more generally. However, in the newly configured children's services arrangements, social work was simply one of a range of roles to be carried out – it had neither a central nor a pre-eminent position and its focus was clearly with those children and young people deemed to be the most vulnerable because they were 'in need', 'in need of protection', 'looked after' and where they may be at risk of crossing the statutory threshold. While children's social work and social care had a vital and important role to play in the transformed world of the new integrated children's services, this was very different to the wide-ranging, community-based role envisaged in the Seebohm Report. These are issues we will return to in the third and concluding part of the book. In Part II we look more specifically at a range of areas where social workers have played a central role in work with children and young people. While their roles and responsibilities have changed, they continue to make an important contribution in these areas.

Part II

Different Service Areas

4

Safeguarding, Child Protection and Children in Need

As we noted in the previous chapter, with the changes being introduced by the *ECM: Change for Children* programme social workers were to play 'a distinct and vital role in safeguarding children from harm' (DfES, 2004b: 5). The notion of 'safeguarding' is closely related to ideas about child protection and trying to prevent child abuse, activities which the media and general public have closely associated with social workers for many years (Franklin and Parton, 1989, 2001). At the same time, however, 'safeguarding' tries to overcome some of the problems with child protection practice identified in research and public inquiries and attempts to reframe how the issue is conceived. In this chapter we will look at how the idea of 'safeguarding' has developed and, in particular, analyse how it is seen to relate to its sister ideas of 'child protection' and 'children in need'. In doing so, something of an irony becomes evident. For, as we discussed in Chapter 1, ever since the public inquiry into the death of Maria Colwell in 1973 (Secretary of State for Social Services, 1974) social workers have been heavily criticized for various failures in the area of child protection, and public inquiries have provided a key vehicle both for bringing about change and for undermining both the trust in social work and the role and aspirations articulated for it in the Seebohm report of 1968. However, while this has had the effect of both considerably reducing the aspirations and restricting the remit of social work, one of the few areas where social work and children's social care is seen as continuing to provide *the* key role and responsibility is in relation to child protection, now framed in terms of 'safeguarding and promoting' children's welfare. How this has come about and with what implications is a central theme of this chapter.

The Contemporary Child Protection System

In the wake of the tragic death of Maria Colwell and the subsequent public inquiry (Secretary of State for Social Services, 1974), a new system of child abuse management was inaugurated with the issue of a Department of Health and Social

Security circular (DHSS, 1974) and further refined in a series of circulars throughout the decade (DHSS, 1976a,b, 1978, 1980). The primary focus of the system was to ensure that a range of key professionals were familiar with the signs of child abuse and that mechanisms were established so that information was shared between them. Coordination between agencies and professionals in relation to particular children was seen as key for improving practice, and the roles of paediatricians, GPs, health visitors and the police were seen as vital. However, it was social service departments that were constituted as the 'lead agency' and local authority social workers who were identified as the primary statutory professionals for coordinating the work and operating the system.

There were a number of key elements. *Area Review Committees,* subsequently retitled *Area Child Protection Committees* (ACPCs) (DHSS, 1988), were established in all local authority areas as policy-making bodies in order to: coordinate the work of the relevant agencies; develop interprofessional training; and produce *detailed procedures* to be followed where it was felt a child had been abused or might be at risk of abuse. In such situations there was to be a system of *case conferences* so that the relevant professionals could share information about a particular child and family, make decisions on what to do and provide an ongoing mechanism for monitoring progress. Where it was felt a *child protection plan* was required the child would be placed on a *child protection register.* The register could then be consulted by other professionals to establish whether the child was currently known.

From 'The Protection of Children from Abuse' to the 'Safeguarding and Promotion of Children's Welfare'

Central government guidance on 'Working Together' was revised on two occasions during the 1990s. A brief comparison of the two documents clearly demonstrates how official thinking about the nature of the problem and the best way of addressing this changed significantly during the decade. The 1991 'Working Together' (Home Office et al., 1991) was published to coincide with the implementation of the Children Act 1989 and had many similarities to the version published at the time of the Cleveland Report (DHSS, 1998; Secretary of State for Social Services, 1988) and, following the aims of all the guidance since 1974, was framed in terms of responding to child abuse and improving the child protection system. This was very evident in the document's subtitle: *A Guide to Arrangements for Inter-Agency Co-operation for the Protection of Children from Abuse.* The emphasis was on the importance of maintaining a balance between protecting children from abuse and protecting the privacy of the family from unnecessary intrusion. While working in partnership with the parents and child was seen as important, the focus was 'children at risk of significant harm', such that the whole document was framed in terms of when and how to carry out an 'investigation' in terms of Section 47 of the Children Act 1989. The key 'threshold' criterion to be addressed was whether the child was 'suffering or likely to suffer significant harm' (s31(91)(9)). While the essential principles of the Children Act 1989 provided the legal framework, the focus of the child protection system was quite specific. For example:

> The starting point of the process is that any person who has knowledge of, or suspicion that a child is *suffering significant harm, or is at risk of suffering significant harm,* should refer their concern to one or more of the agencies with statutory *duties and/or powers to investigate or intervene* – the social services department, the police or the NSPCC (Home Office et al., 1991, para. 5.11.1, emphasis added).

There was no mention of any of the more wide-ranging preventive duties that local authorities had in terms of Section 17. The 1999 guidance was very different: *Working Together to Safeguard Children. A Guide to Inter-Agency Working to Safeguard and Promote the Welfare of Children* (DH et al., 1999). Not only was this the first time that the word 'safeguarding' was used in official guidance about child abuse but the subtitle explicitly framed the issue in terms of s17(1) of the Children Act.

The 1999 'Working Together' was revised in the light of *Child Protection: Messages from Research* (DH, 1995a), the 'refocusing' debate and the research on the implementation of the Children Act, particularly in relation to the difficulties that local authorities were having in developing their 'family support' services (DH, 2001), and was framed – as indicated in the subtitle – in terms of the general duty placed on local authorities by Section 17(1) of the Children Act 1989 'to safeguard and promote the welfare of children in their area who are in need'. The guidance underlined that local authorities had wider responsibilities than simply responding to concerns about 'significant harm' and was explicitly located in the wider agenda for children's services being implemented in the early years of the New Labour government. Social exclusion, domestic violence, the mental illness of a parent or carer, and drug and alcohol abuse (Cleaver et al., 1999) were all identified as 'sources of stress for children and families which might have a negative impact on a child's health, either directly, or because they affect the capacity of parents to respond to their child's needs' (DH et al., 1999, para. 2.19).

While the 1999 guidance continued to make it clear that if anyone believed that a child may be suffering 'significant harm' they should always refer these concerns to the social services department, it also stressed that these should be responded to by social services departments in the context of their much wider 'responsibilities towards all children whose health or development may be impaired without the provision of support and services, or who are disabled (described by the Children Act 1989 as children 'in need')' (para. 5.5). In order to develop this more integrated response a more differentiated and holistic approach to assessment was introduced.

The publication of the 1999 edition of 'Working Together' was combined with the publication of the *Framework for the Assessment of Children in Need and their Families* (DH et al., 2000a) and the two documents needed to be read and used together. The *Assessment Framework,* like 'Working Together', was issued as guidance under Section 7 of the Local Authority Social Services Act 1970, which meant that it 'must be followed' by local authority social services departments unless there were exceptional circumstances that justified a variation. It thus had the same legal status, and was incorporated into 'Working Together'. The *Assessment Framework* was supported by the publication of a range of other material which included: practice guidance (DH, 2000a); assessment record forms (DH and Cleaver, 2000); a family assessment pack of questionnaires and scales (DH et al., 2000b); a summary of studies which informed the development of the framework (DH, 2000b); and a training pack consisting of a video, guide and reader (NSPCC/University of Sheffield, 2000).

The *Assessment Framework* replaced the previous guidance on *Protecting Children: A Guide for Social Workers Undertaking a Comprehensive Assessment* (DH, 1988), which had only been concerned with comprehensive assessment for long-term planning where child abuse had been confirmed or strongly suspected. In contrast, the *Assessment Framework* moved the focus from the assessment of risk of child abuse and 'significant harm' to one which was concerned with the possible impairment to a child's development. Both the safeguarding and promotion of a child's welfare were seen as intimately connected aims for intervention, so that it was important that access to services was via a common assessment route. The critical task was to ascertain whether a child was 'in need' and how the child and the parents, in the context of their family and community environment, might be helped. The effectiveness with which a child's needs were assessed was seen as key to the effectiveness of subsequent actions and services and, ultimately, to the outcomes for the child. As Jenny Gray, who had the lead responsibility for developing the *Assessment Framework* at the Department of Health, argued, the framework:

> was developed on the understanding that assessing whether a child is in need and identifying the nature of this need requires a systematic approach which uses the same framework or conceptual map to gather and analyse information about all children and their families, but discriminates effectively between different types and levels of need (Gray, 2002: 176).

The framework explicitly built on the *Looking After Children* (LAC) system, which we discussed in Chapter 1, and was presented in terms of three dimensions: the child's developmental needs; parenting capacity (of both mother and father); and family and environmental factors. It was only by considering all three and the relationships between them that it would be possible to assess whether and in what ways a child's welfare was being safeguarded and promoted.

The different levels of assessment within the framework had different timescales attached to them. It was expected that within *one working day* of a *referral* to the social services department there would be a decision about what response was required. If it was felt that more information was required, this constituted an *initial assessment* and should be completed within *seven working days*. It should address the three dimensions of the *Assessment Framework* and thereby determine whether the child was 'in need', the nature of any services required, from where, within what timescales and whether a further, more detailed *core assessment* should be undertaken.

A *core assessment* was defined as an 'in depth assessment which addressed the central or most important aspects of the needs of a child and the capacity of his or her parents or caregivers to respond appropriately to these needs within the wider family and community context' (para. 3.11). The core assessment should be completed within a maximum of 35 days from the point that the initial assessment ended. While it had a much broader remit, it was seen as fulfilling a similar role to the original 'comprehensive assessment' (DH, 1988).

While primarily a practice tool for social services departments, the *Assessment Framework* also aimed to provide a common language, shared values and commitment amongst a much wider range of agencies and professionals. In addition, the framework would assist the development of 'an integrated children's system' (the ICS), which would provide the basis for a unified approach to collecting and producing management information data for central and local government departments.

Safeguarding: The Birth of an Idea

Thus, while the concept of 'safeguarding' was key to the Children Act 1989, particularly the rationale of Section 17, it was only in the 1999 'Working Together' that it was made central to government guidance in relation to child protection and child abuse. In many respects the importance of the concept was developed in response to the increasing concerns about the abuse of children in public care earlier in the decade, particularly in relation to the vetting and monitoring of staff as being suitable to work with children.

The term 'safeguarding' was introduced into the vocabulary of child protection in 1993 in a report produced by the Home Office, *Safe from harm: A code of practice for safeguarding the welfare of children in voluntary organisations in England and Wales* (Smith and Home Office, 1993), which was concerned with improving the checks voluntary organizations carried out on prospective staff and volunteers. However, it was the report by Sir William Utting (1997), *People Like Us,* often referred to as the *Safeguards Review,* which underlined the importance of the concept for public policy and practice. While the report was primarily concerned with policies and practices in relation to children living in public care, the notion of safeguarding was also seen as a minimum necessary requirement for ensuring every child's physical and emotional health, education and sound social development.

As we noted in Chapter 3, while the *ECM: Change for Children* programme had a complex genealogy, it was presented by government as its policy response to the Laming Report (2003) into the death of Victoria Climbié. It was also a response to a much less publicized, but equally significant, report produced by eight government inspectorates and published in October 2002: *Safeguarding Children: A Joint Inspectors' Report on Arrangements to Safeguard Children* (DH, 2002). The report had similar findings to those in the Laming report. Many services were found to be under pressure and experiencing major difficulties in recruiting and retaining skilled and experienced staff and, crucially, many of the safeguarding arrangements were seen as inadequate. Inter-agency cooperation was poor, there was confusion about when to share information, and there were few formal agreements between agencies as to how this could be done.

Significantly, the Department of Health report could find no clear and consistent definition of what *safeguarding* meant. The term had not been defined in law or government guidance. The concept had evolved from an initial concern about children and young people in public care to include the protection from harm of all children and young people and to cover all agencies working with children. For its purposes the report defined safeguarding to mean that:

- all agencies working with children, young people and their families take all reasonable measures to ensure that the *risks of harm to children's welfare* are minimised;
- where there are *concerns about children and young people's welfare,* all agencies take all appropriate actions to address those concerns, working to agreed local policies and procedures in full partnership with other local agencies (DH, 2002, para.1.5, emphasis added).

Such a definition clearly demonstrated that safeguarding had a much wider scope than earlier notions of child protection, and was the responsibility of a wide range of health, welfare and criminal justice agencies rather than simply that of social services departments.

Working Together to Safeguard Children: A Guide to Inter-agency Working to Safeguard and Promote the Welfare of Children (2006 version)

The most recent 'Working Together' was published in April 2006 (HM Government, 2006c) and had the same title as the previous version published in 1999. However, it was notable that it was authored by HM Government rather than by particular government departments, as previously. It very much built on the central principles and mechanisms established by the 1999 guidance but was updated to take account of the Laming and Joint Inspectors' reports, together with the changes being introduced by the *ECM: Change for Children* programme and the Children Act 2004. It was a lengthy and complex document and the longest 'Working Together' guidance ever produced, totalling 260 pages, being made up of 155 pages of 'statutory guidance', 75 pages of 'non-statutory practice guidance' and an executive summary and preface. While the guidance was said to underpin all of the ECM five outcomes, it was particularly linked to 'staying safe'.

A key element of the government's strategy was to strengthen the framework for single and multi-agency safeguarding practice. Under section 11 of the Children Act 2004 a statutory duty was placed on certain agencies (including the police, prisons and health bodies) to make arrangements to ensure that they had regard to the need to safeguard and promote the welfare of children. In addition, as from April 2006, local authorities were required to replace *Area Child Protection Committees* (ACPCs) with statutory *Local Safeguarding Children Boards* (LSCBs). The core membership of LSCBs was set out in the Children Act 2004 and was to include senior managers from different services, including the local authority, health bodies, the police, any secure training centre or prison in the area and other organizations as deemed appropriate.

The first eight chapters of the guidance made up the 'statutory guidance', while the remaining four chapters were presented as 'non-statutory practice guidance'. There were also six appendices. Not all managers and practitioners who had responsibilities for safeguarding and promoting the welfare of children were expected to read chapters that were 'not necessary under their job title'. However, for 'those with a particular responsibility for safeguarding children such as designated health and education professionals, police and social workers' (xxii) it was felt 'necessary' that they should read the eight chapters of 'statutory guidance' and 'advisable' to read the remaining chapters. In effect, social workers were expected to read the whole document.

The guidance was framed in terms of supporting *all* children and families in terms of the five outcomes that 'are key to children and young people's well-being' (para. 1.1):

> To achieve this, children need to feel loved and valued, and be supported by a network of reliable and affectionate relationships. If they are denied the opportunity and support they need to achieve these outcomes, children are at increased risk not only of an impoverished childhood, but of disadvantage and social exclusion in adulthood. Abuse and neglect pose particular problems (para. 1.2).

Good parenting was seen as key and early intervention by professionals vital if problems were not to get worse. 'Only in exceptional cases should there be compulsory intervention in family life: for example, where this is necessary to safeguard a child from significant harm' (para. 1.5).

The guidance was presented as part of 'an integrated approach'. Effective measures to safeguard children were seen as those which also promoted their welfare, and should not be seen in isolation from the wider range of support and services provided to meet the needs of all children and families. Safeguarding was explicitly located in the wider policy agenda on tackling social exclusion:

> Safeguarding and promoting the welfare of children – and in particular protecting them from significant harm – depends upon effective joint working between agencies and professionals that have different roles and expertise. Individual children, especially some of the most vulnerable children and *those at greatest risk of social exclusion,* will need coordinated help from health, education, children's social care, and quite possibly the voluntary sector and other agencies, including youth justice services (para. 1.14, emphasis added).

For the first time, the guidance provided a definition of 'safeguarding':

> *Safeguarding and promoting the welfare of children* is defined for the purposes of this guidance as:
> - protecting children from maltreatment;
> - preventing impairment of children's health or development; and
> - ensuring that children are growing up in circumstances consistent with the provision of safe and effective care;
>
> and undertaking that role so as to enable those children to have optimum life chances and to enter adulthood successfully (para. 1.18, original emphasis).

While protecting children from maltreatment was seen as important in order to prevent the impairment of health and development, on its own it was not sufficient to ensure that children were growing up in circumstances that ensured the provision of safe and effective care and that could bring about the five outcomes for all children. Child protection had a much narrower focus:

> *Child protection* is a part of safeguarding and promoting welfare. This refers to the activity which is undertaken to protect specific children who are suffering or at risk of suffering significant harm (para. 1.20, original emphasis).

While 'effective child protection' (para. 1.21) was deemed to be an *essential* part of the wider attempts to safeguard and promote the welfare of all children, all agencies and individuals should aim to *proactively* safeguard and promote the welfare of children so that the need for action to protect children from harm was reduced. Child protection was thus specifically related to attempts to assess and intervene in situations where children were suffering or were likely to suffer 'significant harm', and, as we will see, it was in this context that social workers had specific and statutory responsibilities. To keep such interventions to a minimum all agencies, whether universal or targeted, should engage in 'early intervention'. 'Significant harm' continued to provide the key 'threshold criteria' for compulsory intervention and was seen to constitute a sub-category of the overall local authority statutory duty to provide services for children 'in need' under section 17 of the Children Act 1989:

> Some children are in need because they are suffering or likely to suffer significant harm. The Children Act 1989 introduced the concept of significant harm as the threshold that justifies compulsory intervention in family life in the best interests of children, and gives local authorities a duty to make enquiries to decide whether they should take action to safeguard or promote the welfare of a child who is suffering, or likely to suffer significant harm (para.1.23).

The concepts of 'safeguarding and promoting the welfare of children', 'child protection' and 'children in need' were thus seen as intimately related. The way in which these should be operationalized in practice and how professionals should respond to wider 'child welfare concerns' was described in Chapter Five where the guidance described how individual cases should be managed. The chapter very much built on the 1999 'Working Together' (DH et al., 1999) and the *Assessment Framework* (DH et al., 2000a), together with the shorter guidance, *What to Do if You're Worried a Child is Being Abused* (DH et al., 2003), published in May 2003 following the publication of the Laming report.

Chapter 5:

> provides advice on what should happen if somebody has *concerns about the welfare of a child* (including those living away from home), and in particular *concerns that a child may be suffering, or may be at risk of suffering, significant harm.* It incorporates the guidance on information sharing and sets out the principles which underpin work to safeguard and promote the welfare of children (para. 5.1, emphasis added).

The focus is upon trying to differentiate different types and levels of *concern* about children and how these should be responded to. The different processes involved and the relationships between them were complex. What was very clear was that the role of local authority children's social care and the work of social workers were seen as crucial, for 'councils with LA children's social services functions have particular responsibilities towards all children whose health or development may be impaired without the provision of services, or who are disabled, defined in the Children Act 1989 as children "in need"' (para. 5.15). It was children's social care that had the major responsibility for clarifying the nature of *concerns* referred to them and whether and how the concerns might include concerns about child maltreatment. For:

> When a parent, professional, or another person contacts LA children's social care with concerns about a child's welfare, *it is the responsibility of LA children's social care to clarify with the referrer* (including self-referrals from children and families) *the nature of the concerns;* how and why they have arisen; and what appear to be the needs of the child and family. This process should always *identify clearly where there are concerns about maltreatment,* what is their foundation, and whether it may be necessary to consider taking urgent action to ensure the child(ren) are safe from harm (para. 5.31, emphasis added).

Professionals who contacted LA children's social care should confirm the referral within 48 hours, drawing on the *Common Assessment Framework* (CAF). At the end of any discussion both the referrer and LA children's social care should be clear about the proposed action, timescales and who would be doing what. Both parties should record the decision and the local authority should acknowledge the written referral within one working day of receiving it and, if the referrer had not received an acknowledgement within three working days, they should contact LA children's social care again. This was clearly to be a very formalized process of recording within specified timelines.

LA children's social care should then decide and record the next 'steps of action' within one working day. LA children's social care should consider whether the concerns required an 'initial assessment' to establish whether the child was 'in need'. Where it was decided to take no further action, feedback should be provided to the referrer. If consideration was to be given to discussing the case with another agency the parents' permission should be sought, unless doing so might place a child 'at increased risk of significant harm' (para. 5.34).

If no immediate action was required to protect the child, an 'initial assessment' should be carried out in the way outlined in the *Assessment Framework* and 'should be led by a qualified and experienced social worker' (para. 5.39). In the course of the initial assessment LA children's social care should ascertain:

- is this a child in need? (s17 Children Act 1989)
- is there reasonable cause to suspect that the child is suffering, or is likely to suffer, significant harm? (s47 Children Act 1989)

In doing so, however, it was not good enough to consider allocating resources only if the significant harm threshold criteria were substantiated, for the child may still be in need:

> The focus of the initial assessment should be the welfare of the child. It is important to remember that even if the reason for the referral was a

concern about abuse or neglect that is not subsequently substantiated, a family may still benefit from support and practical help to promote a child's health and development. When services are to be provided a child's plan should be developed based on the findings from the initial assessment and on any previous plans, for example, those made following the completion of a common assessment. *If the child's needs or circumstances are complex, a more in-depth core assessment under s17 of the Children Act 1989 will be required* in order to decide what other types of services are necessary to assist the child and family (para. 5.44, emphasis added).

Even if a child was assessed as being 'in need' the processes involved would then differ depending on whether 'significant harm or its likelihood' was suspected or not. Where it was not, 'family group conferences', where the responsibility for decision making was much more shared with the parents, were emphasized. Where, however, 'significant harm' was suspected, LA children's social care had a responsibility for carrying out a *core assessment under s47 of the Children Act 1989*. Again, the outcomes of a section 47 assessment might be that the concerns about 'significant harm' were substantiated, or not. Even where the concerns were substantiated, because of changing circumstances the child might no longer continue to be at risk of significant harm.

However, where the concerns were substantiated *and* the child was judged to be at continuing risk of significant harm, the key elements of the long-standing child protection system were seen to have continuing relevance. There was to be an initial child protection case conference, a child protection plan, a core group and a designated key worker. Not only should the key worker be 'a qualified and experienced social worker' but the responsibilities for managing and coordinating the system were located with LA children's social care.

Staying Safe

These developments became even clearer in mid-2007. One of the first things that Ed Balls did when becoming Minister at the new Department of Children, Schools and Families was to publish a consultation document on *Staying Safe* (DCSF, 2007d). It stated very clearly that:

For some, safeguarding may have a narrow definition, focused on protecting children from abuse and neglect. But *safeguarding used here covers a range of things we all need to do to keep children safe and promote their welfare* (DCSF, 2007d, para.1.9, emphasis added).

Safeguarding had a broad remit and was 'everybody's responsibility'. This was represented in the diagram in the document on the 'roles, responsibilities and principles for improving children's safety' (Table 4.1).

Table 4.1 Roles, responsibilities and principles for improving children's safety

Children and young people, parents and families

Know what acceptable/unacceptable behaviour towards children and young people is, how to identify and manage risk of harm (and, for parents, help their children do so), and whom to approach if they have concerns.

The **general public** help ensure children and young people are safe, including by their own behaviour, identify unacceptable behaviour by others towards children and act on any concerns.

Everyone **working with children and young people**, whether in paid employment or as volunteers, is alert to risks and indicators of harm and knows when and with whom to share information.

Children's social care	Police services	NHS organizations	Services for vulnerable adults	Other services
Act on child protection referrals, assess need, coordinate responses from local agencies to keep children safe and promote welfare	Identify and act on child protection concerns, carry out criminal investigations, enforce road traffic laws and help to prevent harm	Actively promote health and well-being of children, identify and work in partnership with agencies on safeguarding concerns, and provide timely, therapeutic and preventative interventions	Prisons, adult mental health, adult substance misuse, domestic violence intervention projects recognize the links between service users who are parents and risks to their children's safety, and safeguard children	Schools, including extended schools, FE colleges, housing, planners, parks/green spaces managers, road safety officers create a safe environment for children and young people, educate children and young people about how to keep themselves safe, and refer child protection concerns

We should create safe environments for all children and young people to help prevent harm, including employers checking the suitability of those who work with children – but take additional action for vulnerable groups of children. Services should intervene where necessary, in the most effective way, at the most effective point. Actions chosen should be proportionate to the needs of the child, the risk faced by children, and the impact they will have.

Local Safeguarding Children Boards and children's trusts

Lead the whole system locally including safe local environments, providing and promoting child protection training for service providers, safe roads, building effective partnerships, working within specific legislative frameworks, leading enquiries on specific cases and providing services for children in need.

Inspectorates

Ensure regulated services for children have effective child protection and safeguarding policies in place, and an ethos of safeguarding.

Central government

Formulate policy and lead on strategy to safeguard children and young people, ensure a clear national framework is in place, develop the legislative framework, raise awareness of the issues and responsibilities, support local implementation, review policy and performance through inspection, support research and allocate resources

Where it is more appropriate to work in partnership to address concerns, efforts will be co-ordinated across Government and local services, including the private and voluntary sectors where necessary. A culture of evaluation and learning will be embedded in all services. There is no excuse for abusing, exploiting or neglecting a child, whether suggested for cultural or religious reasons, or reasons of income or social exclusion.

Source: Government Consultation *'Staying Safe'* (DCSF, 2007d: 24).
[Crown Copyright, reprinted with permission. License # C02W000670.]

It is particularly interesting for our purposes to note that 'children's social care' was one of just a number of agencies and was positioned to the left of the diagram, and that its role is summarized as to 'act on child protection referrals, assess need, coordinate responses from local agencies to keep children safe *and* promote welfare'.

When *The Children's Plan* (DCSF, 2007b) and the *Comprehensive Spending Review* (CSR), which we will discuss in detail in Chapter 10, were published later in the year these developments were very clear. One of the 30 Public Service Agreements produced as part of the CSR was to 'improve children and young people's safety' and this was integrated with Chapter 2 of *The Children's Plan* entitled 'Safe and Sound'. Eleven areas were identified for new or additional action with various proposals for action. These were wide ranging and were represented in terms of 'universal', 'targeted' and 'responsive' safeguarding (Figure 4.1).

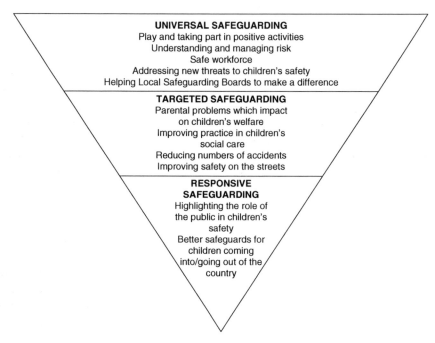

Fig. 4.1 Safeguarding in *The Children's Plan*
Source: The Children's Plan (DCSF, 2007b: 42).
[Crown Copyright, reprinted with permission. License # C02W000670.]

Just four 'indicators' were chosen to measure the success of the strategy:

• percentages of children who have experienced bullying;
• percentage of children referred to children's social care who received an initial assessment within seven working days;

- hospital admissions caused by unintentional and deliberate injuries to children and young people;
- preventable child deaths as recorded through child death review panel processes.

The second indicator is particularly interesting, for it was based on the premise that 'initial assessments', which take place after a child is referred to children's social care, were an important indicator of how quickly services could respond when a child was thought to be 'at risk of serious harm'. Children's social care was clearly identified as *the* child protection agency, and 'initial assessments' were seen as the key gateway or threshold. It was said that in 2007 average performance on the indicator was 68 per cent with a significant variance between authorities of 30 to 100 per cent.

Conclusion

What becomes clear is that while the new systems being set in place to safeguard and promote the welfare of children are far more complex and wide-ranging than the much narrower and forensically driven child protection system of the early 1990s, such a system still inhabits the core of the new arrangements. Similarly, it continues to be local authority children's social care and social workers who are given the lead responsibility for carrying out the key assessment tasks in relation to who may be a child 'in need' and which children may be suffering 'significant harm'. It is 'experienced and qualified social workers' who are given the key responsibilities for decision making at the points of referral, initial assessment and core assessment and who operationalize and coordinate responses under both s17 and s47 of the Children Act 1989. As one of us argued nearly 20 years ago, it is social workers who are given the key role in deciding whether a child is safe or not and negotiating the boundaries between, and respective responsibilities of, the state and parents, particularly where compulsory intervention is being considered into the privacy of the family (Parton, 1991). As we pointed out in the introduction to this chapter, while the *ECM: Change for Children* programme is very ambitious and aims to transform children's services in the light of both research and a range of criticisms from public inquiries, social workers and LA children's social care continue to play the key role in relation to the statutory responsibilities of the state and the specific operation of the child protection system.

Beyond this, however, it seems that many of the principles, systems and processes of the child protection system have been taken up, developed and applied to a much wider proportion of the child population and to those who have responsibilities for them, whether these be parents or other health, welfare and educational professionals. The importance of inter-agency coordination, multidisciplinary work, early intervention and prevention, the 'lead professional' and the sharing of information are now seen as providing the key elements for the transformation of children's services, not just in the operation of the more narrowly focused child protection system but across the continuum of children's services. In many ways, the formalized approaches which have been developed in relation to child protection for over thirty years are now being applied to all children's services. In the process, the mechanisms whereby these various elements will be integrated have become much more complex, and considerable reliance is being placed on new information and communication technologies (ICTs) to make them work.

Not only are such systems aimed to improve and integrate the work of front-line practitioners, but also to provide aggregate data so that the nature of the work can be measured, planned and managed. For example, up until 1988 the only statistics which local authorities were required to collate and return to central government were the annual statistics on the number of children in public care and the nature of that care. After 1988, national statistics were also required concerning children on child protection registers (Corby, 1990). Since 2001, annual statistics have also been collated and published in relation to children 'in need', referrals to social services departments, initial assessments and core assessments. Reviewing these provides a helpful oversight of the nature of the work being carried out by children's social workers and children's social care.

The first point to note is that at any one time the number of children being dealt with by children's social care who are either 'looked after' or on a 'child protection register' make up a relatively small minority of the number of children they are working with and have responsibility for. Figure 4.2 shows that while at any time around 60,000 children are 'looked after' and 26,000 are on a 'child protection register', this is out of a total of 'children in need' of over 385,000. This is not to say that there are not important differentials in the way resources and social work effort and time are allocated, as it is clear that the former two categories are by far the most demanding. However, it is important to recognize that these children make up something less than 20 per cent of the total children for which children's social care attempts to provide a service.

These issues are illustrated further in Figure 4.3, where we have a schematic summary of the nature and distribution of the work over a year, together with the key components of the different processes involved. What is demonstrated is that a major system has been established which aims to filter and categorize cases at key points. From a starting point of 596,300 referrals to children's social care during a year, just 31,500 children are ever entered onto a child protection register. Clearly, only a minority of the initial referrals would explicitly state child protection concerns but it does show that fewer than one in 18, or six per cent, of referrals ever find their way onto a register. A considerable amount of work is

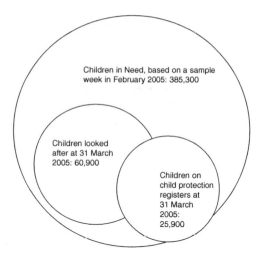

Fig. 4.2 Numbers of children in need, children who are looked after, and children who are on child protection registers in England, and the relationship between them
Note: Total 'Children in Need' includes 151,600 open cases which involved no social services activity in census week. The total for children looked after excludes those subject to an agreed series of short-term placements ('respite care'). The total on the child protection registers includes 310 unborn children.
[Crown Copyright, reprinted with permission. License # C02W000670.]

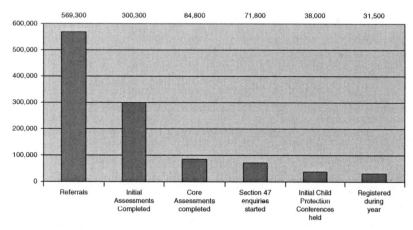

Fig. 4.3 Children in each stage of the referral and assessment procedure, year ending 31 March 2006
Source: Referrals, Assessments and Children and Young People who are subject of a Child Protection Plan or on Child Protection Registers, England, for year ending 31 March 2006.
[Crown Copyright, reprinted with permission. License # C02W000670.]

invested into managing such a demanding and complex decision-making system to ensure that children are safeguarded and their needs met. The decision-making process itself is demanding of resources and professional judgement.

Table 4.2 summarizes how the picture seems to have changed in recent years. It suggests that while the number of referrals to children's social care show a small and uneven decline between 2003 and 2007, the number of initial and core assessments carried out shows a steady increase. The number of referrals where there is no formal assessment activity has been going down. Similarly, the number of child protection registrations has increased slightly.

Finally, when we look at the national statistics on the categories of abuse on child protection registers, a very interesting trend emerges. In Table 4.3 and Figure 4.4 we include alternate years 1994–2006 plus 2007 as these are the most recent figures. The salient points are as follows:

1)   The absolute and percentage increase in neglect registrations from 7,800 (27 per cent) in 1994 to 14,800 (45 per cent) in 2007.

2)   A noticeable, though not as dramatic, increase in emotional abuse registrations from 3,500 (12 per cent) in 1994 to 7,800 (23 per cent) in 2007.

3)   A significant decline in physical abuse registrations from 11,400 (40 per cent) in 1994 to 5,100 (15 per cent) in 2007.

4)   An even more significant decline in sexual abuse registrations from 7,500 (26 per cent) in 1994 to 2,500 (7 per cent) in 2007.

5)   Putting these figures together, registrations for neglect and emotional abuse accounted for 11,300 registrations (39 per cent of total) in 1994 but 22,600 (68 per cent of total) in 2007.

Table 4.2 Children in each stage of the referral and assessment procedure, 2003-07[1]

	Numbers				
	2003	**2004**	**2005**	**2006**	**2007**
Referrals of children to SSDs	570,200	572,700	552,000	569,300	545,000
Initial assessments completed	263,900	290,800	290,300	300,200	305,000
Core assessments completed	55,700	63,600	74,100	84,800	93,400
Registered during the year	30,200	31,000	30,70	31,500	33,300

[1] Year ending 31 March.
Source: Referrals, Assessments and Children and Young People who are subject of a Child Protection Plan or are on Child Protection Registers, England, for year ending 31 March. Issued by Department for Children, Schools and Families, 20 September 2007, SFR28/2007. [Crown Copyright, reprinted with permission. License # C02W000670.]

Table 4.3 Registrations to Child Protection Registers during alternate years ending 31 March 1994 to 2006, by category of abuse, in England

Category of Abuse	Numbers (%)							
	1994	1996	1998	2000	2002	2004	2006	2007
Neglect	7,800 (27%)	9,400 (33%)	11,600 (39%)	14,000 (46%)	10,800 (39%)	12,600 (41%)	13,700 (43%)	14,800 (45%)
Physical abuse	11,400 (40%)	10,700 (38%)	9,900 (33%)	8,700 (29%)	5,300 (19%)	5,700 (19%)	5,100 (16%)	5,100 (15%)
Sexual abuse	7,500 (26%)	6,200 (22%)	6,100 (20%)	5,600 (18%)	2,800 (10%)	2,800 (9%)	2,600 (8%)	2,500 (7%)
Emotional abuse	3,500 (12%)	4,000 (14%)	4,800 (16%)	5,500 (18%)	4,700 (17%)	5,600 (18%)	6,700 (21%)	7,800 (23%)
Mixed/Not recommended by *Working Together*	500 (2%)	400 (1%)	700 (3%)	310 (1%)	4,100 (15%)	4,300 (14%)	3,300 (11%)	3,200 (10%)

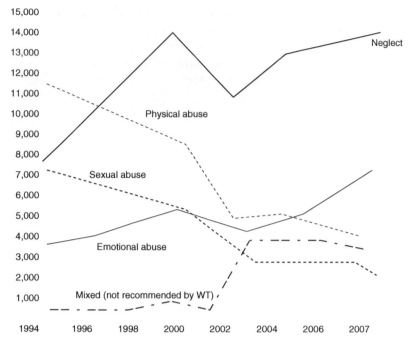

Fig. 4.4 Registrations to Child Protection Registers (alternate years) ending 31 March 1994–2007, by category of abuse, in England
[Crown Copyright, reprinted with permission. License # C02W000670.]

6)   On the other hand, physical and sexual abuse registrations accounted for 18,900 registrations (66 per cent of the total) in 1994 but 7,600 (22 per cent of total) in 2007.

These are significant changes over a 13-year period. For whatever reasons, they suggest that it is now neglect and emotional abuse which are posing the major challenges for professionals in a way that was not the case in the mid-1990s. One might anticipate that this could be a major priority for the newly established Local Children's Safeguarding Boards. If LCSBs have responsibilities for trying to 'prevent the impairment of children's health or development' rather than only 'protecting children from maltreatment', the issue of child neglect moves centre stage. In doing so the need for a range of health, welfare, education and criminal agencies to work together is underlined. Issues around thresholds and how these are operationalized consistently take on a particular significance, especially where there is an expectation that agencies work together to assess and respond to children with both 'additional' and 'complex' needs.

While much of the difficult history of children's social care over the last 35 years has been intimately connected with concerns about failures to respond appropriately to cases of child abuse, particularly where physical and sexual abuse are concerned, it now seems that in the new world of 'safeguarding' it is child neglect and emotional abuse that are posing the major challenges.

5

Youth Offending: Early Intervention, Prevention and Tough Enforcement

One of the areas where the tensions and contradictions in relation to transforming children's services have become most apparent is with policies in relation to 'youth offending'. The purpose of this chapter is to critically review contemporary developments in policy and practice in this area and assess how far they are consistent with the aims and philosophies that underpin the *ECM: Change for Children* programme. In the process it will become apparent that over the past thirty years official conceptions of and responses to youth offending have been subject to considerable change. From the mid-1990s policy and practice have been framed almost exclusively in terms of responding to criminality rather than responding to the welfare of the child, such that the role of children's social work and social care more generally has become of almost residual significance.

While *ECM: Change for Children* and the Children Act 2004 provided for the possibility that Youth Offending teams could be included as part of the integrated Children's Trusts arrangements, this was very much left to local areas to decide. *Every Child Matters: Next Steps* (DfES, 2004b) acknowledged that there was a real danger that youth justice was in peril of being detached from children's services. In particular, the document was concerned that the 'welfare of the child' would not be an integral part of the Youth Justice system and that 'young offenders' would be seen differently from those with other social care needs (DfES, 2004b: 9).

Such concerns were clearly well founded in the light of *Youth Justice – The Next Steps* (Home Office, 2003), published at the same time as *Every Child Matters* (Chief Secretary to the Treasury, 2003). For, while presented as companion documents, they were quite different. The 'basic approach' outlined in *Youth Justice – The Next Steps* was to 'operate a distinct youth justice system broadly on present lines, with a clear and visible response to offending behaviour from age 10 onwards' (HO, 2003: 3). While there was clearly no attempt to see the welfare of children as a central consideration, it was offending behaviour that was the overriding concern.

For example, while:

> Currently the sentencing of young people is subject to several different statutory aims and principles – preventing offending, taking account of welfare and just deserts. *We now propose a single main sentencing purpose of preventing offending* (HO, 2003: 4, emphasis added).

The only time a child's welfare was mentioned was in relation to the need to improve protection for children in custody, which was particularly ironic, as we will see below, in the light of the increased numbers of children and young people who were being incarcerated.

While it would be incorrect to argue that all concerns with the welfare of children and young people in trouble have disappeared (Smith, 1999, 2003), there is no doubt that since the mid-1990s the emphasis in policy and practice has been heavily tilted towards control, regulation, correction, punishment and the prevention of offending. Such changes sit very uncomfortably with the principles of the Children Act 1989, particularly the focus on providing services to children 'in need' (Goldson, 2000) and the emphasis on partnership, negotiation and focusing on the 'welfare' of the child – principles which have been taken further with the *Every Child Matters: Change for Children* programme's focus on children's 'well-being' and its requirement that all agencies should prioritize the safeguarding and promotion of the welfare of the child. How this situation came about and with what implications is the prime focus of this chapter. In conclusion, however, we will note that the establishment of the Department of Children, Schools and Families in the summer of 2007 and the publication of *The Children's Plan* in December 2007 and the *Youth Crime Action Plan* in July 2008 suggested that the issues might be addressed somewhat differently.

The Children and Young Person's Act 1969

In Chapter 1 we briefly outlined the thinking that informed the establishment of social services departments and how this was significantly informed by the need to establish a unified 'family service' which would take a major role in relation to 'children in trouble', based on a welfare approach and where local authority social workers would play a central role. In order to understand how policy and practice in relation to young offenders in the subsequent forty years has developed, it is important to say a little more about developments in the 1960s.

The Labour government of 1964–70 had considerable optimism that the twin pillars of state welfare and professional expertise could overcome a range of social problems. More particularly, youth offending was conceived in terms of a number of social and familial deprivations and it was felt important to move away from a more traditional punitive approach to one that tried to address the underlying needs of children and families via a more explicitly welfare set of responses. The influential Longford Committee (1964) clearly identified the causes of youth crime in family or other personal or social problems and this formed the basis for the White Paper, *The Child, the Family and the Young Offender* (HO, 1965), which argued for the need for a new local authority 'family service' to take responsibility for providing a broad-based welfare approach in relation to young offenders. From this the Seebohm Committee (1968) was established and this provided the basis for the Local Authority Social Services Act 1970, which in turn established social services departments the following year.

The Child, the Family and the Young Offender was subject to criticism, particularly from magistrates and the Home Office, which led to a certain watering down of some of the proposals in a second White Paper, *Children in Trouble* (HO, 1968). During the passage of the Children and Young Persons Act 1969 there were further concessions to conservative interests (Bottoms, 1974), in particular in retaining the key role of the courts.

However, the Children and Young Persons Act 1969 provided for a quite radical departure in how to deal with young offenders. This was most evident in relation to children aged under 14. The central feature was the idea of 'care proceedings', a civil procedure that required two separate criteria to be met before the juvenile court could make an order. The first criterion, the 'primary condition', required establishing one of a number of factual situations, including: parental neglect; the child being beyond control; school truancy; or *the commission of an offence*. The second criterion (the 'care/control' test) required the court to be satisfied that the child was 'in need of care or control which he is unlikely to receive unless the court makes an order' (Sec.1(2)), taking into account his/her welfare needs. On its own, therefore, proving the offence alone, as the 'primary condition', was not sufficient for making an order. Only in cases of homicide could children under 14 be subject to criminal prosecution.

With the 1969 Act it was intended that the two main orders would be either the supervision order or the care order and both were to apply in both offence-based and non-offence-based cases. The effect of the care order would be to give the local authority social services department most of the legal powers of a parent over the child. Unless discharged, a care order would last until the child's 18th birthday, and the child could be placed by the local authority wherever it saw fit, including being returned home.

For young people aged 14–17 the intention of the Act for those who had committed offences would normally be that they would be dealt with in care proceedings, and a criminal prosecution would be possible only in certain restricted cases. After a successful prosecution, the juvenile court could continue to impose one of a range of long-standing sentences such as a fine or an attendance centre order. However, a care order would also be available as a disposal following criminal as well as care proceedings. While custodial sentences in prison establishments were initially to be retained, the plan was that these would be phased out in favour of care orders and the use of new welfare-oriented 'community homes'.

However, in 1970, a newly elected Conservative government immediately introduced changes which meant the legislation was never fully implemented. Care proceedings in offence-based cases were to be allowed, but only if the police wished to use them, and criminal prosecutions were to continue to be permitted for all groups above the age of criminal responsibility. As a result, care proceedings were effectively confined to non-offence cases, though both care and criminal proceedings would continue to be dealt with in the same juvenile court. In addition, the intention to phase out custodial sentences for older juveniles was initially postponed and eventually abandoned.

The original intentions of the legislation were thus thoroughly compromised, with the effect that a series of new 'welfare' disposals were provided in addition to (and not instead of) the more traditional custodial system. In the process the care order and the activities of social workers and social services departments became the focus of considerable controversy during the 1970s.

Juvenile court magistrates were particularly critical. The main order that the care order replaced was the 'approved school order', whereby a juvenile court could send a young offender to a reform school for an indeterminate period of up to three years. Unlike the approved school order, the care order did not guarantee a placement in an institution as the local authority had full discretion as to where the child was placed. While it was suggested the numbers were exaggerated (Zander, 1975), it was increasingly claimed that children were being returned home when the magistrate's clear intention was that they should be placed in an institutional setting. As a result, during the 1970s there was a significant decline in the use of the care order in offence-based cases, while custodial sentences for older juveniles increased (Bottoms and Dignan, 2004). For example, detention centre orders increased from 2,228 in 1969 to 5,757 in 1977.

At the same time, while the use of the 'offence-based' care order declined there was evidence that it was being used inappropriately. Research suggested that care orders after criminal proceedings were being made primarily on the basis of recommendations from social workers rather than being used as a remedy of last resort, as had been the case with the approved school order, and were being used for first offenders because they had welfare needs (Giller and Morris, 1981; Rutter and Giller, 1983). As a result, numerous commentators argued that using a welfare response for young offenders was in great danger of employing disproportionate and overly interventionist responses which failed to recognize the rights of young people and undermined the operation of a fair juvenile *justice* system (Taylor et al., 1980; Morris et al., 1980).

An important element of the 1969 Act was the introduction of 'intermediate treatment' (IT), which was intended to provide interventions that were somewhere between full residential care and ordinary supervision in the community.

Intermediate treatment could be a requirement of a supervision order and thereby act as an alternative to care. However, the idea and practice of IT was used much more widely as a preventive measure for children who might be 'at risk' of offending (Bottoms et al., 1990).

David Thorpe and his colleagues at Lancaster University (Thorpe et al., 1980) developed a stringent critique of these preventive uses of IT. Two particular unintended consequences were identified: it encouraged 'net-widening' as young people on the fringes of trouble were being drawn into the formal state juvenile justice system; and secondly, it had the impact of pushing cases 'up-tariff', for courts were more likely to impose an institutional disposal in cases where 'preventive' IT had been previously used and seen to fail. Thorpe et al. argued that to avoid these consequences preventive IT should no longer be offered and that only an offence should warrant an IT intervention. But also, where an offence had been committed, the minimum possible intervention should be argued for in order to avoid future custody and residential care.

The 'Juvenile Justice' Movement

By the early 1980s, therefore, some major critiques had developed, from quite diverse constituencies, that the compromised welfare orientation of the 1969 Act was not simply 'not working' but had some serious negative consequences for children and young people. As a result, the 1980s witnessed a major practice development framed in terms of 'juvenile justice', which was to prove both influential and, according to certain criteria, effective. There was a particular emphasis on the need to 'divert' young people from the formal criminal justice system and to use IT as a clear and rigorous alternative to care/custody, as opposed to an early intervention or preventive measure. There was 'a commitment to minimum intervention', a 'systems management' perspective and an orientation towards dealing with 'offences' rather than 'offenders' (Smith, 2007: 11). A key assumption was that most young offenders would 'grow out' of such behaviour (Rutherford, 1992). The approach emphasized the importance of using the 'caution' as a way of dealing with minor offences, and the growth in its use from the late 1970s to the early 1990s was paralleled by a decline in the number of known juvenile offenders, the use of prosecutions and the custody rate.

> With the exception of 14–17 year-old girls or young women, the official figures show a clear reduction in the number of young people being formally processed by the justice system over this period. While part of the reason for the fall in known juvenile offenders was demographic, the rate of known juvenile offenders per 100,000 of the population could also be seen to be falling, with the period 1980–90 showing a 16% decline.

In addition, the proportion of all detected offences attributed to juveniles fell, from 32% in 1980 to 20% in 1991 (Smith, 2007: 17).

While in many respects the approach was not consistent with the tough 'law and order' approach of the Thatcher government, it was consistent with the government's wish to cut public expenditure, including expensive residential and custodial accommodation. It was also consistent with a government that was ideologically committed to 'rolling back the state' and reserving its functions for where there was clear evidence of serious, particularly violent, crime.

A major organizational consequence was to establish 'juvenile justice' teams as a separate specialism within social service departments. In the process there was often a quite distinct philosophical and cultural as well as an organizational separation between the 'offence-focused' juvenile justice specialists and the more traditional 'needs-based' orientation of the area teams who took the major responsibility for the mainstream child care and child protection work of the departments.

This separation between juvenile justice and child welfare was reinforced by changes introduced by the Children Act 1989. By 1989 care orders were very rarely used in criminal cases and the 1989 Act abandoned the option altogether. It was also decided to separate the long-standing dual crime and care jurisdictions of the juvenile court. In the future 'care' cases would be dealt with by the 'family proceedings court', so that the juvenile court would become exclusively a criminal court. Following the Criminal Justice Act 1991, the latter was renamed the 'youth court' and given a higher upper age of eighteen rather than seventeen for initial jurisdiction.

The official statistics certainly suggested that the aims of diversion and minimal formal intervention were successful. There was a particular emphasis on the importance of 'managing' the local juvenile justice 'system', sometimes at the cost of direct work with the children and young people and their families, and there was not always an investment in developing *positive* alternatives to offending behaviour (Haines and Drakeford, 1998). While the picture varied around the country, there was a real danger that the focus on justice, due process and keeping children out of the 'system' would mean the approach would be open to considerable attack if the policy and political context were to change. This is precisely what happened during the 1990s.

The Birth of 'Authoritarian Populism'

While one of the arguments in favour of the 'juvenile justice movement' was that an inappropriate focus upon welfare concerns had contributed to the growth of a more interventionist form of practice which contributed to more young people being incarcerated in the 1970s, it has also been argued that the decline in concerns with the social and environmental factors associated with offending behaviour via the 'juvenile justice movement' contributed to the punitive backlash of the 1990s (Haines and Drakeford, 1998). Beginning with official concerns about the urban 'riots' of 1991, the early 1990s witnessed a clear change in the political climate and responses to issues about law and order, particularly in relation to youth offending. There was a sudden upsurge in political and media concern about 'persistent young offenders' (Hagell and Newburn, 1994), and the requirement to focus almost exclusively on the current offence in the Criminal Justice Act 1991 meant that it was more difficult to deal more 'severely' with repeated offending.

However, it was the abduction and murder of two-year-old Jamie Bulger in February 1993 by two 10-year-old boys, Jon Venables and Robert Thompson, which prompted a huge media and political response. As Franklin and Petley (1996) have argued, the media and political responses had the effect of 'killing the age of innocence', for media coverage signalled a phenomenon with a significance that extended beyond the tragic death of an individual child; the case helped ventilate a political backlash characterized as 'authoritarian populism' (Bottoms, 1995). The immediate policy response was 'back to basics', which was summarized by the injunction of the Prime Minister, John Major, that 'we should understand a little less and condemn a little more', and the announcement by the Home Secretary, Michael Howard, to the 1994 Conservative Party conference, of a new law and order package which had at its core the pronouncement that 'prison works'. In the wake of the Bulger case, politicians were keen to address public and media anxieties with the promise of ever tougher legislation to police a generation of children and young people who were 'out of control'. The issue of crime, particularly youth crime (Pitts, 2001, 2003), became a major political issue.

As we have noted in both Chapters 1 and 2, we can also trace the origins of the New Labour project for reforming the welfare state and remodelling society to the notion of being 'tough on crime and tough on the causes of crime', which was developed in the wake of the death of Jamie Bulger (Jordan, 1999). The phrase was first coined by Tony Blair soon after he became Shadow Home Secretary in 1993 (Blair, 1993) and had the effect of seizing the political initiative on law and order from the Conservative government. It signalled that if/when New Labour was elected it would quickly introduce new legislation and policies in relation to crime and youth offending in particular.

The Post-1997 Youth Justice System

New Labour came to power in May 1997 and reform of the English youth justice system was one of its key priorities (Bottoms and Dignan, 2004; Gelsthorpe, 2002). There was considerable similarity between New Labour's pre-election consultation document, *Tackling Youth Crime: Reforming Youth Justice* (Labour Party, 1996) and the Audit Commission's influential report, *Misspent Youth* (Audit Commission, 1996), in terms of both the issues covered and the proposals for reform. The Audit Commission report had little positive to say about the youth justice system. It argued that little constructive work was being done with the majority of young offenders apprehended by the police. Three-fifths received a caution without any intervention, and many court proceedings ended in a discharge. It also suggested that too much money was being spent on procedural matters, such as repeated court appearances before a final disposal, instead of concentrating on trying to reduce future offending. The system was seen as uneconomic, inefficient and ineffective and there was a lack of coordination between the agencies.

There was a clear rejection of the 'minimum intervention' approach espoused by the 'juvenile justice movement'. While the system needed to be streamlined and speeded up, there also needed to be better cooperation between the youth justice agencies and greater attention given to early preventive work. The approach was heavily influenced by the research and arguments we discussed in Chapter 1 in terms of the importance of 'early childhood intervention' in order to address the early signs of problems so that anti-social behaviour and youth crime could be prevented. It was argued that the results of longitudinal criminological research had identified the 'risk factors' associated with offending by juveniles (Farrington, 1996; Utting et al., 1993), such that the factors could be used to identify particular areas, families and/or children at particular risk and then interventions targeted to reduce future offending. In addition, both the Audit Commission and Labour Party documents were located within a strong managerialist framework. As Morgan and Newburn (2007) have argued, the analysis and proposals

> were heavily managerialist in approach, emphasizing inter-agency cooperation, the necessity of an overall strategic plan, the creation of key performance indicators, and active monitoring of aggregate information about the system and its functioning. To a youth justice system that had been the site of competing philosophies, approaches and ideologies – notably welfarism, punitiveness, and systems management – New Labour added a further dose of managerialism, together with its own potent blend of communitarianism and populism (Morgan and Newburn, 2007: 1032).

The Crime and Disorder Act 1998 provided the centrepiece of New Labour's approach to youth offending. The new principal aim of the youth justice system was 'to prevent offending by children and young people' (Sec. 37). However, despite the strong research evidence of the extent of family and social problems amongst young offenders, the government's 1997 White Paper, *No More Excuses: A New Approach to Tackling Youth Crime in England and Wales*

(HO, 1997) made virtually no reference to the child welfare system – the focus was upon the prevention of reoffending by young people who had already offended.

The legislation created a new organizational framework, presided over by the national Youth Justice Board (YJB), and each local authority had to establish a new local multi-agency Youth Offending Team (YOT) to coordinate the delivery of youth justice services in its area. Each YOT had to include, as a minimum, a police officer, a probation officer, a local authority social worker, a health authority worker and someone seconded by the education department. While the composition of YOTs was deliberately framed to take a wide view of offending and its prevention, including both health and education issues, and thus required some consideration of both 'justice' and 'welfare', YOTs differed significantly from the pre-1998 juvenile justice teams. In particular, while the latter comprised almost exclusively social workers, though often with seconded probation officers, and were located within social service departments, YOTs were very different. Not only were they explicitly required to be multidisciplinary, they were located outside of social services departments and reported directly to local authority chief executives. YOTs were established not to divert but to target and intervene. Local youth justice plans have been strongly influenced by the performance framework developed by the YJB and the Home Office and it is the Home Office that provides the bulk of the YJB's budget.

An important feature of the post-1997 reforms was a 'stepwise' approach to reoffending, sometimes called the 'automaticity principle'. The old cautioning scheme was abolished and replaced by a new system of pre-court reprimands and warnings. The scheme previously used by some police areas of using informal warnings was to be restricted to 'non-recordable' (very minor) offences (HO, 1999). Under the new scheme, for a first minor offence a formal reprimand would be recorded, while for a second offence (or a first offence that was relatively serious but did not require a prosecution) a final warning would be given. With a final warning the young offender had to be referred to the YOT, who would consider a 'change package', with the expectation that the package would normally be part of the final warning approach. On the commission of a further offence in the two years after a final warning, the scheme required the offender to be prosecuted.

On a first appearance in the youth court, following the Youth Justice and Criminal Evidence Act 1999, a young offender would be given a 'Referral Order', unless the offence was very minor or very serious. This involved referral to a separate and more informal 'Youth Offending Panel', consisting of lay community representatives, with the victim invited to participate. The expectation was that an 'offending behaviour contract' would be entered into whereby a package was constructed to reduce the likelihood of reoffending (Newburn et al., 2002). The referral order was intended as a version of 'restorative justice' with an emphasis on young offenders making amends to their victims for the offence committed (Crawford and Newburn, 2003). For second and subsequent offences dealt with at court, the offender could be given a community or custodial sentence. The 'automaticity principle' thus anticipated that offences by juveniles would trigger a sequence of particular criminal justice responses. As a result the room for the discretionary consideration of welfare needs in individual cases would be strictly limited.

However, while the new system was to be much more formalized, other measures were introduced both 'upstream' and 'downstream' of reprimands and final warnings to try and prevent up-tariff responses. The YJB developed several early prevention schemes, to be operated by YOTs, to try and mitigate crime and anti-social behaviour and generally prevent offending and criminalization. These have included:

- *Youth Inclusion and Support Panels* (YISPs), comprising representatives of police, education, social services and YOTs to work with 8–13-year-olds identified as being at risk of offending. The aim was to support young people and their families in accessing mainstream services in order to address the factors that put them at risk of offending.
- *Youth Inclusion Programmes* (YIPs) aimed to engage the 50 young people in an area whom the key agencies identified as most at risk of offending, and involve them in positive activities such as offending behaviour programmes and improved access to services, particularly education, in order to address the factors in their lives which placed them at risk of offending.
- *Parenting Programmes*, usually voluntary and often as an adjunct to YISPs and YIPs, but also via Parenting Contracts and Parenting Orders, the latter established by Sec. 8 of the 1998 Act.
- *Safer School Partnerships,* whereby the police are attached to schools to try to reduce both crime and victimization and thereby make the school and its environment more safe and secure and reduce truancy and exclusion, both of which were seen as key factors associated with offending.

While such schemes were designed to improve the prevention of offending, all were controversial as they could be seen to increase both the stigmatization of the children and families involved and to widen the net of the criminal justice system.

Not only did the 1998 Act widen the net of offender prevention strategies, it also introduced a number of orders for circumstances where there was no requirement for either the commission or prosecution of a criminal offence. These included the child safety order, the local child curfew and the antisocial behaviour order (ASBO). In addition, and partly spurred on by the Bulger case, *doli incapax* – the common law assumption that a child aged 10–13 does not know the difference between right and wrong and therefore could not be convicted – was abolished. Taken together, these measures have placed England and

Wales considerably out of step with most jurisdictions in the rest of Europe and have been subject to considerable criticism by civil liberty, human rights and child welfare organizations (see, for example, European Commissioner for Human Rights, 2005; Commission on Families and the Wellbeing of Children, 2005; Goldson and Muncie, 2006). Such developments demonstrated that the government was not simply concerned with trying to enhance the prevention of offending based on research evidence about 'what works' but was also keen to be seen as responding to popular and media concerns about 'law and order' and, particularly, that parents and children should take their responsibilities seriously. There has been a strong moralizing dimension to policy.

This is well illustrated in relation to the use of the ASBO. As a result of the 1998 Act applications for ASBOs could be made by social landlords as well as the police and local authorities. Anti-Social Behaviour (ASB) was defined as 'a matter that caused or was likely to cause harassment, alarm or distress to one or more persons not of the same household'. ASBOs last for a minimum of two years and comprise prohibitions deemed necessary to protect people within the area from further ASB. However, while it was a civil order that required a civil burden of proof (on the balance of probabilities), non-compliance was a criminal matter carrying a maximum sentence, in the Crown Court, of five years' imprisonment. Initially there was considerable reluctance to seek ASBOs. However, through the continual encouragement of the Prime Minister and successive home secretaries, together with the addition of extra powers via successive legislation, including the Anti-Social Behaviour Act 2003, the number of orders imposed grew dramatically from about 100/quarter to the end of 2002 to about 600/quarter in 2005. Juveniles accounted for nearly 50 per cent of the total.

Criticism of the ASBO has come from a variety of quarters (see, for example, Gardner et al., 1998; Burney, 2005; Rodger, 2006; Squires, 2006). There are particular criticisms: that the rights of those subject to ASBOs are undermined because of the civil nature of the application; that because of the length of the order and the fact that the number of prohibitions is often excessive, orders are easily breached, resulting in some young people being dragged into custody who would never have previously been there; and that it provides a short-cut to the police to fast-track persistent offenders into custody. Perhaps most fundamentally, for a government which claimed it wanted to tackle social exclusion, the ASBO had the effect of doing the opposite. Children, young people and families were being stigmatized and branded as outcasts, thereby increasing their marginalization and alienation from mainstream society.

The numbers of children and young people in penal custody doubled from 1,415 in 1991 to 2,825 in 2005. By far the biggest increase occurred in the final years of the Conservative government when it was keen to demonstrate that it was tough on criminals, particularly young offenders, and that 'prison worked'. Between 1993 and 1997 the numbers of young people in penal custody increased from 1,374 to 2,574. Since New Labour came to power the numbers have increased to just 2,825. However, young offenders are now more likely to be criminalized as a result of the New Labour reforms than they were before 1998:

> The pattern is clear. Young offenders are today more likely to be criminalized and subject to a greater level of intervention than before the 1998 reforms. If dealt with pre-court their warning is more likely to be accompanied by an intervention. They are more likely to be prosecuted. If convicted they are less likely to receive a discharge or fine. If subject to a community sentence it is more likely to be onerous. And last, but not least, despite the relative *proportionate* decline in custodial sentences since 2002, the *number* of children and young people sentenced to custody is still 35 per cent higher than a few years before the 1998 Act (Morgan and Newburn, 2007: 1047, original emphasis).

Following his resignation as chair of the Youth Justice Board in March 2007, Rod Morgan made it clear that while he felt some of the developments since 1998 were positive he had become particularly troubled by aspects of the anti-social behaviour strategy and the 26 per cent increase in the criminalization of children and young people – developments driven by the government's 'offences brought to justice' target and of which it seemed particularly proud (Morgan, 2007). Success, it seemed, was no longer measured in terms of the numbers kept out of the criminal justice system and penal custody but by the increased numbers brought in. However, his resignation led to a high-profile debate about youth justice policy and the successes and failures of the Youth Justice Board. It also led to a period of nearly 12 months when the Board had no leadership until the appointment of Frances Done in January 2008. An accountant and administrator by background, with no child welfare or youth justice experience, her appointment received a lukewarm reception (O'Hara, 2008).

Conclusion

This chapter has clearly demonstrated that a whole series of tensions have characterized the field of youth justice over the last forty years and that it has become a high-profile political issue. In particular, the tensions between welfare and punishment have been a continual theme. The Children and Young Persons Act 1969 marked the high point for a welfarist approach and, while never implemented in full, it was social services departments and social workers who were to play the central role. While this continued during the 1980s and early 1990s the philosophy and practice changed considerably under the influence of the 'juvenile justice movement' and most local authorities established specialist juvenile justice teams. However, the murder of Jamie Bulger ushered in a quite new political climate which emphasized punitiveness and being 'tough on crime and tough on the causes of crime'.

The election of New Labour in 1997 heralded a whole range of far-reaching reforms and changes, particularly in organization, funding and management, with the establishment of the Youth Justice Board (YJB) and local authority Youth Justice Teams (YOTs). No longer was youth justice to be the responsibility of social services departments where social workers were the key professional group. Youth justice is now an explicitly multi-disciplinary exercise and has quite separate lines of accountability, performance indicators and funding streams.

However, youth justice policy since 1997 is quite difficult to characterize. As John Muncie has suggested, it is an odd 'melange' of contradictory policies and practices (Muncie, 2004), some of which are clearly criminalizing and punitive while others attempt to be more inclusionary, emphasizing restorative justice and making serious attempts to help young people overcome their problems. What is also clear, however, is that the focus of the work is explicitly young *offenders* and the practices are framed within that context, even though nearly all the young people involved experience a range of complex welfare issues and have a wide range of needs. While the possibility does exist for YOTs to be included in the Children's Trusts arrangements under the *ECM: Change for Children* programme, this is not a requirement. As a number of reports have highlighted (DH, 2002; Audit Commission, 2004), the separation of youth offending teams from the mainstream of children's services posed a major challenge for inter-agency collaboration and for ensuring that *all* the needs of children and young people are met (Bottoms and Kemp, 2007). It seems that this was increasingly being recognized.

When the Department for Children, Schools and Families was established at the end of June 2007 it was given joint responsibility with the Home Office for the funding and policy of the Youth Justice Board, and a number of government statements suggested they wished to overcome the separation between 'children in need' and children 'who offend'. In November the Joint Youth Justice Unit was set up, based on a merger between the former Ministry of Justice Youth Justice and Children Unit and the Young Offender Education Team of the Offenders Learning and Skills Unit at the former DfES. The new Minister, Ed Balls, also stated that he saw every ASBO as representing a failure. To reinforce this, the *Respect Unit*, which had played such an important role in encouraging the use of ASBOs, was moved from the Home Office to the new department, and was then closed down altogether in October 2007 and replaced by the *Youth Taskforce*.

The Children's Plan (DCSF, 2007b) stated that it intended to pilot schemes where local authorities would be encouraged to accompany all applications for an ASBO with an Individual Support Order or offer appropriate support in order to address any underlying causes of the behaviour and to ensure the behaviour did not deteriorate (para. 6.73). The plan also stated that it was intended to pilot a restorative approach to youth offending (para. 6.77). Significantly, it was stated that it wanted 'to achieve greater alignment between children's services and the youth justice system, including where necessary pooling budgets to increase reach and impact' (para. 6.74).

In March 2008 the *Youth Taskforce Action Plan* (DCSF, 2008b) was published which stated it aimed to build on the success in tackling antisocial behaviour and planned to spend £218.5m on:

- tough enforcement where behaviour is unacceptable or illegal;
- non-negotiable support to address the underlying causes of poor behaviour;
- better prevention to tackle problems before they become serious and entrenched and to prevent problems arising in the first place.

A key part of the *Youth Taskforce Action Plan* was the introduction of 20 *Intensive Intervention Projects* for the thousand most challenging young people. Young people would have to agree to a contract and would receive an assertive and persistent key worker who would work with them to make sure they got the help they needed to tackle the causes of their bad behaviour. The support would be non-negotiable so that if they refused to comply they would be placed on an Anti-Social Behaviour Order and/or an Individual Support Order to compel them to cooperate; both were court orders with criminal records and sanctions for those who breached them. Children's Trusts were expected to actively contribute to such developments. Clear efforts were being made for trying to bring criminal justice and children's social care closer together in relation to policy and practice for youth offending. Whether this would increase the potential for meeting the needs of young people or increasing the possibilities for their further criminalization is not at all clear.

On 15 July 2008 the Government published its *Youth Crime Action Plan* (HM Government, 2008) for consultation, at a time of huge media and political concern at the number of deaths of young people from knife crime. The *Action Plan* was produced by the Home Office, the Department for Children, Schools and Families and the Department of Justice, and set out a 'triple track' approach of: enforcement and punishment where behaviour is unacceptable; non-negotiable support and challenge where it is most needed; and better and earlier prevention. It was estimated that 5 per cent of young people committed half of all youth crime and that these young people could be identified early on. They came from a small number of vulnerable families with 'complex problems'. For the families at greatest risk of serious offending the *Action Plan* identified £100 million of extra funding to fund *Family Intervention Projects* (FIPs) – an average of forty in each area and reaching 20,000 families across the country by 2010. Local authorities and Children's Trusts were to play the key role in ensuring that a consistent approach to assessment, early identification and targeted support were embedded in all services so that schools, health services and specialist services would share information and work together for young people 'at risk' as well as those who had already been drawn into crime and anti-social behaviour. This included working with their parents, who would need both 'support' and 'challenge'.

Two major themes that ran through the document were to try to reduce the number of children going into custody, and to attempt to give a stronger role for local authorities and Children's Trusts in preventing youth crime. However, at the time of writing, it was unclear how this might be achieved and how far the legal and financial responsibilities of local authorities would change as a result. What is clear is that the government was looking to change the balance between the punitive and welfare approaches to youth crime and that a central priority was being given to intervening early when dealing with children and young people who, potentially, might end up 'in trouble'.

6

Children and the Care System: Reforming Corporate Parenting

Introduction

The aim of this chapter is to provide an overview and analysis of the situation of those children who are cared for by the state – 'children in care', or 'looked-after children' as they were known from 1991 onwards. This has been an area of considerable activity by New Labour. Following the publication of the Green Paper *Care Matters: Transforming the lives of children and young people in care* (DfES, 2006a), and the subsequent White Paper *Care Matters: Time for Change* (DfES, 2007b), this process has culminated in the Children and Young Persons Act 2008. In total this 'Care Matters' reform process is a major landmark in social policy as it relates to children and young people in care (see Table 6.1).

Table 6.1 Numbers of looked-after children in England, 2003–2007

	Year				
	2003	**2004**	**2005**	**2006**	**2007**
All looked-after children	61,200	61,200	61,000	60,300	60,000
Rate per 10,000 children under 18	55	55	55	55	55
Gender					
Male	33,800	33,900	33,700	33,400	33,400
Female	27,400	27,200	27,200	26,900	26,600
Placements					
Foster care	41,000	41,200	41,300	41,700	42,300
Placed for adoption	3,800	3,600	3,400	3,000	2,500
Placed with parents	6,300	5,900	5,800	5,400	5,100
Other placements	10,100	9,700	10,500	10,200	10,100

Source: Children looked after in England (including adoption and leaving care) for year ending 31st March. Issued by the Department for Children, Schools and Families, 20 September 2007, SFR28/2007.
[Crown Copyright, reprinted with permission. License # C02W000670.]

The chapter will explore the response of New Labour to issues facing children in care and will assess the impact and significance of the 'Care Matters' reform process. Broadly, it is argued here that the New Labour initiatives relating to children in care have been progressive in direction, but that we need to assess these reforms in the wider historical, social and policy environment relating to children and young people in contemporary England.

Arguably, three main themes emerge from a historical analysis of child welfare provision for children separated from their parents (Frost et al., 1999). First, the long shadow of the Poor Law, which made the provision that state welfare should be 'less eligible' or, in everyday words, of a lower standard than life in the community, has been influential in terms of the stigma associated with being 'in care'. Second, there has historically been an emphasis on education and training as methods of rescuing children from poverty, or from what we would now perceive as 'poor outcomes'. Finally, there have been tensions between family-based care (fostering and adoption) and residential provision for children. These three themes will help us assess contemporary developments for this group of children and young people.

We begin our discussion by examining the abuse of children in care – an issue that dominated the child welfare landscape as New Labour came to power in 1997.

The Abuse of Children in Care – Two Key Reports

It is now well documented that physical and sexual abuse of children in care took place during the second half of the twentieth century and could be found across the nation. We will examine how the state responded to this most fundamental of challenges: the abuse of children in care represented a serious failure of 'corporate parenting' and a betrayal of the children and young people the state claimed to be protecting and 'looking after'.

In his first commissioned overview report on the subject of safeguarding children in care, published under the then Conservative government, *Children in the Public Care* (1991), Sir William Utting concluded that:

> residential care is an indispensable service: that should be a positive, joint choice primarily for adolescents, who may present challenging behaviour (Utting, 1991: 62).

This is an important statement – residential care had been marginalized and seen as residual through the 1970s and 1980s and, partly as a consequence, had been poorly managed and allowed, on occasion, to become an abusive environment.

However, following the publication of the 1991 report it became apparent that abuse in care remained widespread. In 1997, when the scale of abuse in

North Wales was known but not yet officially reported on, Utting was commissioned again to report on abuse in care, producing the landmark report *People Like Us*. This report concluded that we required a 'protective strategy' that included:

- A threshold of entry into paid and voluntary work with children which is high enough to deter committed abusers;
- Management which pursues overall excellence and is vigilant in protecting children and exposing abuse;
- Disciplinary and criminal procedures which deal effectively with offenders;
- An approved system of communicating information about known abusers between agencies with a need to know (Utting, 1997: 1).

Utting concluded that:

> The best safeguard is an environment of overall excellence (Utting, 1997: 1).

Both the *People Like Us* (1997) report and the earlier *Children in the Public Care* (1991) provide an authoritative and powerful testimony to the extent and impact of abuse in the care system. In his second report Utting refers to the perpetrators as 'abusive terrorists' (Utting,1997: 5) and describes undertaking his second review as 'a crash course in human (predominantly male) wickedness and in the fallibility of social institutions' (Utting, 1997: 7). He argues that nothing other than root and branch reform could resolve this situation. The two reports together provide a blueprint for the future of care for separated children – seeing a powerful role for a reformed system of care, with a wide range of choice, with young people's needs placed centrally, and managed and planned to deliver a high quality experience.

It fell to New Labour to respond to Utting, a response that came in a number of forms, the predominant of which was the 'Quality Protects' (1998) initiative that we discussed in Chapter 2.

However, as 'Quality Protects' was being implemented another key report was published in 2000. For many years throughout the latter half of the twentieth century it was known that there had been extensive abuse of children in care in North Wales. After many legal complications and delays, eventually a full and comprehensive report was produced – the report of the inquiry chaired by Ronald Waterhouse and entitled *Lost in Care* (2000). The lengthy report sifted a considerable amount of material, including evidence from 575 witnesses. Waterhouse summarized the situation as follows:

> It had been known for several years that serious sexual and physical abuse had taken place in homes managed by Clwyd County Council in the 1970s and 1980s. A major police investigation had been begun in 1991, resulting

in 8 prosecutions and 6 convictions of former care workers, but speculation that the actual abuse had been on a greater scale had persisted in North Wales (Waterhouse, 2000: 2.01).

The report outlines the severe abuse of children and young people over an extended period of time. The following evidence collected by Waterhouse gives us a flavour of both the extent and the seriousness of the abuse:

> The allegations of sexual abuse by Howarth span the whole of his period at Bryn Estyn (from November 1973) to July 1984. They were centred mainly on the flat that he occupied there on the first floor of the main building. It was Howarth's practice to invite boys, usually five or six from the main building at a time, to the flat in the evening for drinks and light food: they would watch television and play cards or board games. Invitations to these sessions were by a 'flat list' compiled by Howarth or made up on his instructions and boys who went to the flat were required to wear pyjamas without underpants. ... Howarth was tried in July 1994 in Chester Crown Court on 3 counts of buggery and 9 of indecent assault. These offences were alleged to have been committed between 1 Jan 1974 and 11 May 1984 and they involved 9 boy residents ... he was convicted on 8 July 1994 of one offence of buggery and 7 indecent assaults, for which he was sentenced to 10 years' imprisonment (Waterhouse, 2000: 8.04-07).

Accounts such as this are to be found across the many pages of the Waterhouse report. The report concludes:

> widespread shortcomings in practice and administrative failings in the provision of children's services, including failure to apply basic safeguards provided for by regulation, which must be addressed if local authorities are to discharge adequately the parental responsibilities imposed upon them in respect of looked after children. The Children Act 1989 has provided a springboard for many improvements in children's services but the need for vigilance and further positive action remains if the ever present risk of abuse is to be minimised (Waterhouse, 2000: 55.09).

These three reports – the two from Sir William Utting and the Waterhouse report – provide us with an overview of a disturbing and challenging social problem. This issue had a high profile and was in danger of bringing the entire system of children's social care, in particular residential care, into disrepute.

How can we understand the nature and origins of the abuse of children in the care system?

Understanding Abuse in the Care System

As we have seen, it is now clear that the abuse of children in the care system existed through much of the nation during the latter half of the twentieth century: we have many reports and inquiries, in addition to court cases and convictions, which provide eloquent, trustworthy and moving testament. It fell to New Labour to respond to the eloquent testimony provided by Waterhouse and Utting.

The reports certainly reflected a crisis in the care system – there had been widespread physical and sexual abuse of children in residential care settings, occurrences which reflected a sector that was demoralized, underfunded, poorly trained and inadequately managed. These events tend to reinforce the strong historical theme that residential care is stigmatized and 'less eligible'.

Frost et al. (1999) have provided a typology that allows us to analyse and reflect on these events. They argue that the abuse can be seen as taking four distinct forms: sanctioned abuse, institutional abuse, systematic abuse and individual abuse.

Sanctioned abuse is known to, and thus 'sanctioned' by, the authorities. The abuse perpetrated by Tony Latham in Staffordshire and reported on by Kahan and Levy in 1991, and that by Frank Beck, mainly in Leicestershire, fall into this category. Both men had a public profile that included writing up their regimes for professional magazines and, in Latham's case, his 'Pindown' techniques were recorded in detail in the institutional day book. Both men were given increased responsibility by their senior managers. Their approaches were known of and achieved some managerial recognition (Frost et al., 1999).

How can sanctioned abuse occur? Latham covered up his abuse as a form of 'therapy' that was supposed to reform the young people in his care. Senior managers seemed to welcome someone who would take responsibility for troubled young people who were hard to handle in the care system.

Institutional abuse is more pervasive and has far-reaching implications in the care system. Institutional abuse is defined as:

> the policies, procedures, and practices which create or contribute towards problems of instability, dependency, stigma, identity formation and under-achievement (Frost et al., 1999: 109).

Such practices are abusive in the sense that they contribute to neglect, poor outcomes, low levels of life skills and the institutionalization of children and young people who experience such regimes. These factors are firmly embedded in poor practice and need to be challenged and reformed if care is to be in any way positive and creative for children and young people (Crimmens and Pitts, 2000).

Systematic abuse is defined by Frost et al. as that which involves more than one person who know each other and who plan the abuse together. There certainly was a network present in North Wales, involving people who trained together and who provided references and jobs for each other (Waterhouse, 2000). It should be recalled that much of this abuse existed before the impact of the worldwide web, which is no doubt a tool that could be used to facilitate such abusive networks.

The final category is individual abuse – the presence of isolated individuals who abuse children. Such individuals will often exercise their abuse in the context of one or more of the forms of abuse that are outlined above.

This typology suggests that we require a complex response to abuse in care – a strategy that ensures that all four types of abuse are fully addressed. Abuse in care is a challenging occurrence which involves devising protective strategies if children and young people are to be effectively safeguarded (see Crimmens and Pitts, 2000).

Whilst Frost et al. (1999) suggest a classificatory framework for understanding abuse in care, in contrast, Wardhaugh and Wilding (1993) provide eight propositions which attempt to explain what they call 'the corruption of care'. Their eight points are as follows:

- the corruption of care depends on the neutralization of normal moral concerns;
- the corruption of care is closely connected with the balance of power and powerlessness in organizations;
- particular pressures and particular kinds of work are associated with corruption of care;
- management failure underlies the corruption of care;
- the corruption of care is more likely in enclosed, inward-looking organizations;
- the absence of clear lines and mechanisms of accountability plays an important part in the corruption of care;
- particular models of work and organizations are conducive to the corruption of care;
- the nature of certain client groups encourages the corruption of care.

We can see from official reports that abuse in care has been extensive and difficult for policy makers to address. The theoretical perspectives offered by Frost et al. and by Wardhaugh and Wilding suggest that such abuse has different dimensions and is multi-causal. What emerges powerfully from the literature on abuse in care is the key theme of the abuse of adult power over vulnerable children and young people. There are extreme forms of power differentials between looked-after children and those who are supposed to care for them. Where this power is abused the results are profound and damaging (Ennew, 1986).

Having examined the three key reports and two explanatory theoretical frame-works, we now move on to explore the state response to the challenge of abuse in care.

'Learning the Lessons'

Learning the Lessons (DH, 2000b) was published in 2000 as the government response to *Lost in Care*. It provides a useful summary of the key reforms introduced by New Labour since they came to power during the 1997–2000 period.

The basic argument of *Learning the Lessons* is that many of the necessary reforms are already in place, in the form of 'Quality Protects', a range of legislative changes (the Protection of Children Act 1999, and the then Care Standards Bill and Children (Leaving Care) Bill) and through guidance such as *Working Together to Safeguard Children* (1988, re-issued 1999), together with policy initiatives such as the Prime Minister's Review of Adoption, all of which are discussed elsewhere in this volume.

Learning the Lessons also outlines the Government's immediate response in terms of checks on people working with children, and a training initiative known as the Residential Child Care Initiative (RCCI) aimed at addressing some of Utting's points about staffing and quality.

This then was a comprehensive attempt by New Labour to respond to the challenge of widespread abuse in care. Arguably this was the issue that underpinned the first years of New Labour's policy approaches to children in care, and it also stimulated Tony Blair to take a personal interest in the issue of adoption, which was seen as an alternative to residential care and the associated dangers of abuse. We explore New Labour and adoption later in this chapter, but first we turn to the important issue of leaving care.

Reforming the Care System

The Children (Leaving Care) Act 2000

The issue of young people leaving the care of the local authority became high profile during the 1980s, following pressure brought about young people, their organizations and the publication of the key text, *Leaving Care* (Stein and Carey, 1986). As New Labour came to power it was evident that leaving care issues remained problematic and challenging, despite legal reforms included as part of the Children Act 1989 and radical changes to practice, largely through the introduction of specialist leaving care teams in many local authorities (see Biehal et al., 1992). Leaving care was reframed by New Labour (as were many social work-related issues) as a social exclusion issue. Young people leaving care were seen as vulnerable to a number of indicators of social exclusion – homelessness, unemployment and criminality. For example:

> In the year ending 31 March 2001 37% of care leavers obtained one or more GCSE or GNVQ compared to 94% of Year 11 pupils in England as a whole.
> Unemployment amongst care leavers was around 50% compared to 19% of young people in the country at the time of the survey.
> One in seven young women leaving care were pregnant or young mothers (Action for Aftercare, 2004: 2).

In an attempt to address these issues, the first major piece of legislation relating to children in care steered through by New Labour was the Children (Leaving Care) Act 2000.

The Act is complex and makes some technical distinctions between different types of young people, but in general it aims to encourage local authorities to improve planning for young people leaving care, enhance financial support arrangements, and delay discharge from care until young people are actually ready to leave (see Action for Aftercare, 2004).

How well is the 2000 Act working? Stein, the leading British researcher in this area, argues that we can usefully see the care-leaving population as falling into three categories (Action for Aftercare, 2004: 4).

First, the most successful group is the 'moving on' group. These have usually experienced some stability in care, are highly resilient and welcome the opportunities they are offered for greater independence.

Second, Stein identifies a 'survivors' group, who have experienced more instability and change whilst in the care system. To achieve positive outcomes this group are more dependent on the quality of aftercare support they receive.

Finally, Stein argues that there is a 'victims' group who have experienced the most damaging pre-care experiences. The care system was unable to compensate for these and they may have experienced change and disruption whilst in care. Aftercare support is important to them but is unlikely to be able to help them achieve positive outcomes.

It is important to note that leaving care should not be seen here as a separate category that is independent of the care system. Outcomes for young people leaving care cannot be separated from their 'in care' experiences.

In relation to the 2000 Act, Stein argues that:

> The introduction of the Children (Leaving Care) Act 2000 has led to the development in England of a 'corporate parenting case model' in some areas, better resourcing and, overall, to the increased profile of leaving care services (Stein, 2004: 62).

In evaluating the 2000 Act, the Action for After Care consortium argue that the successes and concerns about the Act can be classified in four categories:

> *Resources* – it would seem that more resources have been dedicated to leaving care services and that as a result there are more workers with specialist skills in the leaving care area. There are concerns that the increase in resources might not be sustainable in the long run, with particular concerns around leisure and housing.
>
> *Roles, responsibilities and strategic planning* – there seems to have been improvements in strategic planning, clearer policies and clearer views of roles and responsibilities. Concerns are mainly focused around the needs of particular groups of young people – for example, young people leaving custody, unaccompanied asylum-seeking children and young people with complex needs and young parents.
>
> *Outcomes* – the report found some limited improvement in outcomes (given the relatively short period since the Act had been implemented). Concerns focused around methods for measuring outcomes, which we return to below.
>
> *Young people's experience* – seemed to have improved in terms of the increased focus on support and planning in the Act. There will still be concerns about income levels and clarity in terms of rights and entitlements (Action for Aftercare, 2004: 6–9).

As can be seen from this evidence, leaving care remains a complex and challenging area for policy makers and practitioners alike. It seems to be the case that some considerable achievements have followed the implementation of the 2000 Act, but that major challenges remain. The main areas remaining for improvement seem to be with specific groups of young people, including unaccompanied asylum-seeking children and disabled young people. The reforms suggested in the 'Care Matters' process once again fundamentally address concerns about leaving care and indeed attempt to reframe the issue as 'transition to adulthood' – we turn to these reforms later in this chapter.

The Adoption and Children Act 2002

Perhaps one of the more notable incidents of the New Labour period relating to children's social care was that the then Prime Minister, Tony Blair, decided to lead personally a review of the adoption process. This initiative was clearly based in 'family values' which New Labour had espoused in *Supporting Families* (Home Office, 1998). Tony Blair expressed his interest as follows:

> It is hard to overstate the importance of a stable and loving family life for children. That is why I want more children to benefit from adoption (DH, 2000d: 3).

The motivation for this review came partially from the incidence of abuse in care we have explored above and also from media and political concerns that adoption was a slow, bureaucratic process. The Prime Minister's review was effectively a two-pronged change process – one led by a series of reforms to the system that did not require legislative change, and the changes enacted through the Adoption and Children Act 2002.

Unsurprisingly, there was also present a New Labour 'modernization' agenda expressed by the Prime Minister – 'the government is committed to modernizing adoption' (DH, 2000c) – and in addition some familiar frustration about the role of local authorities:

> Too often in the past adoption has been seen as a last resort. Too many local authorities have performed poorly in helping children out of care and into adoption. Too many prospective parents have been confused, or put off, by the process of applying to adopt, and the time the procedure takes (DH, 2000d: 3).

The 2002 Act played an important function of bringing adoption law into line with the 1989 Children Act, most importantly by making the welfare of the child the paramount consideration in the adoption process. The Act placed a duty on local authorities to deliver an after-adoption service and introduced an independent review process for people turned down as adopters. The Act also attempted to reduce delay by improving timetabling in the court process. Significantly, it allowed unmarried couples to adopt – opening up the possibility of gay couple adoption, which was later to prove controversial for the Catholic Church.

The modernization process was largely able to precede the 2002 Act through a series of administrative reforms. A National Adoption Register allowed adoption agencies to coordinate and share information across the country; new national standards, including timescales for the process, were established; a taskforce was established to spread 'best practice, tackle poor performance and help all local authorities reach the standards of the best' (DH, 2000d). A scrutiny of children awaiting adoption and those waiting to be adopted was undertaken.

It can be argued that these reforms have been successful in the government's own terms since adoption from care has increased after being more or less stable for thirty years. Before the passage of the Act the figures were roughly stable at around 2,000 per annum (DH, 2000d) but have since increased significantly to 3,500 in 2003 and 3,700 in 2006 (National Statistics, 2007).

The commitment of New Labour to the adoption process reflects a support for the family as the privileged location for children and a fundamental ambivalence about the ability of the state to act as an effective 'corporate parent'. Adoption is clearly seen as more clearly reflecting the perceived strengths of the birth family.

The complexity of the state/family couplet is reflected in the development of post-adoption support. This is a difficult area for the state to negotiate as adoption represents a permanent transfer of parental responsibility to the adoptive parents. In a sense, then, it can be argued that the state should have no role in adoptive families, other than that it would play with any family. Post-adoption support is therefore a complex process for the state to negotiate (Luckock, 2008). Luckock and Hart argue convincingly that the development of post-adoption support can be seen as part of a movement from a 'privacy/autonomy' model of adoption to a 'contract/services' model (Luckock and Hart, 2005). In the former model adoption is seen as a process of transfer of parental responsibility where the adoptive family is as private and autonomous as any other family. In the latter the state retains a key role in supporting the placement, thus placing the post-adoption family potentially and sometimes actually in a different position from other families. Here, according to Luckock and Hart, the post-adoptive family becomes a customer of post-adoption services. Thus the state preference for adoption is supplemented by the provision of services.

There can be no doubt that adoption remains a preferred outcome for looked-after children, in both policy and practice, where rehabilitation with a birth family is seen as impossible.

Having examined two major New Labour reforms, in relation to leaving care and adoption, we now move on to examine an over-arching reform of the looked-after system, a complex process we will refer to, in shorthand as, 'Care Matters'.

'Care Matters'

The Green Paper *Care Matters: Transforming the lives of children and young people in care* (DfES, 2006a) was published in October 2006, and represents the beginnings of a major policy initiative from the New Labour government. A period of consultation followed, and in the Spring of 2007 the White Paper *Care Matters: a Time for Change* (DfES, 2007b) was published. A detailed implementation plan, *Care Matters: Time to deliver for children in care* (DCSF, 2008c) followed. The Children and Young Persons Act, reflecting by and large the content of the White Paper, received the Royal Assent in 2008.

The White Paper emerged with seven chapters relating in turn to: corporate parenting; family and parenting support; care placements; education, health and well-being; transition to adulthood; the role of the practitioner; and implementation. We will not cover each of these but will address the three main themes that emerge from our historical introduction:

- Does the 'Care Matters' reform process represent a break with the stigma associated with the Poor Law?
- What does the process say about education and training?
- How does it address the tension between family-based and institutional care?

To focus on our first historical theme identified earlier in this chapter – does the current reform agenda attempt a real break with the Poor Law? – the 'Care

Matters' process presents a radical vision offering a way forward for a group of children, many of whom have suffered a catalogue of abuse and disadvantage, sometimes supplemented, rather than resolved, by the care system (see Utting, 1991, 1997). The Green Paper argues the point as follows:

> The State has a unique responsibility for children in care. It has taken on the task of parenting some of society's most vulnerable children and in doing so it must become everything a good parent should be (DfES, 2006a: 1.1).

The White Paper makes a related point:

> A good corporate parent must offer everything that a good parent would provide and more, addressing both the difficulties which the children experience and the challenges of parenting within a complex system of services (DfES, 2007b: 1.20).

Here we can see the rhetorical break with the Poor Law – no hint here of 'less eligibility', indeed the highest level of state parenting is called for. The familiar New Labour emphasis on parenting is used to deliver effective care for children in care, and to aim for high levels of parenting and support.

This rhetoric is brought together by 'a pledge' to children in care to ensure that they receive a reasonable level of care (DfES, 2007b: 1.25). The pledge is aimed at providing a guarantee for the good intentions expressed in the proposals. Unsurprisingly, given the emphasis on audit and measurement associated with New Labour initiatives, the changes will be subject to rigorous inspection through Ofsted. The proposal also embeds the participation of children and young people in the process.

The 'Care Matters' process then seems to be a genuine attempt to 'modernize' the care system and to rescue it from the legacy of poor outcomes with which it is often associated (Stein, 2006). It will be argued later in this chapter, however, that this policy shift has to be more strongly associated with wider concerns about children and young people if it is to succeed.

To turn to our second historical theme – the focus on education and training as the way forward for young people in care – it is clear that this theme, which has been with us since the 16th century, is strongly represented in the 'Care Matters' process.

Educational issues have featured in recent legislation, including the Children Acts of 1989 and 2004 and the Children (Leaving Care) Act 2000. Despite this, educational outcomes for children in care, whilst improving slightly in recent years, have been difficult to improve, for reasons we will explore later.

The 'Care Matters' documentation devotes considerable space to education, which is arguably the dominant theme of the reform process. In summary, the 'Care Matters' White Paper proposes the following in relation to school age children:

- High quality early years education for children in care
- A requirement to ensure that care planning decisions do not disrupt education and that moves in years 10 and 11 should only be in exceptional circumstances
- Ofsted review of the position of children in care in 2008/9
- Children in care should only be excluded from school as a last resort
- Alternative provision for excluded children in care from day one
- Improvements in national minimum standards for foster and residential care relating to education
- A strengthened role for the designated teacher
- A virtual school head for children in care in each local authority
- Personal education plans for children in care
- Funding to pay for extra help for children in care not reaching their targets
- Specified extended services for children in care
- Improved home–school agreements
- An improvement in services for children with special educational needs (DfES, 2007b: 4.10-4.56).

This brief summary hardly does justice to the width and depth of the 'Care Matters' proposals relating to the education of children in care. In addition, there is a range of proposals relating to further and higher education. One would have to be very cynical indeed to suggest that this is not a fundamental attempt to address poor educational outcomes for the care population. As we have seen, education and training as a route out of poverty and poor outcomes has long been a theme of law and policy for children in care. Whether this will be successful we return to below in our discussion of outcomes.

In relation to our third theme, the debate between family-based care and institutional care is again present but is more hidden than the clear emphasis on education.

It can be argued that fostering has a much higher profile than residential care in the Care Matters reforms. *Care Matters,* as one would expect, has much to say about foster care, as foster care provides the major site where children in care are looked after; according to the Green Paper, 68 per cent of the care population are in foster care (see Table 6.1). The government clearly sees the reform of fostering as a key, if not the key, to the future of the care system. The Green Paper argues that the status of fostering and the range of placements must be increased:

> We believe that the proposals in this Green Paper to improve the recruitment and status of foster carers, alongside the increasing expertise in local authorities to manage the local market of placements, will enable more and more local authorities to offer such a choice (DfES, 2006a: 4.11).

The vision of the Green Paper and the White Paper is of a modernized, professionalized, tiered and trained foster care workforce. This is to be achieved through enhanced training as:

> We know there is a shortage of skills and qualifications in both foster and residential care (DfES, 2006a: 4.27).

Both the Green Paper and White Paper are keen to promote a particular model of care:

> we are supporting the development of the Multi-Dimensional Treatment Foster Care for young children, using lessons from pilots for adolescents to make more effective use of parenting interventions to support the successful return home of children from care or to support effective permanence arrangements in a new family (DfES, 2007b: 3.21).

In contrast to the high level of focus on foster care, residential care receives less attention – despite Utting's (1997) plea that choice and diversity in this sector is central to maintaining quality. The main proposal in relation to residential care is the introduction of the social pedagogue, a new form of professional, modelled on European systems. The emphasis on parenting and the family as the preferred option seems to have marginalized residential care:

> our expectation is that most children will benefit from being in a family setting, as has been the thrust of government policy in recent years. As a result more children then ever are in foster care placements. Nevertheless, residential care has an important role to play as part of a range of placement options (DfES, 2007b: 3.57).

This negative, residual perspective on residential care is always in danger of becoming a self-fulfilling prophecy. In contrast, young people and their organizations often express positive views about residential child care, some of which are reported in the Consultation reports on 'Care Matters'. Young people have commented that they sometimes choose residential care because they enjoy living with groups of young people (see Mills and Frost, 2007). Crucially, some young people also say they enjoy having a number of adults to relate to in ways that are different to a parent. Linked to this last point, young people say they do not have to feel disloyal to their own parents if they become close to a member of staff because the latter is clearly not a parent substitute. Some young people have also said that being in foster care can be too difficult, as it can remind them how difficult family life was for them (Page and Clarke, 1977; Frost et al., 1999). Thus we can argue that foster care and residential care should be seen as a continuum of care, providing young people with both choice and diversity.

This vision could be situated more clearly within the 'Care Matters' agenda.

'Care Matters': A Way Forward?

We can detect many of the recurrent themes of New Labour policy in the 'Care Matters' proposals: the need to reform and 'modernize'; the introduction of choice and markets into social care; the attempt to tackle social exclusion; and an emphasis on outcomes, audit and 'what works'. Whilst in general the Care Matters initiative has been broadly welcomed by lobby groups and voluntary organizations, two key critiques have emerged that will now be explored.

The Critique of Social Work Practices

First of all, Polly Toynbee, the *Guardian* commentator, has criticized the 'privatization' element of the Green Paper (see also Garrett, 2008). Toynbee is critical of the proposals that Directors of Children's Services (DCS) should become commissioners of services and that these services could be purchased from small, private or independent practices of social workers. These practices seem to operate in a similar way to general practitioners' practices, and will be known as Social Work Practices. The 'Care Matters' documentation paints a sympathetic picture of social workers – struggling to do the best for children in the context of bureaucracy and a strong emphasis on emergency child protection work. The challenges of acting as an advocate whilst working in a large organization and of recruitment and retention issues also suggest to the government that a new way forward is required.

The Green Paper therefore argues that:

> There must be much greater scope for independence and innovation for social workers (DfES, 2006a: 3.17).

The White Paper proposes that a way forward is to:

> Pilot 'social work practices': to test whether partnership with external agencies can improve the child's experience of care by small groups of social workers undertaking work with children in care commissioned by but independent of local authorities (DfES, 2007b: 14).

Polly Toynbee is critical of this proposal on three main grounds:

a)   There is enough reform happening at the moment – 'Every Child Matters' is a demanding agenda, is working out relatively well and should not be disrupted or sent off course.

b)   The reforms create extra costs, as there still has to be a service plus a body of commissioners.

c)   Similar experiments in the NHS have largely failed.

For Toynbee then the system should be left largely as it is, with the Every Child Matters reforms being given a chance to work. She argues that in addition we need a wider focus on family support and childcare in order to address the root causes of the challenges faced by the care system. One could add that such a proposal arguably fragments the service, creating barriers between the practices and the rest of the local authority service, when the more general shift is towards 'joining-up' services (see Frost, 2005).

The Outcomes Critique

Mike Stein (2006) has produced a telling and influential critique of the basic assumption of 'Care Matters' and the associated 'folk wisdom' that the outcomes for children in care are overwhelmingly poor. He argues that:

> the political and professional consensus that the care system is to blame for society's woes is wrong.

Stein gives five reasons, summarized below, for arguing that this is the case.

First, many young people spend only a brief period in care and this cannot be expected to have any significant impact on outcomes.

Second, many of those who leave care between the ages of 16 and 18 come into care between 10 and 15, often from disadvantaged backgrounds and with already disrupted educations. To expect any significant impact in outcomes for this group is again flawed.

Third, we need to distinguish between three groups of care leavers, as previously explored: those who 'move on' – and often have successful outcomes; those who 'survive' and may do well if adequately supported; and those who are highly vulnerable, who form perhaps 5 per cent of the care population but are strongly associated with a 'failing' care system (see Action for Aftercare, 2004).

Fourth, outcomes may improve as young people mature, having come through the usual challenges of youth transitions. More longitudinal work is required to explore these issues.

Fifth, current outcomes are too crude as they detach young people from their backgrounds and fail to take into account their starting points. This point reminds us of the debates about 'value-added' league tables to assess the performance of schools.

Stein concludes that we need a progress measure – that would be more realistic than the sad litany that the Green Paper commences with. He argues that we need to see young people's problems more in the context of social challenges such as poverty, family problems and poor education. It is unrealistic to expect the care system to compensate for wider social problems and challenges, as if it existed in isolation. In many ways this is a similar conclusion to that reached by Polly Toynbee.

Thus far, then, we have argued that the proposals are broadly to be welcomed – but with two key 'Achilles' heels' identified by leading commentators.

Children in Care in the Wider Context

As the 'Care Matters' documentation recognizes, children and young people in care are not a homogenous group and, as with all young people, their lives represent rich and diverse childhoods. As such, the dimensions of gender, ethnicity, disability, sexuality and socio-economic status, alongside the particular and specific care experiences, are crucial to understanding the care experience. We need to place debates about the care system in a wider context of debates about difference and diversity.

We cannot separate being a child in care from being a child in the wider social context. As one of us has argued elsewhere:

> The care system always bears a relationship to wider social and political themes – we cannot understand the care system without relating it to issues of social class, gender, disability and ethnicity, for example (Frost et al., 1999: 25).

In England we are currently facing a profound paradox around being a child under New Labour. On one side of the paradox we have a government that is profoundly interventionist in its approach to childhood. The ECM programme and the 'five outcomes' are arguably the most interventionist approach to childhood in the world – aiming to shape and mould modern childhood in a particular direction.

On the other side of the paradox we have childhood that is in crisis. A crisis that is present in the news every day – as this chapter is being written there is a concern about a spate of stabbings in the London area, but at any other given time this crisis might be manifest in concerns about childhood and sexuality, or consumption, or diet. The Children's Society has been so concerned about this that it has set up an inquiry into what a 'good childhood' might look like. In 2007, UNICEF has produced a detailed, if controversial, paper that demonstrates that the UK comes bottom of a table that aggregates a number of indicators concerned with the well-being of children (UNICEF, 2007).

We cannot expect the care system to act as a remedy for these profound and widespread social problems. The care system acts as the safety net for children and young people whom the wider social system has let down, but it is unrealistic to expect it to act as a magic wand that can wish away the broader ills and inequalities. Thus an understanding of the care system must be located in a wider debate about contemporary childhood, and, as Stein and Toynbee argue, policies are required to address the serious social problems facing the modern child in England.

In summary, the 'Care Matters' process has many positive points to be valued and supported. We have seen how the New Labour themes of modernization, choice and measurable outcomes are embedded in the reforms. Two major critiques have emerged that we have identified, concerning the fragmentation of the service and outcomes.

In conclusion, we have argued that the care system needs to be fully understood in a wider social and political context. It cannot alone compensate for the serious challenges facing children and young people in society. In order to address the problems facing young people in care, we need to address simultaneously and seriously the issues and problems facing young people in general in an ever-changing world.

7

Sure Start and Children's Centres: A Jewel in New Labour's Crown?

Early intervention in families and the growth of early years provision arguably rests at the heart of New Labour's childhood policy (DCSF, 2007b). The development of services aimed at parents and their young children connects a number of New Labour policies explored elsewhere in this volume – the anti-poverty agenda, equal opportunities policies in relation to women in the workforce, and preventive agendas regarding safeguarding, youth crime and social exclusion (see Fawcett et al., 2004). For these and other reasons, as we will see, there has been enormous financial and political investment in early years services. Over £20 billion has been invested in such services between 1997 and 2006, together with around £1.8 billion per annum being spent on Sure Start and related programmes in 2007–08 (DfES Press release 2006/0140). These interventions will be explored and critically examined in this chapter. Our analysis will demonstrate how the Sure Start and children's centres initiatives connect three major New Labour agendas – namely, 'joined up thinking', 'what works' and 'early intervention'. We will uncover a narrative of considerable achievement and some serious challenges, based in a powerfully interventionist ideology in relation to childhood and parenting. In the conclusion we reflect on the relationship between these initiatives and children's social care.

The Origins of Sure Start

Early in their period of government New Labour established the Cross-Departmental Review of Provision for Young Children. Officials from a wide-range of relevant departments met to drive the review forward (see Glass, 1999). A ministerial steering group was established to oversee the review – led significantly by a Treasury minister. It was agreed that a series of seminars should be convened, aimed at exploring which interventions might be most successful in the early years. The Cross-Departmental Review of Provision for Young Children seminars involved academics, civil servants, politicians and the voluntary sector gathering together to consider the evidence around interventions with young children (see the account by Eisenstadt, 2007).

What emerged from these seminars and the related review process was a major policy initiative that was to lead, and arguably dominate, British child welfare throughout the New Labour period – Sure Start. Sure Start was underpinned by the three major connecting ideological mantras – 'joined-up' thinking, 'what works' and 'early intervention'.

The Sure Start initiative was influenced by a large and high-profile body of research from the United States. In the US the so-called 'gold standard' methodology of randomized controlled trials (RCTs) had been used in relation to early intervention programmes and demonstrated the benefits for children of high-quality interventions in the early years (Meadows, 2007). The most high profile of these was the Perry Pre-school Project (Schweinhart et al., 1993). It was argued that small-scale controlled programmes led to evidence of significantly improved outcomes for children in later life. The Perry research programme involved a 27-year follow up – evidence that was used to argue that every one dollar invested in such services saved seven dollars in later state interventions (by reducing the rate of imprisonment, for example). In addition, Olds and colleagues have, over a number of years, produced a large body of evidence that demonstrates long-term positive outcomes relating to home visiting by qualified visitors, particularly where the programme was clearly structured (Olds et al. 1998). This research was clearly influential in guiding the birth and evolution of Sure Start. But the research could only have had this policy impact where the political climate was supportive: the research chimed home with a new government keen to make an impact, to modernize, to invest in social programmes and motivated by a strongly interventionist ideology in relation to childhood and families.

The project that emerged from these early discussions was known as Sure Start. The original idea was that Sure Start would function in small areas – initially defined by the concept of 'pram-pushing distance' – that would cover the 10 per cent most deprived electoral wards in the country, covering 250 areas initially. A funding package of £450 million was announced to cover the first three years (1999–2002) of Sure Start. Sure Start could thus be identified as 'an area-based initiative' (Eisenstadt, 2007: ix). It would work with parents and their children until their fourth birthday and would mobilize a wide range of children's services. All Sure Start Local Programmes (SSLPs hereafter) would offer a range of services including family support, health, education and child care services – thus exemplifying the 'joined-up' agenda. In 2000 it was announced that Sure Start would be doubled to cover 500 local areas, thus covering the 20 per cent most deprived areas in the country (Melhuish and Hall, 2007: 11).

The purpose of Sure Start was officially summarized as follows:

> Sure Start local programmes form a cornerstone of the Government's drive to tackle child poverty and social exclusion, based on firm evidence of what works. They are concentrated in neighbourhoods where a high

proportion of children are living in poverty and where Sure Start local programmes can help them to succeed by pioneering new ways of working to
improve services (Sure Start Unit, 1998: 37).

Clear aims and outcomes were articulated as follows:

Sure Start aims to achieve better outcomes for children, parents and communities by:

- increasing the availability of childcare for all children
- improving health, education and emotional development for young
  children
- supporting parents in their role and in developing their employment
  aspirations.

This will be achieved by:

- helping services develop in disadvantaged areas, while providing financial help to enable parents to afford quality childcare
- rolling out the principles driving the Sure Start approach to all services
  for children and parents (Sure Start website, 2002).

Importantly, SSLPs would be defined partly by difference. The lead civil servant for Sure Start, Norman Glass, was keen that the projects should respond to
need in their area and that local people should be involved in the design and governance of the SSLPs – a system that Glass would later refer to as being a form
of 'anarcho-syndicalism'(Glass, 2005). Any visitor to SSLPs would note this
difference – some in shiny new buildings, others working out of local community buildings, some emphasizing health care, others built on outreach and community work. Thus, we have an important 'joined-up' intervention, albeit one
connected by difference – containing within it some of the inevitable tensions
between a central drive and localized programmes. Importantly, though, all
would attempt to articulate the following principles:

1. Working with parents and children

Every family should have access to a range of services that will deliver
better outcomes for both children and parents, meeting their needs and
stretching their aspirations.

2. Services for everyone

But not the same service for everyone. Families have distinctly different
needs, both between different families, in different locations and across

time in the same family. Services should recognise and respond to these varying needs.

3. Flexible at point of delivery

All services should be designed to encourage access. For example, opening hours, location, transport issues and care for other children in the family need to be considered. Where possible we must enable families to get the health and family support services they need through a single point of contact.

4. Starting very early

Services for young children and parents should start at the first antenatal visit. This means not only advice on health in pregnancy, but preparation for parenthood, decisions about returning to work (or indeed, starting to work) after the birth, advice on childcare options and on support services available.

5. Respectful and transparent

Services should be customer driven, whether or not the service is free.

6. Community driven and professionally coordinated

All professionals with an interest in children and families should be sharing expertise and listening to local people on service priorities. This should be done through consultation and by day-to-day listening to parents.

7. Outcome driven

All services for children and parents need to have as their core purpose better outcomes for children. The Government needs to acknowledge this by reducing bureaucracy and simplifying funding to ensure a joined up approach with partners (Sure Start website, 2002).

The diverse structure and organization of the SSLPs was to represent a major challenge to another significant New Labour agenda – 'what works'. The 'what works' agenda was to be represented through the largest social science evaluation programme ever undertaken in the UK – the National Evaluation of Sure Start (NESS). Following competitive tender, the evaluation was awarded to a team drawn from a number of research institutions, but clustered around Birkbeck College. Initially led by high-profile American researcher Jay Belsky and later by longstanding British researcher Edward Melluish, the team faced many well-documented challenges in evaluating a high-profile, locally variable programme within a limited timescale. As we shall see later, NESS has a key role to play in the story of Sure Start (Belsky et al., 2007).

The Growth of Sure Start

The first SSLPs were launched in 1999 – just two years after New Labour was elected. It is important to recall this was a period of high political excitement: New Labour had been welcomed widely across a range of progressive opinion. The new government fairly immediately launched a wide range of programmes including political devolution, fiscal reform and an 'ethical' foreign policy. In relation to children and young people – as we see elsewhere in this volume – reforms included the introduction of Early Years Partnerships, youth offending teams, and the introduction of Connexions and the Children's Fund.

Sure Start had a key part to play in this continuum of intervention – arguably it was the jewel in the crown. But SSLPs almost inevitably took some time to be fully established – local authorities had to devise a complex system of local competitive bidding. Once they were selected, the areas had to find suitable premises and staff – a process documented by NESS as a long and complex one, often with two steps forward and one step backwards. The SSLPs were introduced in waves: by 2002 there were some 350 SSLPs across the nation, involving a total budget of over £500 million.

Reflecting yet another key theme of New Labour policy, the SSLPs were structured around targets – a complex, and often changing, set of targets against which they would be measured. As we have suggested, there is a key contradiction between targets and local governance that was to lead to some conflict and difficulties in evaluation. The targets themselves were often changed – a study of the complex nature of these changes and their drivers remains to be undertaken. The following targets were those initially established and aimed to be achieved by 2004:

Objective 1: Improving social and emotional development

Reduce the proportion of children aged 0–3 in the 500 Sure Start areas who are re-registered within the space of 12 months on the child protection register by 20 per cent by 2004.

Objective 2: Improving health

Achieve by 2004 in the 500 Sure Start areas, a 10 per cent reduction in mothers who smoke in pregnancy.

Objective 3: Improving children's ability to learn

Achieve by 2004 for children aged 0–3 in the 500 Sure Start areas, a reduction of five percentage points in the number of children with speech and language problems requiring specialist intervention by the age of four.

Objective 4: Strengthening families and communities

Reduce the number of 0–3-year-old children in Sure Start areas living in households where no one is working by 2004 (Sure Start Unit, 2000).

The establishment of these objectives reflects many of the problems with the audit culture in general (see Power, 1997) and more specifically in child welfare (see Jeffery, 2001).

We can see how the overall objectives above would probably command universal support. But however laudable and positive objectives such as 'Improving social and emotional development' were, they became reduced to technical, measurable and ultimately arbitrary figures. Targets allow innovative and imaginative projects, such as SSLPs, to become measurable, knowable and amenable to monitoring (Power, 1997). As is widely recognized in the health service, targets can also encourage forms of practice that may not necessarily be desirable. Thus, arguably, re-registration on the Child Protection Register, something theoretically to be reduced by Sure Start intervention, is not always undesirable and often can reflect good professional practice. In fact the levels of re-registrations in any given SSLP areas were so small that the 20 per cent reduction desired was effected by events in one or two families. An SSLP told one of us that they had no re-registrations in the index year and were therefore bound to fail! All the Sure Start targets represented such challenges, and programmes struggled to gather relevant and accurate data. The tension between a nationally target-driven programme and local innovation is clearly visible (see Rutter, 2007).

Nevertheless, SSLPs represented a vibrant area of child welfare development during the 1999–2006 period. Local programmes were exciting, innovative, embedded in local communities, often employing local people and spawning numerous narratives of change for parents, children and staff (see Seacroft Sure Start, 2006, for example).

Evaluating Sure Start

As we have seen, the National Evaluation of Sure Start (NESS) was the largest social science evaluation ever undertaken in the UK. NESS faced a number of serious challenges. The Treasury had been fundamentally influenced by the US-based Perry High Scope evaluation, and the figure that for every one dollar invested in Perry High Scope seven dollars had been saved in later state expenditure on welfare, prison and health services. The Treasury was obviously keen to see some sort of replication of this figure – but unsurprisingly did not have the political patience to wait 27 years!

NESS launched a series of related studies, outlined in full on their website (www.ness.bbk.ac.uk) – an elaborate body of work that we cannot hope to explore fully in this context. Here we draw on Sir Michael Rutter's (2006, 2007) effective and authoritative summary of this complex body of work. He highlights a number of methodological, logistical and ideological problems facing the NESS team. Rutter argues strongly that the failure to use a randomized controlled trail (RCT) design for the research made it difficult to measure change, but that the model that was adopted by the NESS team was the best available given the absence of an RCT. Rutter outlines the actual model used as follows:

> the comparison was between families in 150 SSLP areas (where the SSLP had been instigated 3 years earlier) and those in 50 comparison areas (due to have the intervention later), the focus being on those with 9-month old and 36-month old children (Rutter, 2006: 136).

Detailed data was collected from families through home visits and utilized in relation to outcome measures. Rutter outlines the 'key steps' taken to avoid artificial differences before moving on to examine the key findings. The first was the surprising finding that the Sure Start areas were less deprived than the comparison areas. The second key finding was that there was only one significant difference between the two types of areas for 9-month-olds, and no difference at all on the other fourteen measures. For the 36-month-olds two measures showed a difference: 'there was no evidence of any difference (for the better or worse) with respect to children's behaviour or health' (Rutter, 2006: 136). Rutter outlines how the NESS team then devised a composite measure of change in relation to SSLP effectiveness: 'Just over one-fifth [of SSLPs] were performing substantially better than expected and about the same were performing substantially worse' (Rutter, 2006: 137).

The NESS team then attempted to find any associations between features of SSLPs and their effectiveness. These findings are complex, but being a 'health-led' SSLP seemed to lead to better outcomes, as did, to an extent, being led by a local authority (as opposed to the voluntary sector). A further measure used 18 domains to assess effectiveness in relation to 'implementation efficiency':

> When the 18 domains were considered together, they significantly differentiated between the most effective and the least effective SSLPs (Rutter, 2006: 137).

The NESS team went on to assess whether SSLP effectiveness varied according to family characteristics. No variation was found for 9-month-olds but significant differences were found for 3-year-olds. Rutter describes a 'tendency for

SSLPs to have adverse effects for the disadvantaged families' and small beneficial effects in relation to teenage parents (Rutter, 2006: 137).

Rutter outlines and summarizes his views of the NESS research. He makes
eight key points which are worthy of detailed consideration in this context:

1. Rutter is confident that the NESS methods were robust, given the absence of
   his preferred RCT methodology.
2. He speculates that the outcome changes may be slight as not much time had
   passed before measures were taken, especially as programmes often took
   some time to be fully implemented.
3. He considers the adverse findings and concludes that 'a prudent reading of
   the evidence suggests that it would be wise to pay at least as much attention
   to possible adverse effects as to possible beneficial ones' (Rutter, 2006: 135).
4. He argues that the diverse nature of SSLPs means it is difficult to make any
   sense of 'what works' at all.
5. He argues that the aims to eradicate child poverty and social exclusion were
   too vaguely formulated for research to say much that was very sensible for
   them. He also notes the tendency of universal services to increase social
   inequality through differing provisions of access.
6. The features of SSLPs meant that necessary steps were not taken to ensure
   their effectiveness.
7. He outlines research from the United States that argues that positive outcomes are associated with 'carefully constructed protocols' which were
   clearly absent from SSLPs.
8. Finally, Rutter argues the lessons for research approaches to such
   projects and concludes that 'political considerations [should] not be allowed
   to torpedo the opportunity for rigorous research evaluation' (Rutter, 2006:
   138–40).

These issues meant that the NESS team found it problematic to find out 'what
works' in terms of Sure Start. This rather undermines some of the original 'what
works' agenda that underpins Sure Start. However, this story demonstrates the
uneasy relationship between political projects and evidence-based approaches,
which one of us has explored the reasons for elsewhere (Frost, 2003). Rutter
concludes his contribution to the National Evaluation of Sure Start book with the
following devastating conclusion:

> I am forced to admit that I doubt that [the government] has the slightest
> interest in research evidence when dealing with its own policies (Rutter,
> 2007: 207).

A more positive perspective emerges in the later NESS work. This optimistic
perspective is presented in a colourful and engaging form in the publication

The Sure Start Journey: a summary of the evidence (DCSF, 2008a). Here we are informed that the later findings of the NESS process suggest that:

> Parents of three-year-old children now show less negative parenting and provide their children with a better home learning environment (DCSF, 2008a: 7).

This optimism is explained as being related to the longer term impact of Sure Start:

> The report states that it is reasonable to conclude that both longer exposure to SSLPs, and the continued development of such programmes in response to the growing body of evidence, has been responsible for more positive results (DCSF, 2008a: 7).

The End of Sure Start?

Regardless of the evaluation agenda, as Sure Start developed certain tensions and issues emerged – the most powerful of these being around the localism. This had been a real strength of Sure Start – but also ultimately, to paraphrase Lenin, it contained the seeds of its own destruction.

The local agenda had been a powerful and impressive aspect of Sure Start. New Labour had been keen that the SSLPs should have an identity separate from that of the local authorities – who, as Jordan (with Jordan, 2000) has argued, suffered from an over-political identification with 'Old Labour'. Sure Start was to have a locally autonomous character and, whilst sometimes sponsored by the local authorities, the 'lead agencies' were often based in the health or voluntary agencies. Sure Start was clearly 'badged' as separate from local authorities, the Sure Start identity being powerfully led from the Sure Start central unit and with the logo featuring expensively in and around SSLPs.

But, associated with this powerful localism and identity there were also problems and significant challenges. Whilst they covered the most deprived 10 per cent of local areas they bordered onto other deprived areas, often areas with their own serious social problems and a glaring lack of resources. This position was hard to justify – not least to local people in the neighbouring 'non-SSLP' areas.

A powerful lobby grew for Sure Start to cover the whole country, thus overcoming the problems of the notorious 'postcode lottery'. Some ten years earlier Harriet Harman had headed a commission that called for an extensive network of multi-purpose, 'joined-up' children's centres across the country. This vision was eventually announced by the Children's Minister, Margaret Hodge, who stated that there would be a national network of 3,500 children's centres covering the whole country by 2010. This was, self-evidently, a programme even more ambitious than the SSLP programme: it represented considerable expenditure, a political investment and an ideological commitment unprecedented in British child welfare.

This policy shift stimulated a powerful critique from the now retired lead civil servant of the Sure Start programme, Norman Glass. In this context his argument is worthy of analysis as it addresses some of the key policy tensions in New Labour child welfare policy. Glass was evidently furious about the shift from Sure Start to children's centres:

> My contention is that little will remain except the brand name. As a result, the extraordinary enthusiasm for Sure Start among parents and those who work in the programme is likely to be dissipated (Glass, 2005).

Glass argued in *The Guardian* that there were a number of reasons that led to the 'abolition' of Sure Start. First, the issue we have already discussed about local areas with Sure Start projects bordering other equally deprived areas with no such service. Second, because of the careful nurturing of local involvement, a real strength of SSLPs:

> the 'local' Sure Start programmes have always been behind schedule, and – a mortal sin under New Labour – underspent (Glass, 2005).

Margaret Hodge, the first Minister for Children, responded to Glass in the same newspaper with the following:

> I remember those wondrous moments when I first cared for my own babies, and I remember the irrational sense of betrayal when they quickly started to develop identities of their own. This strikes me as precisely how Norman Glass feels about the coming of age of Sure Start (Hodge, 2005).

Her more serious point was perhaps:

> We want Sure Start in every community because there are disadvantaged children in most communities. But many challenges facing families transcend class. Mothers from many backgrounds can experience postnatal depression, or seek good quality early years education and care, and they want all the services built around children's needs (Hodge, 2005).

Clearly, New Labour was ready to move on from SSLPs eventually to a national network of children's centres. The tensions in having a locality-based programme had become overwhelming and the agenda moved on to delivering a new philosophy, 'progressive universalism', for children and families.

The Children's Centre Project

The children's centre idea was first promoted in the *Report of the Inter-departmental Childcare Review* (HM Treasury, 2002b) and initial start-up guidance was produced in February 2003:

> By 2010 there will be a network of 3,500 children's centres across the nation. It is these children's centres that carry the legacy of the SSLP – they are known as Sure Start children's centres and are steered by the national Sure Start Unit (Sure Start Unit, 2003).

This was an incremental approach which was later outlined as follows:

> In phase 1 (2004–06) children's centres were developed to serve families living in the 20% most disadvantaged wards. In phase 2 (2006–08) local authorities are planning to ensure all of the most disadvantaged families will have access to children centre services i.e. families in the 30% most disadvantaged areas. Centres will also be developed to serve families outside the most disadvantaged areas bringing the total number of centres to 2,500 by March 2008. In the longer term, there will be a Sure Start Children's Centre for every community – with 3,500 centres planned by 2010 (Sure Start Unit, 2005: 4).

This was an ambitious programme of developing a national programme of 3,500 centres over an 8-year period. Clearly, the Sure Start 'badge' was seen as successful and was maintained. In the spirit of SSLPs, the 'joined up' approach is again central:

> Children and families will be able to receive an integrated service from the centre across early education, childcare support services and health advice (Sure Start Unit, 2003).

Children's centres share some of the diversity that signified SSLPs – they can be single centres, multi-centres, 'virtual' or mobile centres, new builds or based in existing buildings. They can be private, public or voluntary sector. What they share is a core offer – the key services which they must offer and which help to give a unity to the children's centres concept. This 'core offer' differs according to the location of the children's centre but, for the most deprived 30 per cent local areas, includes:

> integrated early learning and childcare (early years provision) for a minimum of 10 hours a day, 5 days a week, 48 weeks a year and support for a childminder network (DfES, 2007c: 16).

This varies for centres in the other 70 per cent of areas, which may elect not to offer early years provision but must offer 'drop-in activity sessions for children, such as stay and play sessions' (DfES, 2007c: 16).

Additionally all centres must offer:

> Family support, including support and advice on parenting, information about services available in the area and access to specialist, targeted services; and Parental Outreach;
>
> Child and family health services, such as antenatal and post natal support, information and guidance on breastfeeding, health and nutrition, smoking cessation support, and speech and language therapy and other specialist support;
>
> Links with Jobcentre Plus to encourage and support parents and carers who wish to consider training and employment; and
>
> Quick and easy access to wider services
>
> (DfES, 2007c: 16).

There are a number of key differences between SSLPs and children's centres, as well as some evident points of continuity. The crucial and most politically important difference is obvious: whereas SSLPs covered only selected neighbourhoods, children's centres are universal – every community will be covered by a children's centre. This clearly overcomes the 'postcode lottery' argument used against the design of SSLPs.

The core offer for children's centres is underpinned by *National Standards for Leaders of Sure Start Children's Centres* (DfES, 2007d) and by a volume of governance guidance (DfES, 2007c). The National Standards, practice guidance, a performance-monitoring framework, all monitored by OFSTED inspection, are all aimed at delivering a high-quality programme of integrated services.

Building Children's Centres – Training and Leadership

Children's centres demanded a new breed of leaders. Whilst inevitably such leaders would come from the established professions – mainly early years, social work and health – they were to be 'joined-up' leaders having to leave behind the baggage of the previous profession and move on to become visionary leaders of the new future. As part of the children's centres movement the government introduced the National Professional Qualification in Integrated Centre Leadership (NPQICL). The NPQICL is based at the National College for School Leadership (NCSL) which hosts the National Professional Qualification for Headteachers. (NPQH). Participation in the programme is 'strongly recommended' in the official guidance (DfES, 2007c: 4). The programme content was developed and piloted by a team based at the innovative and well-regarded Pen Green Centre in

Corby, Northamptonshire. The pilot took place in 2004–05, with national implementation taking place in 2005–06. The programme is designed for managers of Sure Start designated children's centres. Aimed at Master's level, the professional qualification also carries academic credits weighted at half of a Master's degree. NPQICL takes one year to complete and involves attendance at sessions, mentoring, written and work-based assessment. It is a demanding programme aimed at developing 'transformational leaders'. The programme is aimed very specifically at early years leaders, is based in feminist and transformational values, and aspires to the development of individuals, drawing deeply on self-reflection and personal change. The first-year roll-out was positively evaluated (Williams, 2006) and after three years of practice was redesigned for the 2008–09 intake to ensure the programme was sustainable and viable on a long-term basis.

This is a significant development in many ways. First of all, the embedding of the programme in the NCSL is important. The NPQICL holds equivalence with the NPQH – a great step forward for an early years service that is often regarded as a Cinderella service, led almost exclusively by women. Second, it is a progressive programme – drawing on radical theorists and activists such as Paulo Friere – which carries the imprint of both the NCSL and the DfES. It has created a cohort of new leaders willing and motivated to take forward the children's centres movement, while also creating an influential underpinning lobby group (Aubrey, 2007).

Children's Centres – Delivering for Children and Families?

We need to step back and consider the scale of the Sure Start/children's centres achievement: by 2010 there will be a network of 3,500 centres, many newly built, covering the entire country. They exemplify the concept of a 'one-stop shop' for parents, delivering 'joined-up' services to localities and attempting to overcome the issues of stigma by offering universal services. There can be little doubt that this is a considerable achievement and a massive state investment in parenting and childhood.

Underpinning these developments is an approach that state documents identify as 'progressive universalism':

> Those children and young people who need it should receive additional support to address the persistent gap in outcomes between the lowest and highest socio-economic groups. This means offering a continuum of support according to need with greater personalisation of services to meet every child's and family's requirements (DfES, 2007a: 5).

The use of universalism here is that we would expect in social policy discourse – that is, services available to all on the basis of need. However, 'progressive' is used in a different way here: it refers not to a political or redistributive ideology as one might expect, but to the progressive delivery of services to those in more need. This underpins the children's centre approach. There are two types of children's centres, with different 'core offers' – one aimed at centres in the 30 per cent most deprived areas and another aimed at the remaining 70 per cent. Thus all parents may want the 'universal' offer of day care for three-year-olds, but only some would need the progressive services targeted at, say, lone fathers. Thus progressive universalism encompasses a traditional social democratic approach of universal welfare services combined with a more interventionist, targeted approach aimed at tackling social exclusion.

Conclusion

This chapter has examined perhaps the most significant development in child welfare under New Labour – the Sure Start project which will evolve into a network of 3,500 children's centres by 2010. We will now reflect on the implications of this development for children's social care.

Sure Start is a quintessentially New Labour initiative. It reflects, as we have seen, major themes of New Labour ideology, including 'joined-up thinking', early intervention and 'what works'. It was clearly 'badged' with a specific Sure Start identity, one distinct from social services departments, which initially served to distance it from local authorities. . Thus clearly, although concerned with many social work issues, particularly around prevention and family support, Sure Start was not a social work initiative.

However, social work and children's social care remain part of the of Sure Start/children's centres initiative. Some social workers and social care projects are based in children's centres. In addition, many children's centre managers are social workers by professional background. A recent study of the 354 participants who began the NPQICL in 2005 found that the largest group were teachers (104), followed by 91 nursery nurses, and 62 with professional social work qualifications (Clouston, unpublished). They bring with them social work values and approaches within the children's centre agenda.

Thus we have a paradox that permeates this book and that we examine in detail in our two concluding chapters. Social care is both absent and present in the children's centres agenda. In theory, given the approach suggested by the Seebohm Report (1968) we explored earlier, Sure Start and/or children's centres could have been social services departments' preventive initiatives. But for New Labour this would have implied an association with the deadweight of bureaucracy and the negative implications that social work is perceived to carry with it. Thus Sure Start was clearly distanced from social care and social work. Despite this, social work and social care values permeate the initiative. Social workers are based in children's centres, often manage centres, social work students have practice placements in centres and social workers work closely with children's centres.

Thus the paradox is clear. Sure Start was an initiative that simultaneously could never have been a social care project, but equally would be unsustainable without the involvement of social care staff. During the post-war period (1945–97) child care, as opposed to childcare (as in day care), was predominantly a social work concern. Subsequently child care has become a much more diffused concern – a 'joined-up' responsibility located across children's centres, schools, extended services and social care offices. Social care, although remaining central to child care and child welfare, now has a more specific role. It has been displaced from the universalist role envisaged by Seebohm into more specific concerns with safeguarding, looked-after children and children with complex needs, as we shall see in our concluding two chapters.

8

Working with Children and Young People with Complex Needs

Introduction

It has been argued throughout this book that the role of social workers – and that of related social care workers – has been profoundly restructured in recent years. As a result of this, in what we can characterize as the 'Every Child Matters' era, children's social care is largely focused on the two key areas of child protection and 'looked-after' children. In addition to these roles it is also crucially the case that social workers are involved in work with 'children with complex needs' – for example, children with severe special needs, and those with complex health issues, mental health issues and/or disabilities.

The role of social care in such situations is complex and demanding. Social care workers will often act as the cement that holds the services together by assessing, coordinating and supporting. Often, in undertaking these roles, they may find there are tensions between 'social' and 'medical' models that the social worker will have to work within and between (see Anning et al., 2006).

The social model of disability, often adhered to by social care staff and user-based movements, is defined as follows by the British Council of Disabled People:

> Disability is the disadvantage or restriction of activity caused by society which takes little or no account of people who have impairments and thus excludes them from mainstream activity (Morris, 2003: 2).

The social model allows disabled people to move away from a 'personal tragedy' narrative towards a model that allows them to take control and exercise power over their own lives (see Barnes and Mercer, 2003). The social model has been influential in developing and shifting services for children and young people, although many challenges remain to make services fully inclusive and responsive.

This chapter explores some of the policy context of social care work with children and young people with complex needs. As the field of 'complex needs' is wide ranging and arguably ill-defined we have chosen to examine, in some detail, two groups of children who can be seen as having 'complex needs'. First, in this chapter, we explore the issues arising from practice with disabled children and how New Labour has perceived and responded to their needs. It will be argued that policy is broadly progressive in this arena, but that there is evidence of uneven provision and of structural barriers to full equality that mean that policy aspirations are difficult to implement effectively. Second, in the following chapter, we examine a group who clearly have 'complex needs', although they are not always included in this category; that is, unaccompanied asylum-seeking children. Here again provision is uneven, but in contrast to the situation with disabled children, where discrimination is unlawful, there are clear legal and policy barriers in the way of ensuring that 'every child matters'.

Policy Background

Specialist provision for disabled children and young people emerged in the early nineteenth century in the form of charitable provision. The Poor Law Amendment Act, 1834, encouraged Boards of Guardians to pay fees directly to charitable institutions to educate such children. In 1889, however, a Royal Commission on the 'blind, deaf and mentally handicapped' reported that these powers had not been sufficiently utilized, and that such a lack of investment would lead to such children and young people becoming 'not only a burden to themselves, but a weighty burden on the state' (in Frost and Stein, 1989: 26). The concerns of the Commission led to the Elementary Education (Blind and Deaf Children) Act of 1893 and later to the 1899 Act relating to 'defective and epileptic' children, which initiated compulsory education for this group but which also left an 'uneducable' group, who were left in institutional care or worse (see Topliss, 1979, for a full account). Thus a pattern of separate provision for disabled children was established which was to set a pattern of provision which even today is difficult to eradicate.

Today, disabled children are more likely to be looked after in the care system than non-disabled children: around 6 per cent of disabled children are in care, whilst the figure for the remainder of the population is around 0.6 per cent (Fawcett et al., 2004: 115). Twenty-eight per cent of looked-after children have a statement of Special Educational Needs, compared to 3 per cent of the general population. About 13,300 disabled children are in long-term residential placements (DCSF, 2007a). Additionally, many children with severe special needs remain in residential care in segregated settings, but may not be included in the 'in care' statistics.

Disabled children face the barriers faced by all disabled people – those relating to issues such as transport and leisure – which act as a form of social exclusion. A major step forward has been taken through the implementation of the

Disability Discrimination Act 2005. This obliges public bodies and others to make 'reasonable adjustments' to ensure that disabled people can participate fully in social life. This and other policy shifts have followed pressure and campaigning by disabled people's groups.

Fawcett and colleagues have argued that there are three tensions in New Labour's approach to disabled children. These are briefly summarized below:

1. A tension between work versus 'care'. Fawcett et al. argue that the benefit system prioritizes paid employment and places pressures on young disabled people. 'The paradox between the promoted goal of social inclusion and the exclusionary mechanisms of the benefit process can leave young disabled people stranded between positive rhetoric and the dispiriting reality of the current work/benefits system' (Fawcett et al., 2004: 118).

2. A tension between support and surveillance, due to the emphasis on investing through parents rather than to children and young people directly. Fawcett et al. report Tom Shakespeare's study, a key finding of which was:

    that disabled children were subject to a very high degree of surveillance by adults. Such children were found to have very few social contacts outside the family and activities were often dominated by adult presence. Adults also mediated in terms of contact with other children, often serving to compound segregationalist practices, adversely influencing the attitudes of non-disabled children. Whilst disabled children identified with disability in many different ways, adults tended to emphasize the different and special needs of disabled children and to limit their range of responses (Fawcett et al., 2004: 122–3).

3. Investing in children raises tensions between targeting and rights. Here Fawcett et al. argue that:

    the government can be seen to have prioritized a form of targeting ... over rights. Whilst this form of targeting can be used as a means of narrowing the divide between disabled and non-disabled children, it can also further accentuate segregation rather than inclusion on the basis of the special requirements or 'special needs' (Fawcett et al., 2004: 124).

Fawcett et al. conclude that:

    current policy agendas for disabled children and young people can be seen to contain developmental aspects as well as contradictions and constraints (Fawcett et al., 2004: 218).

Fawcett et al. published their work in 2004, well before the shift in government policy reflected in *Aiming High for Disabled Children* (DfES, 2007a). This development in policy will now be outlined, analysed and reflected upon.

New Labour and Children and Young People with Complex Needs – Emerging Policy Developments

New Labour has identified children and young people with complex needs as a particular target for 'modernized' and 'joined-up' forms of intervention (see Hughes, 2007). In relation to disabled children, for example:

> The Government wants all children to have the best start in life and the ongoing support that they and their families need to fulfil their potential. Disabled children are less likely to achieve as much in a range of areas as their non-disabled peers. Improving their outcomes, allowing them to benefit from equality of opportunity, and increasing their involvement and inclusion in society will help them to achieve more as individuals. It will also reduce social inequality, and allow communities to benefit from the contribution that disabled children and their families can make, harnessing their talent and fostering tolerance and understanding of diversity (DfES, 2007a: 5).

Here we see many of the New Labour 'key messages' that have been explored elsewhere in this book: themes such as a focus on outcomes, social inclusion and equality of opportunity feature strongly in the above quotation. Unusually for such a policy statement it refers explicitly to reducing 'social inequality' instead of the usual conceptualizing around 'social exclusion'. The 'Aiming High' policy messages are important as disabled people have often been marginalized in capitalist and socialist societies alike (Oliver, 1983). Both disabled parents and disabled children fear that they will face discrimination – for example, disabled parents may feel that they are more likely to lose their children where there are child protection issues (SCIE, 2007b). It is important then for social workers and social care workers to support policies that challenge discrimination against disabled people by working within the social model.

In the 'windscreen' model (see Figure 3.6) children with complex needs lie at the right-hand side of the continuum, after 'children with no identified additional needs' and 'children with additional needs', indicating a need for more intensive intervention across the full range of professions. Children with complex needs present a major challenge to practitioners across the range of child welfare professions if they are to be truly empowered and enabled to take more control over their lives.

According to the windscreen model, 'children with complex needs' include both those whose issues are explored elsewhere in the study (children in need of protection, adopted children, children in care and youth offenders) and more specifically in terms of this chapter:

- children with severe and complex special educational needs;
- children with complex disabilities or complex health needs;
- children diagnosed with significant mental health needs.

These are groups of young people who are at risk of multiple forms of social exclusion and therefore, as we have seen, they are a primary target of the New Labour reform agenda.

We should note that children and young people with complex needs are people who share many needs, views, wishes and opinions with other children and young people: 'What matters most to them is being able to live at home, go to school, spend time with friends and participate in leisure and community activities with family and peers' (SCIE, 2007b). In other words, children and young people with complex needs are children first – and people with complex needs second.

The concept of 'complex needs' is, arguably, ill-defined with no agreed definition amongst either practitioners or policy makers (SCIE, 2007a). Complex needs certainly include disabled children, children with special educational needs and those with serious health conditions. However, the category of 'complex needs' has to be flexible enough to include other children and young people as well, some of whom may have unique and specific needs.

Work with children and young people who have complex needs will always be multi-disciplinary – often involving doctors, psychologists, other health care staff, educational and social care professionals. Thus meeting the requirements of those with complex needs requires a 'joined-up' approach – a key theme of this book. Again the requirement for integrated services is an overlap with the needs of other young people who also require services integrated through the delivery of the five Every Child Matters outcomes.

What can bring together multi-agency services effectively is a 'key worker' who can play a crucial role in planning and coordinating service provision. The case for such a key worker is made in the Children's Plan (DCSF, 2007b). Families of children with complex needs too often experience services as being distant, bureaucratic and difficult to access (Ward and Tarleton, 2007), an issue that is exacerbated by the need to liaise with many professionals. The key worker can play a fundamental role in working in partnership with families, carers and children to minimize duplication and ensure that services are effectively coordinated.

Official policy makes a close link between an effective multi-disciplinary approach and a 'whole family approach', which is:

> one that enables a coordinated package of support to be provided for everyone in the household even if those delivering it belong to different

teams in an authority, or to services commissioned by different Directorates (Hughes, 2007).

It is also the case that about 12 per cent of the 14.1 million parents in the United Kingdom are disabled, some of whom have disabled children. In addition, the issues around disability are often compounded by challenges arising from poverty and isolation (SCIE, 2007a).

As in all forms of child welfare there is a potential – and often an actual – tension between a focus on the needs of the child and the needs of the family. This tension is well illustrated by the government policy on 'inclusion' in mainstream services for children with special educational needs, which is resisted by some parents who favour specialist provision which more precisely meets what they perceive as the needs of their children. Clearly the needs of children and parents are not necessarily identical, as Fawcett and colleagues outlined in the discussion above.

Services for children with complex needs and their families also need to be flexible and responsive to the diverse life challenges that face people in this situation. They often face unexpected challenges such as a change in health needs, urgent requirements for respite care, or a need to respond to unforeseen events in the family.

The challenges facing services for children and young people with special health and social care needs have been identified to include:

a)   social care services being difficult to access, with the worker's role being seen as over-specialist and restrictive; some workers thus adopt 'rule breaking' as a way of overcoming restrictions;

b)   commissioning and service delivery arrangements are often dominated by 'medical model' concerns, 'meaning that social care needs and services may be overlooked' (p. 24);

c)   more flexibility and responsiveness are required;

d)   short-term funding often affects service continuity and reliability (see SCIE, 2007b).

Genuine consultation and participation by disabled children and young people is an important step in improving the quality of services. This emphasis can be seen in the National Service Framework for Children, Young People and Maternity Services (NSF) in England which stresses the need to consult and involve children. Standard 8, which applies specifically to disabled children and those with complex health needs, states:

> Professionals should ensure that disabled children, especially children with high communication needs, are not excluded from the decision-making process. In particular professionals should consider the needs of children who rely on communication equipment or who use non-verbal communication such as sign language (DH, 2004: 29).

It has been argued that whilst such aspirations exist, ensuring their success has been uneven:

> Evidence suggests that while children are increasingly being involved in decision-making, growth has been slower in respect of disabled children (Franklin and Sloper, forthcoming).

Watson et al. (2007) have demonstrated how children with complex needs can be involved in research about how agencies work with them through multi-agency arrangements. Such work involves sensitivity and flexibility which, the authors argue, can make an important contribution to improving services and informing policy initiatives such as those explored below.

'Aiming High for Disabled Children' – New Labour Approaches to Disabled Children and Young People

In this section we examine the approach taken by New Labour to an important part of the population of children with complex needs – disabled children. In 2007 New Labour published a crucial report (DfES, 2007a) with the ambitious aim of transforming the lives of disabled children. In many ways this is a typical New Labour initiative in terms of children – it is wide-ranging and ambitious, demonstrating a belief that the state can change the lives of children in a positive direction.

Aiming High for Disabled Children argues that disabled children should be seen as 'both a local and national priority' (DfES, 2007a: 6) and the Minister admits that disabled children 'have not been as high on the agenda as they should have been in the past' (Balls, 2007). A target is established in the 2007 Children's Plan of achieving this transformation by 2011. The 'Aiming High' report attempts to address the needs of:

> The 570,000 disabled children in England, around 100,000 of whom have complex care needs, [who] need support from a wide range of services, and so should be benefiting even more than most from these reforms (DfES, 2007a: 11).

The 'Aiming High' report identifies three key areas requiring action if the outcomes for disabled children and young people are to improve:

- empowerment;
- responsive services and timely support; and
- improving quality and capacity (DfES, 2007a: 5).

These are clearly important areas of reform aimed at addressing centuries of inequality for disabled children. We shall examine each in turn. First, in terms of empowerment the intention of the government is outlined as follows:

- a 'core offer' will encompass minimum standards on information, transparency, participation, assessment and feedback, to make it clear what entitlements and services disabled children, young people and their families can expect. Through providing greater transparency, it will be easier to benchmark provision across the country;
- piloting Individual Budgets will give families and disabled young people real choice and control to design flexible packages of services which respond to their needs; and
- spreading good practice on engagement such as parents' forums across the country, underpinned by £5 million of investment over the CSR [Comprehensive Spending Review] period, will give parents of disabled children a voice in local empowerment mechanisms, foster better relationships between service providers and parents, and allow parents to contribute their expertise to help shape services (DfES, 2007a: 6).

It should be noted that the importance of relevant and accessible information has been identified by a number of researchers, particularly for disabled parents (Tarleton et al., 2006, Ward and Tarleton, 2007).

The importance of assessment for disabled children and their families is also recognized by the 'core offer'. *Aiming High* argues that disabled children should also benefit from the Common Assessment Framework, as other children do, and that this should provide 'a gateway to more specialist assessments where necessary, and more high-level multi-agency assessments provided in the same place at the same time' (DfES, 2007a: 17). Research has established that often these more complex assessments are insufficiently coordinated. It is also recognized that this is a process and that children and young people will require 'ongoing and differential assessment, but this should be provided in a coherent, coordinated way'.

The core offer also champions a 'clear and published complaints procedure for all families who are not happy with the services they are receiving' (DfES, 2007a: 34).

The 'core offer' language is now familiar across a range of services, as is the focus on information giving and benchmarking. The personalization theme is also familiar and in this context is to be delivered through 'Individual Budgets'. The Commission for Social Care Inspection (CSCI) reveals that 5,027 parents of disabled children had received direct payments in 2005–06. However, 43 local authorities had not made any payments and direct payments still made up less than £1 in every £100 of social care expenditure (CSCI, 2006). There is clearly still a long way to go in making 'Individual Budgets' a reality. These are

attempts to empower children and their families through transferring responsibilities that have normally been located with state-employed professionals and
transferring them to the service users, using a model of the service user as 'consumer' rather than recipient, active participant rather than passive 'service user'.

Empowerment also takes the form of 'partnership' – a key theme of British
child welfare, at least since the passage of the Children Act 1989. It is formulated here in the organizational form of 'parent's forums' – bringing professionals and parents together to plan services and discuss issues.

Empowerment is defined by New Labour, as we have seen elsewhere in this
book, in terms of rights and responsibilities:

> The concept of empowerment is intimately linked to the principle of **rights
> and responsibilities** for individuals. In this context, empowerment means:
> * *a right* for citizens to 'opt-in' to networks of support to help influence
>   and shape the services on offer. This creates a duty for service commis-
>   sioners and providers to reach out to vulnerable groups and empower
>   them in making their views known and heard; and
> * recognition that with rights come *responsibilities* for citizens: to engage
>   constructively with service providers in shaping service provision where
>   possible, and understand competing priorities and local constraints
>   (DfES, 2007a: 16, original emphases).

This takes a more explicit form later in *Aiming High:*

> supporting disabled children and young people and their parents to shape
> services. This can also mean them playing a part in local mechanisms to
> facilitate citizen pressure to hold front-line services to account, linked to
> the new Local Government White Paper 'Community Call for Action'
> (DfES, 2007a: 16).

Thus the empowering move for disabled children and their families is linked
to the exercise of 'responsibilities', including the rather clumsily phrased
responsibility to 'understand competing priorities and local constraints'. But
later we find a more potentially radical formulation of facilitating 'citizen pressure', which contrasts with the more familiar positioning of the service user as a
'consumer' (Luckock and Hart, 2005).

Alongside these empowering reforms the government has identified the need
for 'promoting more responsive services and timely support'. The government
is keen to measure this through what they identify as 'sufficient incentives'
for providers and commissioners by establishing a 'national disabled children
indicator as part of the new set of priority PSAs to be agreed across Government
at the Comprehensive Spending Review' (DfES, 2007a: 7).

These are familiar mechanisms in the New Labour lexicon of providing incentives and audit mechanisms to steer and measure the performance of local authorities.

In planning improved services for disabled children and young people there is also an emphasis on early intervention. Again, this is a key theme across child welfare policy and in this context is outlined as follows:

> to prevent interventions coming too late at important stages of a disabled child's life or development, the Government will provide specific resource for evaluation and benchmarking good practice on early intervention for disabled children and their families as part of the work of the new Centre for Excellence for Children and Family Services (DfES, 2007a: 7).

The lack of data in this field is also emphasized and thus it is important to:

> develop a clearer picture of the disabled children population at a local level so that disabled children's needs are planned for, Local Authorities and PCTs will improve their data collection for this group, and national and local agencies will work together to develop more co-ordinated data sets (DfES, 2007a: 7)

Another element of policy reiterates the important provisions of the Childcare Act 2006, that is, that:

> the Government will continue to roll out the Early Support Programme to cover all disabled children aged 0–5 to promote wrap around, timely provision for young disabled children and their families (DfES, 2007a: 7).

This will explicitly provide accessibility:

> accessible childcare is vital to help parents work, and to improve children's development. The Government will set up a childcare accessibility project, underpinned by £35m over the CSR through the General Sure Start Grant (DfES, 2007a: 7).

Indeed, this development makes more concrete the provisions of the 2006 Childcare Act which already requires:

> Local Authorities to have particular regard to the needs of disabled children as part of their new duties to assess the childcare needs of families and to secure sufficient childcare to children up to and including age 14 (18 for disabled children) (DfES, 2007a: 7).

The final element of improving service provision in *Aiming High* is aimed at addressing the important issue of transition from childhood to adulthood, and therefore from children's to adult's services:

> The Government will provide £19m over the CSR period for a Transition Support Programme to help disabled young people and their families benefit from intensive, co-ordinated support and person centred planning (DfES, 2007a: 7).

Improving joint working between the services for children and adults was identified in a speech by Beverley Hughes, as Minister for Children, as 'the next big challenge we now face' (Hughes, 2007). Indeed, more effective multi-agency working is regularly identified by researchers as crucial for improving services to families where there are disability issues (see Ward and Tarleton, 2007, for example).

Transitions are seen as 'vital if disabled young people are to gain independence, choice and control over the assistance they need, achieve to aspirations and play a full and active role in society' (Hughes, 2007). This again should be a personalized service that should meet the needs of the individual young person and not take place at 'a specific point in time for all' (Hughes, 2007).

The importance of transitions is highlighted in the Commission for Social Care Inspection report *Growing up matters: better transition planning for young people with complex needs* (CSCI, 2006). The report demonstrates that the transition can be very difficult and often seems to lead to a decline in support and service delivery for the person involved.

The third and final element of the 'Aiming High' programme is to improve the quality and the capacity of services for children with disabilities. This includes a promise of extra funding including 'a specific grant of £280m over the CSR period to deliver a step change in the provision of short breaks for disabled children'. This is expanded upon in *The Children's Plan*, published in late 2007:

> To improve facilities, we will invest £90 million over the next three years in short break provision. This funding for public, private and voluntary sector providers will help improve equipment, transport and facilities and allow more inclusive breaks, where severely disabled young people can take part in activities with their non-disabled peers (DCSF, 2007b: 1.39).

These provisions are made legislative reality in the Children and Young Persons Act 2008.

In addition to these short break measures there is a commitment in *Aiming High*:

> to maximize mobility, help children access schools, leisure and other services, and promote independent living, the Government will deliver a

radical reform of community equipment and wheelchair provision (DfES, 2007a: 8).

An important element of the 'Aiming High' project is to ensure that universal services are more fairly accessible to disabled children. As part of this there is a proposal to address these issues through workforce reform by commissioning 'the Children's Workforce Development Council to research the skills and behaviours required by the workforce and to identify gaps' (DfES, 2007a: 8).

It is often the case that where universal services are developed there is a danger that disabled children are excluded. As a spokesperson for the Children's Society stated in relation to the extended services agenda:

> Many [disabled children] need individual support in schools through the statementing process, but it is common that this individual support isn't provided during extended school time (Taylor, 2007: 18).

This statement highlights that positive policy statements are not always realized in practice. In *Aiming High* the government itself argues that good practice is not found uniformly across the nation. Of course, there are many examples of effective and innovative practice, as is reported in the policy review that foreshadowed the 2007 Children's Plan:

> For example, in some areas, coordinated working, innovative practice in service delivery, and the involvement of disabled children, young people and their parents is fostering services that are more responsive and flexible to disabled children and their families' needs, and families have told the Review that these are making a real difference to their lives (HM Treasury and DfES, 2007a: 2).

But a key challenge is to ensure that good practice is demonstrated across the country. Three key issues for improving practice are identified in *Aiming High:*

- existing data does not present a full picture of the quality of provision in different areas. However, there is evidence that across local authorities, disabled children and families are offered different levels and standards of care, and that those most in need are not always the most likely to get support. Parents and young people in some areas feel that they are not sufficiently empowered, informed, or involved;
- research for the Review also showed that much provision is targeted on high need, high cost interventions, with a lack of focus on intervening early in a child's life, at a key transition point, or change in their condition. Local areas rightly prioritise those in greatest need, however a lack of early support is sometimes exacerbating the numbers of disabled

children and families who reach crisis point and need more complex interventions; and

- despite strong examples of successful coordination in the planning and provision of innovative services, for example through the Early Support Programme which is encouraging multi-agency working, there is more that needs to be done to tackle remaining coordination problems. This includes differing eligibility criteria, differing referral systems and cultures, and differing and inconsistent data about the disabled children population across agencies (DfES, 2007a: 14).

Aiming High for Disabled Children then is a clear and comprehensive policy that attempts to address the discrimination against disabled children which has deep historical roots. As we have seen, the policy is based in a social inclusion framework that we discussed in Chapter 2. It draws on a whole range of the New Labour mantras of integrated services, early intervention and services delivered through a 'core offer'. It is framed in terms of 'rights' and 'responsibilities' and encourages participation in service provision and sometimes presents challenges to service providers.

Whilst the policy is to be welcomed, and is broadly progressive, a key challenge is to make these aspirations a reality. This involves ensuring an even standard of good practice across the country and addressing the structural barriers of poverty and exclusion that often face disabled children and their families (Barnes and Mercer, 2003).

Conclusion

Mike Oliver, a leading author and campaigner in the field of disability, has argued that:

> The social work task is no longer one of adjusting individuals to personal disasters but rather helping them to locate the personal, social, economic and community resources to enable them to live life to the full (Oliver, 1983: 31).

This approach is arguably being strengthened by the 'personalization' model which is currently being vigorously pursued by New Labour across the health, education and social care agenda. The approach here is to move towards services being tailored to personal needs, for example through the provision of direct payments to people, who are then in charge of their own requirements. Such models can be effectively pursued only through the active involvement of service users in all elements of their lives – at the individual, group and strategic levels of service planning and delivery.

Social care workers have a crucial role in the personalization and empowerment agenda. This agenda represents a radical shift away from a patronizing casework model to an empowerment model.

A major challenge for social care workers is to address the transition from children's to adult services. This has been a complex transition for many years (Morris, 1999), but especially since the evolution of all-encompassing, Seebohm-style, social services departments to distinct children's social care and adult social care departments, with distinct managerial arrangements and organizational structures. The government adjunct to 'think family' is a challenging one in this context and one we return to in our concluding chapters.

9

A Challenge to Social Care Practice: Working with Unaccompanied Asylum-seeking Children and Young People

Introduction

It is now a commonplace to say how quickly the world is changing in an age of rapid globalization (Held and McGrew, 2002). In the United Kingdom many citizens enjoy the advantages of globalization, including, for example, cheaply manufactured goods and worldwide air travel. We may therefore expect to pick up some of the costs and responsibilities that flow from these advantages.

Globalization has a profound impact on social problems and social care practice – for example, through the impact of the World Wide Web on child protection, the internationalization of the workforce, and the challenges of working with new migrant populations. The example of the impact of globalization considered in this section is social care practice with unaccompanied asylum-seeking children and young people, which provides a stark and challenging aspect of contemporary social work practice. (For the sake of brevity, and to avoid the de-humanizing abbreviation UASC that is often used, we shall refer to such young people as 'unaccompanied children' from now onwards.) Over the past decade or so social care work with such children has become increasingly important and widespread across the United Kingdom. The impact across the country is uneven – in Kent for example it is reported that 'in September, 2001, the authority was already supporting 500 unaccompanied children and young people but this figure quadrupled the following year' (Kearney, 2007: 98). The impact elsewhere is uneven and is partly dictated by the 'dispersal' policy of the government. The Children's Commissioner reports that 5,515 claiming applications were recorded in 2006 (11 million, 2008: 4). The official estimate is that about 6,000 unaccompanied children are supported by local authorities in the UK and that figure has been roughly similar since 2004 (Border and Immigration Agency, 2008a).

The social theorist Zygmunt Bauman (2003) has written of one of the consequences of globalization: displaced humans – the migrants, refugees, asylum seekers – who suffer at the sharp end of enormous global social change. Unaccompanied children are undoubtedly part of this process. They face all the challenges of the 'separated' children we have explored in Chapter 6 – isolation, challenges to identity and social disadvantage – together with their additional experiences of global dislocation and diverse stories of war, violence and trauma. As Barnardo's have argued more generally in relation to asylum seekers:

> most importantly, the children of asylum seekers should always be treated as children first and as asylum seekers second (Barnardo's, 2008: 2).

This is not to argue that the experience of children in distress crossing international boundaries presents a totally new challenge. Indeed, rather in reverse of the modern situation, England for many centuries practised sending its own children abroad. Child migrants, as they were known, were sent overseas by a range of organizations from the 1640s until the early 1960s. The stories of disjointed lives and fragmented identities have now been reconstructed by a number of commentaries (Bean and Melville, 1990). One key difference is that such children were unwittingly instruments of imperial and racial domination; today, unaccompanied children come to a situation where they experience racism and discrimination.

Our focus here is on unaccompanied children. An unaccompanied child is defined as an asylum-seeking person, under the age of 18, who is not living with their parent, relative or guardian in the United Kingdom (DCSF, 2007e). Such children are often fleeing violence, abuse and exploitation. It should also be noted that many other asylum-seeking children are here with their families – Barnardo's estimate that over 100,000 children could be involved in the backlog of decision-making about their status.

Practice with unaccompanied children represents perhaps the most complex challenge for our social care agencies to work with. But, as Mitchell (2006) has argued, it is important that they are not seen simply as 'problems', and that we understand 'what is happening when the problem is not happening' (Parton and O'Byrne, 2000: 56).

In the next section we go on to examine the legal situation of unaccompanied children, the challenges to assessment practice and the particular role of social care professionals. It is the group of children and young people that most cast into doubt the literal meaning of the 'Every Child Matters' policy stream (Barnardo's, 2008).

A Legal Quagmire – Children or Asylum Seekers?

As we have seen throughout this book, the main mantra of New Labour in relation to child welfare since 2003 has been that 'Every Child Matters'. Whilst this is arguably a rhetorical device, it is also potentially useful in enabling us to make claims for our most marginalized children and attempting to ensure that they really do 'matter' (see Cunningham and Tomlinson, 2005 for a critical commentary on this issue).

Asylum in general is a high-profile political and media issue reflected in the fact that 'there have been six major pieces of legislation over the past 10 years, with the sixth, the UK Borders Act, receiving Royal Assent in October, 2007' (Barnardo's, 2008: 3). The legal status of unaccompanied children is often precarious as the majority are granted 'discretionary leave' to remain, normally until their 18th birthday, and rarely are allowed the more secure status of 'indefinite leave' to remain, or 'humanitarian protection' (Dixon and Wade, 2007: 126).

One reason that social work with unaccompanied children is particularly challenging and complex is because of the underpinning tension experienced by professionals between the Children Act 1989, in which the needs of the child are paramount, and the contrasting treatment of children under immigration law, in which their needs do not always seem to be paramount. This is a key legal, policy and practice tension which has a dramatic impact on the welfare of unaccompanied children. This tension is rooted, partially at least, in the United Kingdom's reservation when it ratified the United Nations Convention on the Rights of the Child. The reservation made it clear that the United Kingdom would not apply the convention to 'those who do not have the right under the law of the United Kingdom to enter and remain in the United Kingdom' (see Dennis, 2007: 20). Partially reflecting these complications, social care policy and practice across the country is uneven (SCIE, 2007c).

The reservation in terms of the UN Convention was, rather apologetically, reinforced by the government in 2005, when it was stated by their official spokesperson in the House of Lords, Baroness Andrew, that, 'I cannot give a commitment to lift the reservation' (quoted by Dennis, 2007: 21).

The tension between child welfare law and immigration law was further expressed in the guidance to the Children (Leaving Care) Act 2000 which states that the Act clearly does apply to unaccompanied children – but that this application has to be seen in the context of immigration law and the 'immigration status' of the child. This tension can be seen, for example, in the DCSF circular on the funding of leaving care arrangements for unaccompanied children, which combines child care and immigration criteria in assessing eligibility for local authority funding (DCSF, 2007d). As Cemlyn and Briskman express it:

> A key issue for social work is that since the early 1990s a main plank of deterrence has been a progressive dismantling of social rights for all asylum seekers, removing them from the usual provisions of citizenship (Cemlyn and Briskman, 2003: 165).

Statements about the 'Care Matters' reform process (see Chapter 6) have been equally confusing. The government has stated that Care Matters clearly applies to unaccompanied children – but that such children also have particular needs 'in order to prepare for a positive return home' (quoted by Dennis, 2007: 22). The Children's Plan attempts to clarify the situation as follows:

> We appreciate the potential vulnerability of unaccompanied children, and the distress they may experience while waiting for a decision on their asylum claim without the support of a family. Government recognises that unaccompanied asylum-seeking children (UASC) are first and foremost children. Many unaccompanied asylum seekers will be supported as children in care by local authorities as, by definition, they enter the country without an adult to take parental responsibility for them and, therefore, the local authority will be responsible for assessing these young people's needs and supporting them to access services. These young people, as children in care, will benefit from the reforms that we are introducing in our Children and Young Persons Bill (DCSF, 2007b: 26).

This seems to be a more empathetic understanding of the situation facing unaccompanied children, but the implementation of policy, and the detail of this policy, have often proven crucial.

The theme of such children returning home is seen in Home Office statements, such as that 'we do not believe that it is a child's best interests to remain in the UK separated from their parents or communities' (Home Office, 2005: 31).

An important policy issue relates to the transition undertaken by such young people at the age of 18. When a new policy was introduced, in 2000, it led to young people being transferred at age 18 from a social-care-based form of care to support through vouchers and dispersed accommodation. Since 2000, however, as policy and practice have evolved, 'many more young people are now eligible for continued social work provision beyond their eighteenth birthday, as care leavers' (Dennis, 2007: 25). This development itself has been effected by the implementation of the Nationality, Immigration and Asylum Act 2002, implemented in January 2003, which has again muddied the waters around exactly who qualifies for which sort of assistance (see Dennis, 2007, for an excellent summary of these complex developments).

In addition to facing this legal quagmire, unaccompanied young people have lived vulnerable lives and have, by definition, escaped from trauma.

Significantly, a section of the 2002 Adoption and Children Act allowed local authorities to provide accommodation for children under Section 17 of the Children Act 1989, without them actually becoming 'looked after' children, thus allowing local authorities to work with unaccompanied children through the family support element of the 1989 Act whilst simultaneously providing accommodation. In a study reported by Dixon and Wade (2007: 126–7), 76 per cent of their sample were supported under community provision and a minority were accommodated.

In 2003 the Department of Health issued guidance that argued that the 'presumption' for unaccompanied children should be that they accommodated under Section 20, that is as looked-after children, unless good practice suggested otherwise. Again, this reflects the legal complexities of the situation.

The Hillingdon judgment of 2003 has been significant here (Nandy, 2005). Four unaccompanied young people challenged the lack of support they had received: they had been supported under Section 17, but not under Section 20. They argued that they should be eligible to receive services under the Children (Leaving Care) Act 2000. The judgment found that Section 17 should not routinely be used to provide accommodation, and argued that the guidance from the Department of Health referred to above should be followed. The judgment found that they should have been supported as if they had been 'looked-after' children.

Another legal issue is that the duty to cooperate under the Children Act 2004, which applies to most agencies working with children, does not apply to the immigration authorities (SCIE, 2007c).

Clearly the law relating to unaccompanied children is extremely complex, and of course is subject to frequent changes. The crucial aspect as far as this study is concerned is the tension between the mainly benign intentions of the Children Act 1989 and related legislation and the harsher provisions of immigration law in a climate that is rather hostile to refugees and asylum seekers in general. This places social care in an invidious and challenging position which many practitioners throughout the country are struggling with.

The government foreshadowed the introduction of new guidance from the Borders Agency in the 2007 Children's Plan as follows:

> The Home Office Borders and Immigration Agency will set out their plans for improving support to USAC in their response to their consultation paper *Planning Better Outcomes and Support for Unaccompanied Asylum Seeking Children*. This will set out proposals for strengthening identification and support for trafficked children; and for improving the quality and time-liness of asylum decision making to reduce the uncertainty faced by UASC, so that planning for their care can support their integration or their safe return to their country of origin (DCSF, 2007b: 26).

Assessment – Judging the Needs of Unaccompanied Asylum-seeking Children and Young People

As well as the legal complications so far explored there are also practice-based dilemmas which rest on the legal situation but which have a direct impact on forms of social work practice. In this section we explore specifically the complex role of assessment in relation to unaccompanied children.

As we have seen, the situation of unaccompanied children represents a real challenge to the interpretation of the Children Act, as Mitchell argues in relation to assessment:

> For many, the quality of the needs assessment and, in light of this, the sections of the Children Act 1989 under which services are provided represent the crux of the controversy that surrounds the provision of services and support by social services to unaccompanied minors (Mitchell, 2003: 181).

In their report published in 2000 the Audit Commission noted that unaccompanied children were not always offered an assessment of their needs (see also Mitchell, 2006). A number of research reports in the early part of the twenty-first century found that most unaccompanied children were worked with under Section 17 of the 1989 Children Act, without a full assessment having been made. This section of the Children Act was originally intended to promote support for families. One consequence of this practice, reported by Dennis (2007), was that such children only see a social worker to get their 'voucher', or indeed have no allocated social worker as such. Apart from not offering a full and rounded form of support, this practice also has profound implications for the placement of the child and for leaving care practice, as we shall see later. Stanley has argued that at the beginning of this decade policy was being made at 'grassroots' level, with the need for assessment being widely ignored, and that effectively services were being provided according to age rather than need (Stanley, 2001).

There can be little doubt that all aspects of assessment practice are complex when working with unaccompanied children:

> Social workers may have to deal with a number of difficulties in undertaking assessments. The gathering of information in itself may be problematic given that the young people are displaced and therefore cut off from their social and familial networks. Social workers seldom have any recourse to gather information from anyone other than the young person him or herself. Young people themselves may be reluctant to talk to social workers, as perceived authority figures, or due to a limited understanding of the social work role (Mitchell, 2003: 183).

In fact the basics of assessment, such as the child's date of birth, might be a difficult factor to assess accurately in the case of unaccompanied children. The official guidance from the Home Office and ADSS points out the complexities of assessing age, arising from the following factors:

> Not all countries and cultures attach the same importance to chronological age, and birth records are therefore afforded less importance.

Recording conventions and calendars are different in other countries and may not be easily reconciled with UK systems.

Adults may wish to avail themselves of asylum processes and support arrangements made for children, as they are perceived to be more favourable.

With other children there may be a need to assess their age for protection or care reasons e.g. traffickers may present young people as older or younger in order to avoid immigration controls or social services checks (Immigration and Nationality Directorate of the Home Office and Association of Directors of Social Services, nd).

The complexities of age assessment are clear here and this is clearly a fundamental base for any effective assessment.

Official policy, as outlined in the *Framework for Assessment of Children in Need and their Families* (DH et al., 2000a), makes it clear that unaccompanied children should be assessed, and their particular vulnerability is recognized in a section headed 'Assessment of Children in Special Circumstances'. Mitchell reports a study of 212 cases, based in three local authorities, that were subject to an assessment and finds that assessment had taken place in 88 per cent of these cases and in only 32 per cent of these were the assessments 'adequate or better', using a researcher-based judgment (Mitchell, 2006: 49). Mitchell finds that qualified social workers and those based in children's teams undertook assessments that tended to take an 'exchange' approach – that is, based on a constructive exchange of information between the participants. Young peoples' experience of these was that they were generally sensitive and responsive. This contrasted with a more procedural approach located in some specialist asylum teams, which young people did not always experience positively.

Mitchell also reports, in common with other commentators in the field, that practitioners have to cope with 'the uncertainty and ambiguity that surrounded young people's accounts of their past lives and experiences' (Mitchell, 2006: 53). This contained challenges to professional practice and sometimes led to atmospheres of suspicion and mistrust in teams. Kearney describes how one team planning placements coped with the experience of dealing with unaccompanied children's narratives:

> Even where contradictions existed we found it was important to bear in mind that multiple narratives of a family's history could exist. In our experience, it was only in a few cases that it was not possible to establish a connection and the gaps or inconsistencies were extreme enough to suggest that it may not be appropriate to recommend a placement (Kearney, 2007: 103).

Mitchell's (2003) views on these challenges have been explored above.

The Children's Commissioner for England undertook an unannounced visit to a screening unit established to assess asylum applications from people claiming to be under the age of 18. The report outlines the challenging nature of the process:

> Children need to have their basic needs for accommodation, food, cleanliness and rest met before they undergo this intense and lengthy sequence of events. They also require legal representation and information to help them understand the process better.
>
> The oppressive nature of large parts of the asylum process makes it difficult for children to give full and accurate account of themselves. This may have implications for the decision made on their asylum claim (11 million, 2008: 12).

These observations are brought to life by a direct quote from a young Ugandan woman aged 16:

> No one told me what was happening. I had nothing to eat or drink, not even water. I went to the toilet, that's where I got water to drink because at the time you don't have any money ... it was really bad. It's how they treat you and deal with the other people and ignore you like you are not there. Then they ask you the same questions over and over again (11 million, 2008: 4).

The Border and Immigration Agency (BIA) published proposals to reform this system in 2008. Amongst their 'five key reforms' is one to put 'in place better procedures to assess age' through the development of specialist regional centres who develop specialist skills in this area. Interestingly the primary motivation of the BIA here is to ensure that 'children and adults are not accommodated together' because of the associated child protection concerns (BIA, 2008a: 11).

We can conclude therefore that a basic social work skill, such as assessment, has particular dimensions and challenges in the context of practice with unaccompanied children. Practice skills are challenged and practice and policy seem to be uneven across the country, although research does give us some directions for a more positive practice. Certainly effective assessment must lie at the heart of providing quality services for unaccompanied children and young people.

Practice: Working with Unaccompanied Asylum-seeking Children and Young People

Having explored some aspects of the law and challenges relating to assessment, we now move on to examine some of the practice challenges that exist in work with unaccompanied children. Social work with children and young people always provides a series of political and value challenges for social workers. These aspects of social work are particularly apparent in work with unaccompanied children as their very status and existence in the country are subject to an overt political agenda. The use of legal, ideological, social, financial and political forms of discrimination against asylum seekers and refugees in general means that the political aspects of social care practice with unaccompanied children are particularly sharp, apparent and challenging.

Whilst unaccompanied children share many needs, issues and strengths with the other children and young people referred to in this study, they also face a set of particular issues that mean they require specific help and intervention:

> Many studies have found that refugee children and young people are often not seen as children first, but are dealt with as refugees. These studies point out that refugee children face the same issues as any other children, but that there are also specific and extra issues that need to be taken into account when thinking about appropriate service provision (Hek, 2005: 1).

Actual social care practice with unaccompanied children is complex and challenging, partially as a result of the tensions around the legal position of unaccompanied children, as:

> Asylum raises huge issues for those seeking it, but also considerable challenges for social work (Cemlyn and Briskman, 2003: 173).

Professional encounters with unaccompanied children are often challenging, producing what Kohli has identified as complex and 'thick' narratives which re-construct multi-layered stories (some of these are sensitively re-constructed by Kohli, 2007).

To deliver the five ECM outcomes effectively for these children and young people is a major challenge to our social care and related services. It will involve accepting them as legitimate settlers and then ensuring that they receive a full range of services, such as support when leaving care. Kohli outlines three ways of working with unaccompanied children:

> first practical assistance in the social world, second as a way of therapeutic helping that allows distress to be managed, and third, as a way of providing long-term companionability and friendship for unaccompanied minors (Kohli, 2007: xiv).

Underpinning such practice are the experiences of unaccompanied children. First, they are often separated from parents, relatives and siblings. As with other separated children, this implies all the trauma of being torn apart from a birth family. This experience is compounded by distance and the subsequent problems in communicating with home.

Second, many unaccompanied children have experienced the additional trauma of war, starvation or persecution – or often some combination of all these issues. These traumas may well have had a significant psychological and/or physical impact on the child or young person. In Mitchell's sample:

> Almost half of all the young people came from countries undergoing armed conflict or serious disturbances. A significant proportion (over two-fifths) were victims of direct or indirect forms of persecution (as defined in the 1951 UN Convention on the Status of Refugees). Similar proportions (around one-eighth) of the young people had left as a result of serious deprivation and poverty or had been trafficked for exploitation, or had been tortured (Mitchell, 2003: 180).

Third, unaccompanied children have specific cultural needs that local authorities may find hard to meet. These challenges have not always been helped by the dispersal policy pursued by the British government. This has led to unaccompanied children, and refugee families, being dispersed across the country in order to reduce the concentration of displaced people in the South Eastern area of England.

The three points made above are well illustrated by the following example, which is worthy of quoting at length:

> I am very depressed because I miss my own country, I miss my family. I have lost contact with all of them. There are problems in the house: it's cold and dirty and the landlord doesn't care about us, there is also the problem of not knowing how long I am going to be living here, I can't put down roots, I can't try and make a future when I don't know how long I am going to be here and I do want to go back eventually, although I know that my own country is in a state of turmoil. I grew up with war around me and I have never really known normality; in fact this is quite strange coming here and not having to deal with some of the issues I was dealing with in my own country. I have witnessed war since I was a child. I learned to play with pistols and guns. I have seen people dead on the side of the road and now I am reliving it. This makes it really difficult for me to concentrate on learning English. I need to be in a good mood to learn. I need to have a steady life (Marriott, 2001, in Hek, 2005: 24–5).

Unaccompanied children then have experiences grounded in certain global factors – wars and conflict that have a profound impact on such children. In a world where time and space are compressed, they have used their resilience to find refuge in another country and culture.

The actual care experience of unaccompanied children varies considerably and is affected by a number of factors which include:

> type of placement and the nature of the support that different placements offer; the location of a placement; the frequency and nature of the contact between a young person and the social services department; and the type and level of financial assistance provided to a young person (Mitchell, 2003: 186).

Mitchell's judgment is verified by SCIE (2007c), who refer to uneven and often poor levels of service. As one young person put it:

> What you get depends on what social services department you are with; things are definitely getting more difficult as I get older' (Boy aged 18) (Stanley, 2001, in Hek, 2005: 45).

Where unaccompanied children and young people have been consulted it is clear that they value practical help and assistance:

> They have talked about how important it was to find a placement where they would be welcomed: a reliable legal representative who could deal speedily with their application for asylum and someone who could assist them with their language skills, settling into school or college, and accessing health services (Hek, 2007, p.116).

Other aspects of policy and practice have also been found helpful:

> A few aspects of UK policy and provision have been acknowledged as helpful for these children, including the independent Panel of Advisers for Unaccompanied Children, specialist assessment of children's claims by the Home Office, and access to independent legal representation (Ayotte and Williamson, 2001).

In terms of social care, positive examples can also be given where research has indicated:

> the importance to young people of regular, committed and informed contact with social workers, who may need to extend well beyond their usual roles to support young refugees' rights to other services. Such an approach is most likely where local authorities have included asylum seeker issues in strategic planning and networking, provided sufficient training and resources, and based specialist refugee workers within mainstream children's services (Cemlyn and Briskman, 2003: 168).

Leaving 'care' is a crucial issue for unaccompanied children given that their age profile on entering the country is largely over 14, and with some 62 per cent being 16 or 17 (see Dixon and Wade, 2007).

However, as a result of the legal complications discussed above, in addition to the fact that many young people have been supported through Section 17, Dixon and Wade conclude that:

> for most unaccompanied young people, therefore, social services support has ceased at 18 and there has been an expectation that they would make their own way in the world as young adults (Dixon and Wade, 2007: 128).

Hek summarizes young peoples' views as follows:

> Young people express anxiety about this transition, and say that they have little information and what information they do receive is unclear and confusing (Hek, 2005: 49).

Whilst we know relatively little about outcomes for unaccompanied children leaving care, there is limited evidence that their outcomes may be better than those of other care leavers. Certainly Wade et al. (2005) argue that those supported under Section 20, or who have been placed with extended family, seem to be more effectively prepared for leaving care than those cared for in the community.

The interplay between pathway planning and immigration status is extremely complex, and therefore Dixon and Wade suggest that 'multi-dimensional' planning is required that can take account of a number of different scenarios that may face the young person. Again, and inevitably given the legal complications, Wade et al. (2005) find that pathway planning for unaccompanied children is 'highly variable'. This reflects wider patterns of uneven practice:

> Young people's experiences appear to vary greatly and may be influenced by a number of factors. These include: the type of placement and the nature of the support that different placements offer; the location of a placement; the frequency and nature of the contact between a young person and the social services department; and the type and level of financial assistance provided to a young person (Mitchell, 2003: 186).

Dixon and Wade (2007) conclude by arguing that the situation for unaccompanied children leaving care might be improving during the post-2005 period – they identify the organic development of services such as specialist teams, fewer unaccompanied children arriving in the country, improved central government guidance and some improvements in placement options as reasons for some optimism. Certainly some authors such as Kearney (2007) and Hek (2007) provide examples of effective placement practice for unaccompanied children, and many accounts from the young people themselves provide remarkable narratives of resilience and courage. Indeed, there is mounting evidence that outcomes for unaccompanied children once they are looked after are positive:

> They tend to enter the system later than others; they come from minority ethnic groups; they are less likely to display behaviour that is experienced as difficult by carers; they make comparatively good progress at school (Sinclair et al., 2007: 79).

Conclusion

At the time of writing, the Border and Immigration Agency is suggesting five reforms of practice in this area:

1) Ensuring that the BIA, in exercising its functions, keeps children safe from harm whilst they are in the UK
2) Putting in place better procedures for identifying and supporting unaccompanied asylum seeking children who are the victims of trafficking
3) Locating unaccompanied asylum seeking children with specialist local authorities to ensure they receive the services they need
4) Putting in place better procedures to assess age in order to ensure children and adults are not accommodated together
5) Resolving immigration status more quickly and, in turn, enabling care planning to focus on integration or early return to the country of origin (BIA, 2008b: 6).

These reforms are being implemented during 2008, as this book is being completed. The reforms continue the tension between attempting to meet the needs of children and the emphasis on 'early return', which as we have seen creates a tension in child welfare practice.

It is clear that social care practice will remain central to attempting to promote the welfare of this vulnerable and often resilient group of young people. It seems that the tensions between the best interests of the child and the pressures of immigration law will be with us for some time to come. Social care workers will be at the front line of attempting to address these seemingly irresolvable tensions.

Part III

Current Issues and Future Prospects

10

The Current State of Children's Social Care in England

In the light of our analysis of a number of key areas in which children's social care operates in Part II, the main purpose of this chapter is to begin to take stock of the current role and possible futures for children's social care. In doing so we will: (1) begin by returning to a number of themes introduced in Part I of the book, in terms of the changes that have taken place since the publication of the Seebohm Report in 1968; (2) summarize the implications of the *ECM: Change for Children* programme for children's social care; (3) discuss the debates and policy changes that have taken place since the re-election of New Labour in May 2005; (4) analyse in some detail *The Children's Plan,* published by the Department for Children, Schools and Families in December 2007 (DCSF, 2007b); and, finally, (5) review the publication of *Think Family: Improving the life chances of families at risk* (Cabinet Office, Social Exclusion Task Force, 2008). Throughout, our central concern will be to analyse the implications of these developments for children's social care.

What will become evident is that there are a number of important tensions and challenges which pervade current policy and practice developments. These will be discussed in an extended conclusion. In the process we are presented with something of a conundrum, for just at the point when social services departments have been dismantled and social work has been allocated a very particular and, potentially, marginalized role in the new children's services departments, there is an increasing policy recognition of the importance of addressing issues in the context of 'the family' and that practitioners require a range of skills in order to engage 'families' – skills which look remarkably like those associated with social work. While the context is very different, it is as if we have come full circle, so that much of the vision that lay at the heart of the Seebohm Report is precisely what is now being called for to address the current challenges. It is thus with the Seebohm Report that we begin.

The Seebohm Report and the Establishment of the Unified, Community-based, Family Service

The appointment of the Committee on Local Authority and Allied Personal Social Services, chaired by Frederic Seebohm, in December 1965, was prompted by a recommendation in the White Paper *The Child, the Family and the Young Offender* (Home Office, 1965) in August of that year that in order to address the increasing concerns about the growth of juvenile delinquency and to improve the prevention of crime, and with regard to the treatment of offenders more generally, it was important to improve the structure of local authority services concerned with various aspects of supporting the 'family' and thereby reduce the risk of 'family breakdown'. In particular, it was felt there was a failure of coordination between related but separately administered services and a failure of services to reach all who were in need of them. The central recommendation of the Seebohm Report (1968) was the establishment of a new local authority department which would provide:

> a community based and family oriented service, which will be available to all. The new department will, we believe, reach far beyond the discovery and rescue of social casualties; it will enable the greatest possible number of individuals to act reciprocally, giving and receiving service for the well-being of the whole community (Seebohm, 1968, para. 2).

The new department would thus be universal in nature, with a focus upon the family and the community. While by far the smallest, it would constitute the fifth social service alongside health, education, social security and public housing, and provide a key and distinctive contribution to the welfare state (Townsend, 1970). As we demonstrated in Chapter 1, at its centre would be the new generic profession of social work:

> The basis of the department, in our view, should in most parts of the country be teams of upwards of a dozen social workers, each team serving a population of between 50,000 and 100,000, and with the maximum of responsibility delegated to them from the headquarters of the social service department. For the time being, the social service department should be run by a separate committee of the local authority, with a separate principal officer reporting directly to the council. We envisage that in the course of time most of the principal officers at the heads of the new departments would be professionally qualified social workers with training in management and administration or administrators with qualifications in social work. We emphasise the importance of close links between the social services departments and other departments, notably the health, education and housing departments (Seebohm, 1968, para. 19).

Social service departments were established in April 1971, following the 1970 Local Authority Social Services Act, as stand-alone unified local authority departments with social work as its hallmark. They would provide the personalized, humanistic dimension of the welfare state where its operation would be crucially dependent upon social workers' understanding and ability to work with relationships. Not only would the department provide a range of services, it would also attempt to coordinate the efforts of the other state services in order to meet the needs of particular individuals, particularly those of a small number of families who were seen as causing a disproportionate number of problems and were often referred to as 'problem families' (Philp and Timms, 1962).

However, as we saw in Chapter 1, the new departments were never able to fulfil the ambitions outlined for them (Stevenson and Parsloe, 1978). In particular, a series of high-profile child abuse public inquiries portrayed social workers and social services departments in a very negative light. While the Barclay Report (1982) into the role and tasks of social workers underlined the importance of the generic model and promoted a community social work approach, from the early 1980s onwards social work roles became more and more specialist.

By the 1990s, following the 1989 Children Act and the 1990 NHS and Community Care Act, most departments were organized in terms of at least two parallel sets of structures – one focusing on adults and one upon children and families. The idea of the community-based generic area team had all but disappeared (Stevenson, 2005) and, certainly in relation to adult services, the key role was framed in terms of a care or case manager who might or might not be a social worker. The public and political image of social work by the late 1990s was inextricably interrelated with failures in relation to children, particularly in terms of child abuse.

An analysis of press reporting of social work in England in national daily and Sunday newspapers between 1 July 1997 and 1 July 1998 (the first year of the New Labour government) is particularly instructive in this respect (Franklin and Parton, 2001). There were nearly 2,000 articles, measuring 97,932 column centimetres (ccm), of which 6,995 ccm were devoted exclusively to discussions of social work and social services. The 15 most common messages, accounting for 80 per cent of the total, were negative with regard to social work and included: 'incompetent', 'negligent', 'failed', 'ineffective', 'misguided', 'bungling'. Over 75 per cent of the stories were related to children where the dominant concerns were about child abuse, paedophiles, adoption and fostering. Media stories about the nature, purposes and efficacy of social work were, almost without exception, negative and critical. While expenditure on children made up only 25 per cent of the budgets of social service departments, it was this area of the work which was perpetually in the media and political spotlight (Hill, 2000).

In such a context it is perhaps not surprising that departments increasingly adopted a procedural mentality, which emphasized the need to follow administrative protocols, to ensure that practice was made accountable. While the technical demands on social workers increased, the space for professional discretion and judgment reduced (Howe, 1992, 1996) and, by the late 1990s, morale in the profession seemed at an all-time low (Jones, 2001).

A useful framework for understanding the changes in social services departments is provided by Jim Ife (1997), who analyses the operation and balance of power in the organization and delivery of human services in terms of a contest between the competing discourses and practices of: managerialism; professionalism; community; and market. Whilst clearly the changes on the ground are complex and uneven, what we broadly witnessed in the period from 1971 to 1997 was a significant shift away from an emphasis on professionalism and community towards an emphasis on managerialism and the market in the way social services departments were organized and operated and in the way priorities were identified and decisions made.

By the time New Labour came to power in May 1997, the optimism within social work about trying to establish a strong generic community-based social services department had long disappeared. In addition, while social services departments could be seen to have gone along with the changes in social care produced by the Conservative governments of Margaret Thatcher and John Major, their roots were closely associated with the worst aspects of local authority 'Old Labour'. In the context of its very poor media image, it was thus unlikely that 'New Labour' would want to give social service departments and social work a central role in its attempt to launch a series of new initiatives to tackle social exclusion and to refashion welfare services.

That is precisely what happened; for the launch of Sure Start, the Children's Fund and a variety of New Labour initiatives was led by central government and provided via a range of new governance networks and partnerships, while social services were limited to playing a central role in relation to 'looked after' children, child protection and 'children in need'. In addition, they were subject to a range of new systems of inspection, monitoring and audit to try and improve their performance.

Ian Kirkpatrick has analysed a variety of pieces of primary and secondary evidence on the changes in social services departments since the 1970s, including the early years of the New Labour government, and concluded:

> There has been a marked retreat from the ideal of universal provision based on citizenship rights, towards services that are increasingly targeted and means tested. The focus of attention is now on the most deprived and least privileged groups within society. While SSDs were not abolished they were no longer to be substantial providers of care in their own right. The focus has been on extending the market for social care and transforming the management arrangements of SSDs to bring them closer to the practice of private firms (Kirkpatrick, 2006: 7).

He also concluded that while the number of social workers employed in local authorities grew during the 1990s and the introduction of professional registration would further consolidate the process, this had been achieved in the context of a much reduced institutional autonomy for the profession. Central government and employers were much more able to prescribe the process and content of social work education and training and there had been a raft of tightly drawn legislation, guidance and procedures, particularly in the area of children's services, so that social work had become an increasingly case-accountable and procedurally regulated activity. From the beginning New Labour had a fundamental mistrust of local authorities' capabilities to *modernize* and an ambivalence about the future of social services departments, which reflected severe doubts about the value of social work as a professional arm of social policy, in which social workers would act as autonomous practitioners, exercising professional judgment based on knowledge, expertise and experience (Jordan with Jordan, 2000).

While the process of change had started under the auspices of the Conservative government from the late 1980s onwards, since 1997 the changes invoked by New Labour have been even more rapid and intensive. In particular, the promulgation of a whole range of new performance targets, inspection regimes and various systems of audit have had the effect of both rationalizing on the one hand and centralizing on the other. As Stephen Webb has argued, the years leading up to the new millennium witnessed 'a double discursive alliance of *scientism* and *managerialism* in social work which gears up to systematic information processing operations to produce regulated action. We thus have the assimilation of a form of "scientific management" in social work' (Webb, 2001: 74, original emphasis). In the process we have been presented with something of a paradox whereby, while government demands greater certainty, at the same time there has been a denial that achieving certainty is possible. The net result seems to have been that the various changes introduced have acted to sidestep the paradox and have substituted *confidence* in systems in place of *trust* in individual professional practice (Smith, 2001). This has been most starkly illustrated by the numerous public inquiries into child abuse over the years where practitioners have been subject to considerable criticism. The official response to these failures has been to increase the procedural requirements placed upon practitioners and the promulgation of a variety of detailed systems for the assessment, monitoring and review of cases.

The Implications of the *Every Child Matters: Change for Children* Programme for Children's Social Care

As we saw in Chapter 2, while there were a number of continuities with the previous Conservative government's approach, New Labour aimed to introduce a quite distinctive approach to social policy in the way it attempted to combine an emphasis on both liberal individualism and communitarianism. From the outset it placed a high priority on trying to attack social exclusion and tried to shift the role of state welfare away from a model whose prime aim was *compensating* people for the 'diswelfares' they may have experienced as a consequence of the market, to one which saw its prime role in terms of *investing* much more directly and strategically in improving the quality of human capital, so that individuals could compete and engage with the market. It was education and health that were to be the priorities, rather than social security.

In a context where social investment for the future in order to compete in the global market was a top priority and where it was important to address social exclusion, policies in relation to children and childhood lay at the heart of the New Labour project to refashion the welfare state.

As we saw in Chapter 7, a new priority was given to developing childcare and early years services and one of the distinctive features of the first New Labour government was the launch of the Sure Start programme, which emphasized the importance of a multi-disciplinary, community-based and preventive programme for parents and young children living in the 20 per cent most deprived sections of the population. While local authorities were expected to participate, the projects were explicitly established outside of the structures of social services departments and were administered and funded directly from central government. A smaller but similar model was used for the launch of Children's Fund projects in 2000.

However, it was clear, soon after New Labour's re-election in June 2001, that the government wanted to extend the process of reform to include much more directly the mainstream services, and a framework for the 'transformation' of children's services was outlined in the *2002 Spending Review* in a chapter entitled 'Children at Risk' (HM Treasury, 2002a). As we argued in Chapter 3, while the Green Paper *Every Child Matters* was presented by the government as a response to the Laming Report (2003) into the death of Victoria Climbié, it was primarily concerned with bringing forward the government's proposals for changing the organization and rationale for the delivery of children's services.

However, rather than only be concerned with 'children at risk', as suggested by the *Spending Review,* the intention was to ensure that all children were included. The emphasis was to integrate services both vertically (in terms of the integration of universal, targeted and specialist services, see Figure 3.2) and horizontally (between different services and specialisms). Universal services were conceptualized as offering early (primary) intervention to prevent the emergence of specific risk factors. The vision was of 'a shift to prevention whilst strengthening protection' (DfES, 2004b: 3), so that the changes were designed not only to ensure that children did not fall through the 'nets' designed to protect them from abuse but also to ensure that all children received early help so that they could fulfil their potential.

As we outlined in Chapter 3, the *Every Child Matters: Change for Children* programme (DfES, 2004a) and the Children Act 2004 introduced a number of changes which would have the effect of reconfiguring the governance, organization and delivery of children's services in England and aimed to introduce integrated strategies, processes, front-line delivery and governance in order to focus services on improving the outcomes for all children. The introduction of the 'Common Assessment Framework' (CAF), the 'Lead Professional' and 'Contact Point' were seen as three key changes which would help bring about the changes in practice.

Perhaps the most significant change was the requirement to appoint a Director of Children's Services and a councillor with lead children's services responsibilities in each local authority. This heralded the end of social services departments. While the changes had to be in place by mid-2008, most local authorities introduced the changes during 2006 and 2007. Each local authority with education and social service responsibilities had, at a minimum, to bring together the local authority education department and the children's social care from the social services departments into one department. Local authorities could bring other of its services into the new department and were also strongly encouraged to establish 'Children's Trusts' with the local NHS-run community health services. The changes had the effect of splitting social service departments, with children's social care being taken into Departments of Children's Services and the remainder of its services going into the newly established Department of Adults' Services.

In the process, social work has been clearly dislodged from being the core profession in the new arrangements. Not only are there only about 25 per cent of the new Directors of Children's Services who have a background in social services and social care, but social workers are tremendously outnumbered by educationalists as being the pre-eminent profession in the new departments. Similarly, the budget allocation for children's social care pales into insignificance in the context of the budget for schools and other education services.

The role of children's social care, as we saw in Chapter 3, was to be restricted to work with the most vulnerable children, particularly 'children in need', including those in need of protection, 'looked after' children and disabled children. The more preventive and early intervention developments were to be located primarily in the new children's centres and extended schools. As we will see later, children's centres were to play a key strategic role in the new developments; and while those with social work and social care backgrounds were not excluded from working in these settings, they were clearly conceptualized within a broadened early years/educational paradigm as opposed to one based on social work or social care. The net result of the changes, rather than providing social work with an opportunity to re-establish the vision set out for it by the Seebohm Report (1968) 40 years previously, has been that the role and tasks of social workers in the new departments are likely to tie them even more into the narrow statutory and very formalized work which had been their hallmark for many years in the old social services departments (Jordan with Jordan, 2000; Jordan, 2001).

Building on *Every Child Matters:* Developments from 2005 to 2007

While the *Every Child Matters: Change for Children* programme can be seen as the culmination of a variety of policy developments and debates in the second New Labour government of June 2001 to May 2005, the serious process of implementation in local authorities did not start until mid-2005. By then New Labour had been re-elected for a third term of office and very quickly the Prime Minister, Tony Blair, started making statements that he felt the pace of change, particularly in relation to health, education and social welfare generally, had been too slow and that more radical changes were needed. It was also a period when the divisions within the party and the government became more obvious between the 'Blairites' and the 'Brownites'. While part of these divisions arose from personal animosities and difficulties, we can also detect policy differences. These are particularly evident in relation to policies in relation to children, young people and families. We can perhaps characterize the period from May 2005 to June 2007 in terms of 'Blairism', with the period from July 2007 as being distinctively associated with Gordon Brown, the new Prime Minister, and his close political ally Ed Balls, who became the Secretary of State at the newly created Department for Children, Schools and Families. We will examine the latter in the next section when we analyse the 2007 *Children's Plan* (DCSF, 2007b).

Following his re-election in May 2005, Tony Blair made it clear that he felt progress in relation to overcoming social exclusion and anti-social behaviour had not been as successful as he had hoped. On 10 January 2006 he launched the *Respect Action Plan* (Respect Task Force, 2006), which was supported by nine government departments, headed by the Home Office. It aimed to tackle the underlying causes of anti-social behaviour, to intervene earlier where problems occurred, and to broaden the efforts to address new areas of poor behaviour. It aspired to build 'stable families and strong, cohesive communities', and argued that while it was important to address the causes of problems it was also important to challenge poor behaviour where it existed. Poor parenting and 'problem families' were seen to lie at the root of the problems.

These themes were made more explicit when, on 11 September 2006, following a speech by Tony Blair the previous week to the Joseph Rowntree Foundation, the government launched *Reaching Out: An Action Plan on Social Exclusion* (HM Government, 2006a). The *Action Plan* examined the reasons why, despite the considerable amount of investment and reform, including the disappointing early results of the Sure Start initiative (Ormerod, 2005; Belsky et al., 2006; Rutter, 2006), there were still individuals and families who were cut off from the mainstream of society:

> About 2.5 per cent of every generation seem to be stuck in a lifetime of disadvantage. Their problems are multiple, entrenched and often passed down through generations (HM Government, 2006a: 3).

As John Welshman (2006, 2007) has argued, in both the *Action Plan* and the speech by Tony Blair that launched it, the explanations of the problems and the proposals for policy and practice were very similar to Sir Keith Joseph's ideas about the 'Cycle of deprivation' in the early 1970s. The emphasis of government policies seemed to be shifting to a more muscular interventionist stance toward those who seemed more 'hard to reach' by the earlier programmes, particularly where they were perceived as being members of a hard-core underclass. Policy seemed to be heading in a direction increasingly consistent with Ruth Levitas's 'moral underclass discourse' (MUD), which we discussed in Chapter 2, where the focus of attention should be on trying to change the behaviour, culture and values of a small number of families where the problems were passed between generations. The language used was very reminiscent of a pathological 'cycle of deprivation', such as:

> 'intergenerational cycle of deprivation', along with the 'transmission' and 'inheritance' of disadvantage. Moreover, alongside the focus on social exclusion has been the parallel rhetoric of anti-social behaviour, with its explicit problem family vocabulary (Welshman, 2006: 475).

However, whereas Sir Keith Joseph saw a central role for social workers and health visitors in helping to break the 'cycle of deprivation', Tony Blair and the *Action Plan* mentioned only health visitors and midwives. Importantly, for our purposes, the *Action Plan* said it aimed to build on the *Every Child Matters: Change for Children* programme. However, it was felt that progress was patchy and generally slow. In particular, the Plan argued that rigorous evidence about 'what works' was not always informing how services were operating and that there was 'a lack of appropriate data on outcomes from identifying those at risk and from intervening' (HM Government, 2006a: 10–11).

While the central principles of the *Every Child Matters: Change for Children* programme, particularly the emphasis on early intervention and sharing information, were also central to the *Action Plan,* there was a much tougher and authoritarian ring to the plan. There was a particular concern about those who were 'hard to reach', not so much because they were not known to services but because they were 'hard to engage' and 'hard to help effectively'. Four groups were considered particularly hard to reach: looked-after children; families with complex problems; teenage pregnancies; and adults with mental health problems. 'There is not going to be a solution unless we are sufficiently hard-headed to say that from a very early age we need a system of intervention' (Blair, 2006). It seemed that social inclusion was going to mean both tough policies and tough practices. In autumn 2006 Naomi Eisenstadt was appointed as Director of the newly established Social Exclusion Taskforce, based in the Cabinet Office, to drive the initiative forward. One of the first jobs for the new taskforce was to carry out a 'Families at Risk' review to report later in 2007.

However, the success of New Labour's policies for children and families, particularly in relation to the 'socially excluded', surfaced as a significant political issue in February 2007 following the publication of the UNICEF Report (2007), which placed the UK bottom out of 21 economically advanced nations in terms of the overall 'well-being' of children and young people. The publication of the report coincided with the murder of a 14-year-old boy in South London amidst escalating concerns about young gangs and knife and gun crime. Political and media comment was considerable, and very similar to that in 1993 following the murder of Jamie Bulger, and suggested that childhood was in crisis and a terrible reflection on the state of British society. At his monthly press conference on 27 February, Tony Blair spoke at length about social exclusion and launched *Reaching Out: Progress in Social Exclusion* (Cabinet Office, Social Exclusion Task Force, 2007a) in an attempt to address some of the concerns raised and to demonstrate the progress that New Labour had made since coming to power.

Essentially he argued that New Labour policies had proved successful and that since 1997 the bottom 20 per cent of society had seen their incomes rise faster than the richest 20 per cent, though he accepted that this did not apply to the very rich. He also argued that while 1.6 million children had been lifted out of poverty, there still remained a small number of families with multiple problems who were proving particularly 'hard to reach', and that it was these who would need special attention in the future.

As we will see a little later in the chapter, this renewed emphasis on the importance of engaging the 'hard to reach', identifying and working with 'families at risk' and trying to break the 'cycle of deprivation' have had an impact on policy. However, the political context changed, for on 27 June 2007, Gordon Brown took over from Tony Blair as Prime Minister and one of his first decisions was to establish a new government department – the Department for Children, Schools and Families (DCSF) – and appointed his close political ally, Ed Balls, to become its first Secretary of State. It was clear that this was to be a central plank of Gordon Brown's attempt to renew the New Labour project and at the same time put his own brand on policy in this now central and high-priority field. Ed Balls's first decision was to establish a process of consultation in order to produce a 'Children's Plan' which would provide the aims and framework for policy change until 2020; and it is to this we now turn.

The Children's Plan: Building Brighter Futures

On 11 December 2007 Ed Balls launched the government's *Children's Plan* (DCSF, 2007b). *The Guardian* reported its publication with the headline 'Fitter, happier and better educated: the hope for 2020', and wrote:

> The government has set a 13-year deadline to dramatically reduce illiteracy and antisocial behaviour and eradicate child poverty in a children's plan which makes a promise from the heart of government that children will be happier by 2020.
> The sprawling 170-page document places schools at the hub of an array of measures designed to boost support for parents and provide children and young people with better play and activities to steer them away from crime (Curtis and Ward, 2007: 6).

In many respects this quotation from *The Guardian* captures the most significant elements of the Plan: it came from the heart of government; it was very wide ranging and ambitious; it placed schools at the hub; and it signalled a new and more active relationship between the state, parents and children. As Ed Balls said in his Foreword:

> The Plan and the New Department mean that more than ever before families will be at the centre of excellent, integrated services that put their needs first, regardless of traditional institutional and professional structures. This means a new leadership role for Children's Trusts in every area, a new role for schools at the centre of their communities, and more effective links between schools, the NHS and other children's services so that together they can engage parents and tackle all the barriers to the learning, health and happiness of every child (DCSF, 2007b: 3).

While the Plan was particularly concerned with addressing the needs of the most deprived and vulnerable and reducing the wide disparities in children's performance at school, it was also very much concerned with maximizing the potential of every child.

The work informing the Children's Plan had started well before Ed Balls established the process of consultation in July 2007. In the Budget of 2006, the then Chancellor, Gordon Brown, had announced a policy review of Children and Young People to inform the 2007 Comprehensive Spending Review (CSR). It was to consider how services for children, young people and their families could build on the principles identified in *Support for Parents: the best start for children* (HM Treasury and DfES, 2005). Following an interim report published in January 2007 (HM Treasury and DfES, 2007a), the final report was published in March 2007 as *Aiming high for children: supporting families* (HM Treasury and DfES, 2007b).

The final review report identified four areas where, over the period 2008/09 to 2010/11, it would take particular action: (1) a new emphasis on building resilience by promoting good social and emotional skills and positive parenting; (2) greater personalization to ensure that all services are more responsive to the needs of families; (3) proactive support, recognizing that public services need to reach out to those who need it most but who may be less willing or able to articulate their needs; and (4) help for families to break out of the 'cycle of low achievement'. The ideas were consistent with much in *Reaching Out: An Action Plan on Social Exclusion* (HM Government, 2006a), but the language was perhaps less authoritarian and muscular in tone. It is notable that social work and children's social care were not mentioned anywhere, except when used as an example of where a professional, as well as fulfilling his or her main role, may also need to act as the 'lead professional' in order to ensure that services were providing a proactive integrated response (para. 5.21) when trying to work with families 'caught in a cycle of low achievement'.

The government also announced an early CSR settlement for the then Department for Education and Skills as part of the 2007 Budget in order to carry forward the recommendations of the review. This would see education spending in England rise by 2.5 per cent a year in real terms between 2007/08 and 2010/11. When the full CSR was published in October 2007 it identified 30 Public Service Agreements which would operate during the period and provide the key focus for driving forward and performance-managing the developments.

Six of these applied specifically to children and young people:

- Halve the number of children in poverty by 2010–11, on the way to eradicating child poverty by 2020 (PSA Delivery Agreement 9).
- Raise the educational achievement of all children and young people (PSA Delivery Agreement 10).
- Narrow the gap in educational achievement between children from low income and disadvantaged backgrounds and their peers (PSA Delivery Agreement 11).
- Improve the health and well-being of children and young people (PSA Delivery Agreement 12).
- Improve children and young people's safety (PSA Delivery Agreement 13).
- Increase the number of children and young people on the path to success (PSA Delivery Agreement 14).

These PSAs were referred to throughout the *Children's Plan* and were reflected in the six strategic objectives of the new DCSF to improve children and young people's lives. Each chapter in the *Children's Plan* referred to one of the DCSF's strategic objectives.

Five principles were said to underpin the Plan:

- Government does not bring up children – parents do – so government needs to do more to back parents and families.
- All children have the potential to succeed and should go as far as their talents can take them.
- Children and young people need to enjoy their childhood as well as grow up prepared for adult life.
- Services need to be shaped by and responsive to children, young people and families, not designed around professional boundaries.
- It is always better to prevent failure than tackle a crisis later.

The government did not see the Plan as an end 'but as the beginning of a new engagement between Government, children, families and experts', all of whom were involved in the process of consultation and would continue to be consulted, including the production of a report on progress after the first year. It is notable that the Plan, and the title of the new department, made quite explicit reference to families and the introductory chapter was framed in terms of a discussion of family policy in the twenty-first century; there was an explicit attempt to locate policy and practice in relation to children in the context of 'family policy'. However, the Plan recognized that the nature and context of family life were now much more diverse and complex than previously:

> Our family policy will support families with whatever level of information and support they need, when they need it. This will include lone parent families, step families, and families where children are being brought up by their grandparents.
> This means recognising that life is more complex than it ever was. Employment patterns are changing, and more women than ever and an increasing number of men too are juggling family life with paid work. More parents are providing support and care to elderly relatives as well as bringing up children (DCSF, 2007b: 19).

While the Plan said that it aimed to build on *Every Child Matters*, it stated that it was important that services worked together 'not just to provide a safety net for the vulnerable, but to unlock the potential of every child' (pp. 143–4). The government wanted:

> to build a system that provides opportunity and delivers services to meet the needs of children and young people, supports parents and carers, and intervenes early where additional support is needed to get a child or young person back onto the path to success (p. 144).

But while the emphasis was upon integration it was clear that education, schools and children's centres lay at the heart of the plan. The government clearly felt that education – in its broadest sense – was the best way of both maximizing opportunities and addressing the large inequalities in outcome, for:

> Attainment is the biggest single predictor of a successful adult life, but a successful education is not a product simply of what happens in schools and colleges. As our experts and the parents and children we asked told us, we can only succeed by looking at all aspects of a child's life in the round (p. 144).

It was hoped that, whenever possible, services could be co-located, and schools, extended schools and children's centres were seen as both central to the plan and, usually, the most accessible places for children and parents. It was vital that universal services – particularly schools – were thoroughly integrated into the system so that prevention and early intervention could become a reality. In a section entitled 'universal services' and referring to a preventive system, the rationale for this was made clear:

> Almost all children, young people and families come into regular contact with early years settings and with schools and colleges. That means that early years settings, schools and colleges must sit at the heart of an effective system of prevention and early intervention working in partnership with parents and families. They are the places where children and young people build the breadth of experience that makes for a rounded childhood. If these services are not integrated with more specialist provision, by looking for early warnings that children might need more help and by providing facilities for specialist services to operate so they can be easily reached by children and families, we will be hamstrung in achieving our broad ambitions for children and young people (p. 144).

The Plan had considerable ambitions for the '21st century school'. Not only was it to provide excellent education but it was to actively contribute to all aspects of a child's life in terms of health and well-being, safety, and developing the wider experiences and skills that were seen to characterize a 'good childhood' and set a young person up for success as an adult. In addition, schools were a vital community resource which should make a major contribution to maximizing community cohesion.

Under local authority leadership Children's Trusts were vital in taking the Plan forward and maximizing the integration between services and reflecting local needs. There was a clear expectation that Children's Trusts should 'look beyond direct local authority or other statutory provision to a wide range of potential providers, in the voluntary and community sector and in the social enterprise and private sectors'. While the Plan clearly looked to build on many of the ideas and changes initiated in the *Every Child Matters: Change for Children* programme, the increased emphasis on the central role to be played by early years, schools and colleges and the strong educational paradigm which informed the whole document was much more explicit.

Apart from the introductory and concluding chapters, which set out the overall approach and how the Plan would be taken forward, there were four substantive chapters. 'Excellence and equity', 'Leadership and collaboration', 'Staying on', and 'On the right track' were taken up, almost exclusively, with setting out the various elements which were seen as key for refashioning and developing early years, schools and colleges, together with the other services which they would work with in their new role. Children's social work and social care were not mentioned. Where it was discussed was in Chapter 1, entitled 'Happy and healthy', and, to a lesser extent, in Chapter 2, entitled 'Safe and sound'.

Chapter 1 made it clear that the government was determined to try to improve the situation for accommodated children and young people, as we outlined in Chapter 6 earlier, and would be publishing further details on the implementation of *Care Matters*. It also briefly outlined and confirmed what it had previously said about improving services for young carers, unaccompanied asylum-seeking children, disabled children and in relation to adoption.

The only explicit mention of 'the children's social care workforce' and 'children's social workers' was in paras. 1.44 and 1.45, when it was stated that the government planned to: (1) pilot a newly qualified status from 2008/09 offering a year of guaranteed induction support as well as introducing quality standards and assessment; (2) develop and pilot a fast-track, work-based route into children's social work aimed at mature graduates; and (3) establish a framework for professional development. However, no explicit statement was made about the role and tasks of social workers and how it was thought they would contribute to the overall vision for children's services. It seemed to be assumed that this would be related to 'children in need', particularly those in need of protection, children looked after and some children with disabilities, particularly where these children were deemed to have complex needs. In effect, children's social work and social care would be limited to what had been the reality for many years and the role outlined previously as part of the *Every Child Matters: Change for Children* programme.

Think Family: Improving the Life Chances of Families at Risk

Perhaps the most glaring example of how thinking had moved on since the 1970s and how children's social work and social care had become marginalized, was when *The Children's Plan* discussed the proposals for 'reaching the most vulnerable families'. It was felt that 'effective home visiting and other outreach services can make a real difference to families who cannot or choose not to access services, providing important information and access to services such as childcare and family support' (p. 21). To address this it was planned to expand outreach so that there was a minimum of two outreach workers in all Children's Centres in the most disadvantaged areas. Core principals and standards for such outreach work would be developed together with funding to support the training of some 5,000 practitioners. In addition an extra £13m of funding had already been announced to strengthen the intensive support to the neediest families by piloting a key worker approach.

However, at no point did the document discuss the contribution that social workers and other children's social care workers could make to these areas of work which were seen as so vital to the success of *The Children's Plan*, and which had been signalled previously in *Reaching Out: An Action Plan on Social Exclusion* (HM Government, 2006a). *The Children's Plan* also said that it would fund 12 to 15 Family Pathfinder projects which were to be announced in the forthcoming government's 'Families at Risk Review' and which was published as *Think Family: Improving the life chances of families at risk* (Cabinet Office, Social Exclusion Task Force, 2008) in January 2008.

As we saw earlier, *The Children's Plan* was framed in terms of making a significant contribution to a 'family policy for the 21st century'. This emphasis on family was even more evident in *Think Family*. Ironically, just at the point when social services departments – based originally on the Seebohm Report idea of a generic, community-based, family service – were being dismantled, *Think Family* argued that it was crucial that managers and practitioners in the new children's and adult services departments 'think family':

> From local policy-makers, practitioners, professionals and families, the Families at Risk Review has heard a clear message: excellent children's services and excellent adults' services are not enough in isolation. *To transform life chances, and break the cycle of disadvantage, services must go further. They must 'think family'* (Cabinet Office, Social Exclusion Task Force, 2008: 4, emphasis added).

An earlier report from the 'Families at Risk Review' (Cabinet Office, Social Exclusion Task Force, 2007b) had identified the key themes to be addressed and provided the background for developing the idea of 'think family'. 'Families at risk' was used as a shorthand term for families with multiple and complex problems such as worklessness, poor mental health or substance misuse. The focus was those who already had complex and ongoing problems as well as those who were at risk of developing them. The context was the belief that against a backdrop of rising prosperity and improved outcomes for the majority of families there was a small minority of about two per cent of families who experienced multiple problems. However, children's services could only ever mitigate the impacts of parental problems such as domestic violence, learning disability or substance misuse. It was important therefore that adults' services not only joined up better with children's services to provide support for the needs of 'the whole family', but adults' services needed to consider the parental roles and responsibilities of their clients. In a system that 'thinks family' both adults' and children's services needed to join up around the needs of the family.

Four characteristics were identified as key to the 'think family' approach:

- Have no 'wrong door', so that contact with any service would offer an open door into a broader system of joined-up support.
- Look at the whole family.
- Build on family strengths.
- Provide support tailored to need.

To ensure that this took place it was important that 'think family' informs every level of the system. In order to demonstrate how this could be conceptualized, the same diagram of concentric circles we reproduced in Figure 3.4 was used but this time with 'families' at the centre. While much of the previous 10 years had seen a process whereby, for conceptual, policy and organizational reasons, families had been deconstructed into the constituent parts of children, parents and adults, in *Think Family* (Cabinet Office, Social Exclusion Task Force, 2008) they were put back together again.

It was recognized that work in this field demanded particular skills:

> Practitioners should be given the *confidence and skills to work assertively and creatively* to engage families who are reluctant to accept support. Families with entrenched problems may be wary of services and it can be hard for them to motivate themselves and engage with support. Therefore, failing to meet appointments or declining help should not mean that the family is forgotten. Practitioners who are proactive and persistent have had considerable success in engaging some of the most excluded families (Cabinet Office, Social Exclusion Task Force, 2008, para. 3.16, original emphasis).

The only time when social workers were mentioned was when it was stated that, along with district nurses and health visitors, they already took a 'family-based approach' (para. 3.11). In fact no professional group was particularly highlighted. The emphasis was upon identifying a 'lead professional', working as part of a 'multi-agency team', sharing assessment, developing 'a whole family assessment' and sharing information. In order to develop the model the government committed £16m to fund a number of Family Pathfinders to explore different approaches and to identify what worked and what needed to change. *Think Family* had many similarities with the recommendations of the Seebohm Report, but with one important difference: it did not place social workers at the centre of the development.

Tensions and Challenges in Children's Policy

In this chapter we have reviewed policy developments in relation to children's services since the re-election of the New Labour government in May 2005, with particular reference to their implications for children's social work and social care. What seems particularly ironic is that just at the point social services departments had been dismantled there was a renewed call to emphasize the family context of service planning and delivery and to 'think family', but in a context where social work had become fairly marginalized. We will return to these issues shortly. Before doing so, however, we wish to provide an overview of the current state of policy in relation to children's services, particularly in the context of *The Children's Plan,* which aims to set the framework for developments up until 2020.

While there has been a continual process of change in this area ever since New Labour came to power in 1997, and this has had a considerable impact upon the creation of new services and the reconfiguration of organizations, there has also been considerable continuity in the way the challenges have been identified and the broad policies developed to address them. An emphasis on attacking social exclusion, early intervention and prevention, and trying to ensure that all children achieve their potential has been central, and is driven forward by a strong performance management approach. The main reason for the continual attempts at reform and change has arisen from a dissatisfaction with the progress made, and increasingly this has been focused on the major challenges posed by the 'hard to reach, high risk families'.

While New Labour has said that it is determined to reduce child poverty, this has only been very partially successful and it seems very unlikely it will reach its target of halving child poverty by 2010 (Seager, 2008). Throughout it relied heavily upon a combination of what Ruth Levitas (2005) has called the *social integrationist discourse* (SID) and the *moral underclass discourse* (MUD). Both were very evident in *The Children's Plan*, which placed a particular emphasis on the importance of education and schools to ensure children fulfilled their potential but also as key to ensuring that a range of social problems could be identified and addressed. In addition there was a renewed emphasis on the importance of trying to provide more assertive efforts to address the small number of families who had multiple problems and who accounted for a disproportionate amount of public sector resources. The commitment to the *redistributionist discourse* (RED) was confined to improving the position of those just at or below the poverty line. Throughout, New Labour has been comfortable with trying to attack poverty but not inequality.

It is not surprising, therefore, that there is growing inequality between those on the highest and lowest incomes. The inequality is due not simply to the poor falling further behind but because the rich, particularly the very rich, have been getting richer. Brewer et al. (2004) have argued that under New Labour the UK has experienced an unusual combination of slightly rising income inequality and falling relative poverty. This is attributable to two trends: the gap between the very rich, particularly the richest 500,000 individuals, and the rest of the population has got wider since 1997; while, at the same time, many lower-income families have seen their incomes rise faster than average. It now seems clear that while the gap between those near to the top and those near to the bottom has reduced slightly, the gap between the very top one percent and 0.1 per cent in particular and the rest has increased (Sefton and Sutherland, 2005; Brewer et al., 2008). This contrasts with both the post-war period until the late 1970s, which saw both declining poverty and declining inequality, and the period 1979-97 which saw both poverty and inequality increasing. As Orton and Rowlinson (2007) have argued, it seems that 'New Labour's combination of falling poverty, increasing riches for the wealthiest and high levels of inequality, perhaps suggest a "Third Way" is evident' (p. 62).

The question arises, however, whether the issue of increasing inequality really matters if poverty is reducing, particularly as it is the latter which has the most direct implications for those working in the children's social care field. The person who has made the clearest case that inequalities cause social problems is Richard Wilkinson (1996, 2005), particularly in terms of their impact on health and violence in society. He has accumulated a range of evidence which suggests that it is material inequality rather than poverty which is key and that societies that are poorer but more egalitarian have relatively high levels of good health and less violence because of a higher degree of social cohesion. The *relative* distribution of income, wealth and lifestyle are seen as central factors in influencing an individual's sense of worth and whether they feel valued. Societies which are becoming wealthier but more unequal, for example the US and the UK, perform poorly as a result. These were just the findings that were evident in the UNICEF report (2007).

Wilkinson argues that in more equal societies: there are stronger bonds between people; public space is treated more as social space; there is more involvement in social and voluntary activities outside the home and in civic society more generally; and there is less aggressive behaviour. There is evidence of high self-esteem, and less stress, insecurity and depression. Clearly, absolute levels of poverty are important in determining life chances, health outcomes and behaviour, but it is increasingly evident that the relative inequalities of income and wealth within any society are particularly significant.

If this is the case, it seems that the ambitious plans that New Labour has set out in both *Every Child Matters* and *The Children's Plan* can only ever be partially successful. The plans put a particular emphasis on the importance of education and the role of schools. However, this brings us to another major tension in the New Labour approach. For while it sees schools as, amongst other things, providing a vital contribution to maximizing community cohesion and social inclusion, it also wants schools to become more autonomous, flexible and business-like. The White Paper *Higher Standards, Better Schools for All* (DfES, 2005b,d) emphasized that schools should have greater freedom in order to respond to parental 'demand' in terms of both the substance and scale of what they offered. Schools should develop their strengths such that the range of provision would become more diversified. The emphasis is upon competition and a neo-liberal set of individualized market relations (Ball, 2007) rather than ideas about cooperation, partnership and integration on which *The Children's Plan* is based. Those state schools deemed to be failing will be made into academies or trusts. On 10 June 2008 Ed Balls announced that there were 638 schools attended by poorer, disadvantaged or unselected students where only around 30 per cent achieved five GCSEs at A-C level, including mathematics and English. He said that he intended to close up to 270 schools and merge and replace them with academies or the newly created 'national challenge trusts', some grouped under the 'extra mile' initiative (Wintour and Curtis, 2008).

Not only are these very different rationales for what the primary purposes of schools are about, they also set up some potentially major practical difficulties. With so many different potential agents running schools it becomes difficult to encourage cooperation and cohesion and it undermines the role of the local authority. If schools become semi-independent business-like operations it becomes very difficult to include them at the 'heart' of the new children's services if they do not wish to participate. Similar issues apply to health trusts, and in particular to GP practices which have similarly been set up as pretty independent, business-like units (R. McDonald, 2006). Such tensions place considerable pressures upon local authorities and the emerging Children's Trusts to deliver what is expected of them.

As the House of Commons Children, Schools and Families Committee (2008) argued, while the DCSF was given lead responsibility for putting *The Children's Plan* into operation it was very dependent on other central and local government departments actively cooperating in order to bring this about. In addition, the Committee felt there was a failure to identify clear priorities with a timetable for action. While the Plan's strategic objectives were similar to the *Every Child Matters* five outcomes, they were not the same and it was not clear how the two might be linked.

Beyond this, however, there are further tensions which pervade both *The Children's Plan* and the thinking behind it. These include: implementing a very top-down agenda while trying to engage the views of the various stakeholders, including children and young people themselves; and attempting to introduce policies and practices which are concerned with a version of social justice and social inclusion, alongside those which are more concerned with children and young people seen as social threats and trying to ensure parents fulfil their responsibilities (Gillies, 2008).

A major issue relates to the potentially changing nature of the relationship between children, parents and the state. *The Children's Plan* went out of its way to argue that the government was not looking to replace or undermine the role of the family but to enter into a new relationship in order to support parents. However, it is not easy to increase the support to families and encourage early intervention, prevention and the integration of services without creating the image of a 'nanny state' which both encourages dependence and increases surveillance.

Part of the way in which this has been addressed is to re-emphasize a much more holistic and benign view of the family. In doing so there is a real danger that some of the major complexities involved in conceptualizing, representing and then responding to the diverse realities of contemporary family life will not be recognized. For over the last 30 years research, public inquiries and the efforts of various campaign groups have demonstrated that the views and interests of 'family' members can be quite different, particularly in terms of children, men and women, and that these vary between different ethnic, cultural and class groupings. Developing trust, flexibility and responsiveness while working with authority and being able to negotiate are clearly key if the work is going to be successful.

Of course, working with such ambiguities and tensions has been a central part of the nature and purposes of social work since it emerged in the second half of the nineteenth century. It is the key territory in which social work has operated throughout its history. However, social work and children's social care have been marginalized in the brave new world of children's services, reduced to a narrowly defined statutory role.

This throws up one of the biggest tensions which is evident in the structural arrangements whereby the new departments are organized. For while the emphasis is upon integration and moving out of traditional 'silos', the lines of accountability within the new departments often run quite separately. In particular, children's social care and the work of children's centres are often organized in parallel with each other, with quite different philosophies and systems of operation. While children's social care is responsible for 'children in need', including child protection, children 'looked after' and children with complex needs including disabilities, it is children's centres and other parts of the new departments of children's services which have the prime responsibility for developing the preventive, early intervention, community outreach parts of the work. Trying to ensure these sectors operate consistently and in harmony with each other poses a major challenge.

What is not clear is whether the development of attempts to improve prevention and early intervention, such as the CAF, ContactPoint and the role of 'the lead professional', together with children's centres, will have the effect of increasing or decreasing the demands upon children's social care. For example, while one study of the impact on referrals to social services and child protection registrations showed that the presence of a Sure Start programme made no discernible difference (Carpenter et al., 2007), another has suggested that referrals to social services increased (Tunstill and Allnock, 2007). This is an important issue, for the quality of work that can be carried out in the narrow and prescribed roles in which children's social care operates crucially depends on the amount of time and resources that can be allocated to its core tasks.

Finally, we cannot forget that the role and tasks as well as the morale of the children's social work and social care workforce have been crucially affected by the poor image it has had in the media and portrayed in child abuse public inquiries over the past 35 years. There is no sign that this is going to go away (Devo, 2007).

We thus have something of a conundrum. For, compared to the vision outlined for it originally in social services departments, the role of children's social work and social care is now much clearer, but very narrow and restricted. In many ways social work has become marginalized in the work of the newly reconfigured children's services. But at the same time it is also clear that many of the principles and aims of the Seebohm Report are now seen as key to improving the situation and outcomes for children and young people. It is to these issues that we turn in the final chapter when we look at the role of the social worker in an integrated world.

11

Being a Social Worker in an Integrated World: Social Care Work with Children and a Positive Future of Social Work

Introduction

As we have seen throughout this book, social work with children and young people has been fundamentally reformed and 'modernized' in many ways since the election of New Labour in 1997. We have witnessed the demise of generic social services departments and the emergence of more specific children's and adult's social care services, a related reform of the organizational framework in which social care practice with children and young people takes place, the development of the General Social Care Council (GSCC), the introduction of professional registration and the emergence of social work as a graduate profession (Cree and Davis, 2007). Many child care social workers find themselves working in multi-disciplinary teams within integrated organizations – a trend that is likely to increase in the future. This chapter reflects on the current state of children's social care in this new, and still emergent, context and argues the case for a positive role future for social care.

Whilst, at least since the formation of children's departments in 1948 (Packman, 1981), social work has represented a specific form of practice with 'marginalized' children and young people, its contemporary role is unclear. In Chapter 10 we have presented a coherent argument that social work has become increasingly narrow and restricted, and perhaps marginalized, but also a coherent argument can be made that the influence of social work has become broader and increasingly pervasive (see Frost and Robinson, 2007, for example). In this chapter we will explore the latter argument – that social work has a clear and confident role to play in this new integrated world and that it can build and develop the skills and approaches embedded in the traditions of social work. Here we take an optimistic view similar to that taken by Blewett et al. (2007):

> Far from sharing the pessimistic view in some quarters, that social work is 'a profession in crisis' the paper is based on a conviction that social work as a profession is well placed to meet the challenges of a complex and rapidly changing policy context, and to make an important and unique

contribution to all of the new service configurations in respect of children and adult services (Blewett et al., 2007: 2).

Social Work – Towards a Confident Profession in a Multi-disciplinary World

Under the children's trusts arrangements, initiated by the Children Act 2004, state-employed social workers are, by definition, working in a closer relationship with other child- and family-related professions. The exact organizational nature of this relationship varies considerably – for example, some social workers will work in fully integrated, co-located teams, whilst others remain in exclusively social care teams. Regardless of the day-to-day location of the individual social worker, their leadership and strategic planning will be situated as part of a children's trust arrangement aimed at enhancing integrated working in children's services.

In the remainder of this chapter we explore the implications of such arrangements for the future of social work in terms of:

- developing a positive professional identity;
- social care perspectives on social problems;
- working in a integrated world – issues of professional status and power.

By addressing these issues we will be able to assess the degree to which the current organizational framework has enhanced or diminished the role and status of the social work profession.

Developing a Positive Professional Identity

Social workers, in common with other professions, have traditionally been trained in a way that developed a strong sense of professional identity, with a commitment to social work as a profession and to its specific values and techniques (Frost, 2005). It is a paradox then that, once they are qualified, much contemporary practice is focused on developing integrated working and a shared sense of identity with other professionals – often through the children's trust arrangements we have outlined previously. Thus, newly trained social workers with a strong sense of professional identity enter a working environment where they are asked to collaborate and integrate.

In integrated settings professional identity is always dynamic and changing. Professionals in such integrated settings are involved in a complex and continuous process of negotiating both their identity and their forms of practice (see Anning et al., 2006). As one of us has argued elsewhere (Frost, 2005), social workers can maintain a strong sense of social work identity, which we might label as a 'core' identity, whilst simultaneously changing and developing new forms of identity. A social worker quoted in a study undertaken by one of the current authors puts this well:

> I've retained my identity as a Social Worker but I've gained an awful lot more knowledge about other agencies and about the way they work, how to access different things (Anning et al., 2006: 194).

Thus it can be argued that we can hold on to a strong sense of our professional identity, even whilst this is changing, evolving and being challenged.

The issue of shifting skills and identities is well illustrated by the emergence of the Common Assessment Framework (CAF), which we explored in Chapter 3. Prior to the introduction of the Common Assessment Framework (DfES, 2006e,f) the social assessment of children was almost exclusively the concern of social workers. Now the skill of undertaking such assessments is spread across a number of professions, as long as they have undergone the specific training required. Thus the emergence of the CAF provides an example of social work identity being challenged and changed.

At the same time, however, the social work profession retains a privileged position in relation to initial and core assessments (DH, 2000a) and when reporting to courts. This is where social work reports play a crucial role and where children's guardians, who are key officers in family proceedings, often hold professional social work qualifications. Thus a core form of the identity of social work, around the ability to undertake complex assessments, is retained.

When working in integrated settings social workers are often able to develop new ways of working and contribute to building their teams, even where they face challenges or conflicts. Professionals in such settings can utilize methods that highlight what they have in common, whilst emphasizing that well-functioning teams thrive on respect for diversity. There is evidence that a real commitment to integrated working forms the basis for effective multi-disciplinary teams in practice (see Anning et al., 2006). Thus it is possible to argue that the shift towards integrated working can provide a positive professional identity for social workers. They can claim specialist skills, in the field of looked-after children for example, whilst contributing more widely to a multi-disciplinary team development.

A Social Care Perspective on Social Problems

One of the underpinning assumptions of this book is that social problems and indeed childhood itself are 'socially constructed' (Jenks, 1996). Social construction is relevant here because our political and social understanding of the issues faced by children and their families is shaped by social forces and discourses – and these issues cannot be understood independently of these discourses.

The differing professions engaged in contemporary integrated children's agendas construct 'their' service users within their own professional approaches that will have been developed during qualifying training. These professional 'ways of knowing' come together in the varying organizational structures under children's trusts. In many ways these differing discourses will be complementary, but also sometimes they will come into conflict.

Anning et al. argue in their study of five integrated teams that:

> All the teams shared what we might call complex models of understanding: we saw no evidence of crude, uni-causal or over-deterministic models being utilised. However the teams had a tendency to hold a dominant mode of explanation – although this dominant model was not always shared by the entire team, and was often accompanied by a secondary or complementary model of explanation (Anning et al., 2006: 52).

What emerges is a complex picture where different models exist and interact side-by-side. Where teams work well this diversity can be celebrated and can improve the quality of professional work, although it can also be a source of conflict and difference.

Social care as a profession has always been eclectic in nature, perhaps uniquely so. We can find social workers who would describe themselves as Marxist, radical, feminist, behaviourist, task-centred or, indeed, eclectic (Payne, 2005). Modern social care work draws on a range of explanatory models and leads to diverse forms of practice – at community, group or individual level. But it also has an intellectual and practical unity that gives social work a professional identity. The French theorist Donzelot (1980) has demonstrated that 'the social' has a key role in enabling the state to intervene with some families whilst maintaining the perceived autonomy of the family as a social institution (Parton, 2008b). This locates social work in a specific relationship with families – and explains why it is often controversial and subject to the often critical form of media coverage that it generates (Franklin and Parton, 2001).

Philp (1979) has argued that social work carries out three characteristic tasks: these are the creation of human subjects, the integration of objective characteristics and speaking for the subject. By this Philp means that social workers help people confronting social problems to be seen as human; for the situation they are facing to be seen as a human, subjective situation; and then the social workers give voice to this subject (see Parton, 2006a). Thus, whilst social work may be eclectic in drawing on a range of influences it creates a clearly identifiable form of knowledge and professional identity.

When social workers find themselves in integrated settings the nature of their role and the tensions of their functions come to the forefront. They promote particular forms of explanation of the social problems they confront. A challenge for integrated teams is to reflect together on the models underlying their practice engagement with service users. Each model will have its own unique professional frame of reference. These models are theories, in the sense that they are abstract, but they matter in the real world as models have to have a practical value in the realm of practice. They have to 'work' in the day-to-day practice of each profession. Often these tensions between models are found where social work and medical staff work together. In Chapter 8 we reflected on this issue in relation to disabled children.

One reason why social work is arguably a key profession in the new integrated world is that it takes a holistic approach, that is, the task of understanding the human subject and giving a voice. This approach arguably sits well with the new integrated agenda, where the five outcomes assist professionals in seeing children and young people in this holistic way rather than only as 'pupils', or 'patients', or indeed 'cases'. The value of this approach has been demonstrated by research undertaken by Beresford, who demonstrates that:

> Service users placed a particular value on social work's 'social' approach, the relationship and the positive personal qualities they associate with social workers. The latter included warmth, respect, being non-judgemental, listening, treating people with equality, being trustworthy, openness and honesty, reliability and communicating well (Beresford, 2007: 5–6).

Social work has traditionally played a key role is seeing the person in their wider family, community and social context. This is illustrated by the Assessment Framework (DH, 2000a), where social work assessments are able to present this holistic view to the court, or other settings, that make crucial decisions in relation to the child.

The social worker also attempts to work in partnership with the child and/or family and represent their perspective, wherever this is possible, thus providing a clear, positive role for social work. Thus it can be argued that social work has maintained a clear role and identity in the new world of integrated working.

Issues of Professional Status and Power

For many years social work has been described as a 'semi-profession' (Etzioni, 1969) – those taking this position would argue that social work meets only some of the criteria that sociologists and others identify as defining a profession. Social work was seen as being without a clear knowledge and research base, and also without clearly defined entry criteria to the profession. It is argued here that this has changed in recent years, at least in the United Kingdom, following a number of reforms, including:

• graduate entry level to the profession; social work becoming a 'restricted title', with a register of social workers; the establishment of a code of practice (see Cree and Davis, 2007).

It can be argued here that social work has been strengthened as a profession in the full sense of the term, with a status comparable with other 'social' professions such as teaching. How this status is deployed in the actual field of policy and practice is a much more complex puzzle to unravel.

The tensions between professions are often expressed through power and status issues. This is often transmitted through the use of language used to communicate knowledge across professional boundaries. According to a hospital social worker in the previously cited study, the team she worked in utilized a professional discourse that was used to exclude:

> I found it very hard to go in to that … meeting … what is daunting is we don't even speak the same language … they know that I don't know things because I constantly try and express that, I get quite embarrassed at having to repeat myself so often (Robinson et al., 2005: 191).

The social worker here feels that she is having power and higher status exercised over her, but, of course, social workers sometimes exercise power over other workers. Foster carers and day-care staff, for example, will often feel that they are dominated by social workers and their professional status.

Professional power and status differentials found in integrated teams and children's trusts arrangements cannot simply disappear. Issues of difference and power represent a major challenge for the integrated working agenda in terms of how different professionals exercise power and status.

A fundamental challenge of working in an integrated setting is for professionals to engage with power differentials and to embrace change and diversity while not losing those core professional values and modes of understanding that underpin their sense of identity.

Children's social care does face a serious challenge due to its location in children's trusts, which we can conceptualize as 'stigma' through association. This is arguably because social work is linked with the most marginalized children and young people – abused children, looked-after children and youth offenders. Thus social care work is always associated with problems and to a degree with failure (Ferguson, 2004). This makes the location in children's trusts challenging as social care sits alongside universal services such as children's centres, education and health with are more easily linked with 'excellence' and 'success'. Thus children's social care is always in danger as being seen as a largely 'problematic' element of children's services.

Reforming the Children's Workforce

To understand social work and social care in the contemporary climate involves making links with the wider workforce reform agenda. The Department for Children, Schools and Families (DCSF) agenda for reforming the workforce remains a dynamic and changing one. Central to our concerns here are the workforce development document *Building Brighter Futures: Next Steps for the Children's Workforce* (DCSF, 2008d), and a series of initiatives emerging from the Children's Workforce Development Council (CWDC). In addition, the General Social Care Council has published its review of the future of social work *'Social Work at its Best'* (GSCC, 2008). All these initiatives have implications for workforce development and all have something to say about the future of social work.

The main thrust of the DCSF policy agenda locates social work as part of the newly emergent integrated workforce for children and young people. The development of the workforce and the emphasis on integration is a major theme of *The Children's Plan* (DCSF, 2007b) and is outlined in more detail in the *Building Brighter Futures* document (DCSF, 2008d).

The Children's Plan both re-emphasizes and strengthens the focus on integrated ways of working that has emerged so powerfully this century. The Plan, arguably, can be summarized as having a powerful focus on improved outcomes for children and young people that will be delivered by the effective leadership of an integrated workforce and monitored by a rigorous inspection regime. The emphasis on the central role of the workforce could hardly be more powerful:

> The *single most important factor* in delivering our aspirations for children is a world class workforce able to provide highly personalised support, so we will continue to drive up quality and capacity of those working in the children's workforce (DCSF, 2007b: 10, emphasis added).

Thus we can see that the integrated workforce is conceptualized as delivering a profound improvement in outcomes for children and young people. But what is the specific role of social work within this agenda? How can social work's long-standing expertise and particular strengths in relational human work be best employed?

Whilst it is true that integration is the most powerful state agenda, there is recognition by government that the children's workforce remains made up of a range of professions with their own discrete workforce development issues and professional identities. Specifically in relation to social work, *Building Brighter Futures* (DCSF, 2008d) outlines a number of initiatives arising from the investment of £73 million in the future of the social work profession. These initiatives include:

(a) the piloting of a fast-track route for people wanting to transfer professions into social work;

(b) a marketing campaign aimed at encouraging professionals wishing to transfer into social work;

(c) a review of social work education, with a particular focus on practice placements;

(d)   the piloting of a newly qualified social work status, offering a protected caseload and professional development during the first year of practice, which will be led by the CWDC;

(e)   the development and piloting of an ongoing professional development framework;

(f)   the introduction of social work pilots as outlined in the Children and Young Persons Bill, and as discussed in Chapter 6 of this book.

These are a series of initiatives that have implications for the future of the social work profession. The level of official activity demonstrates an ongoing degree of state interest in the renewal and 'modernization' of the social work profession. There seems to be an attempt to develop and secure the development of a social work profession that will maintain a strong sense of professional identity whilst playing a specified role within the integrated workforce. This trend can be seen in initiatives in specific local authority settings which have attempted to reform social work – the most high profile of these perhaps being the 'Reclaiming Social Work' initiative based in Hackney (Gulland, 2008).

A key challenge for the profession is to maintain a focus on the human, relational aspects of its work, especially in relation to prevention and early intervention, within the context of what our respondents described as an increasingly bureaucratic and regulated work environment.

Developing a Positive Role for Children's Social Care

In recent years two major reviews of social work in the United Kingdom context have been undertaken. Asquith et al., in their review of the role of social work in Scotland, identify the following potential roles for social work:

- Counsellor
- Advocate
- Partner
- Assessor of risk or need
- Care manager
- Agent of social control (Asquith et al., 2005: x).

Having undertaken a similar review in the English context, Blewett and colleagues argue that the future of social work can be seen in the tensions between the following roles:

- Assessment and service delivery
- Practice/prevention and reactive/protection
- Centre-based versus community-based social work

- Advocacy and social change versus therapy and individual change
- Care commissioning and care provision
  (Blewett et al., 2007: 35–6).

We can see in both of these reviews that the future of social work, and the potential roles than can be undertaken, are unclear and potentially diverse. The latter review fed into the publication of *'Social Work at its Best'* (GSCC, 2008). This is a disappointing publication that fails to build on the valuable material gathered by Blewett et al. in their preparatory literature review. The GSCC review is poorly presented and lacks the vision and authority to act as a real blue-print for the future of social work. For example, its largely descriptive nature can be seen in the first paragraph:

> Social work is an established professional discipline with a distinctive part to play in promoting and securing the wellbeing of children, adults, families and communities. It operates within a framework of legislation and government policy, set out in Putting People First and the Children's Plan, and contributes to the development of social policy, practice and service provision. It collaborates with other social care, health, education and related services to ensure people receive integrated support. It is a profession regulated by law (GSCC, 2008).

Despite the disappointing nature of this particular document it is possible, as we have seen, to put a strong case for being an optimist in relation to the future of social work. Above, some of the challenges have been outlined. Whilst each is complex, they can all contribute to a process of constructive change. There is no doubt that the social work role is complex and contested, with actual and potential conflicts about professional identity, models of understanding, and about status and power.

Whilst conflicts and contested definitions exist in integrated settings, social workers have developed ways of working together as 'communities of practice' that generate shared meanings and understandings.

Within integrated settings, and in children's trusts more widely, social care has a clear role to play. It works with children in need of safeguarding, children in care, in the field of adoption, and with children with complex needs. In all these fields, many of which involve liaison with the courts, social work has a clear and indispensable role. When Joint Area Reviews take place there is invariably a focus on one or more of these key areas of practice. This helps to maintain the high profile of social care work and ensures that having a positive and thriving social work service is central to the success of a children's trust.

Social workers in multi-agency teams can retain a core identity and core values, whilst engaging in developing 'communities of practice'. In integrated, multi-agency teams, ongoing tensions between sustaining an emerging team and

encountering different professional models and values are inevitable, but positive ways forward can be found. In the wider context, social care work remains
central to the main concerns of children's trusts. The key concerns of children's
social care – safeguarding, working with children with complex needs and those
looked after – will continue to be indispensable in children's trusts.

References

11 Million (2008) *Claiming Asylum at a Screening Unit as an Unaccompanied Child.* London: 11 Million.

Action for Aftercare (2004) *Setting the Agenda: What's Left to Do in Leaving Care?* London: NCH.

Anderson, R., Brown, I., Clayton, R., Dowty, T., Korff, D. and Munro, E. (2006) *Children's Databases – Safety and Privacy: A Report for the Information Commissioner.* Cambridge: Foundation for Information Policy Research; available from http://www.ico.gov.uk (accessed 28/11/06).

Anning, A., Cottrell, D., Frost, N., Green, J. and Robinson, M. (2006) *Developing Multiprofessional Teamwork for Integrated Children's Services.* Maidenhead: Open University Press.

Asquith, S., Clark, C. and Waterhouse, L. (2005) *The Role of the Social Worker in the 21st Century – A Literature Review.* Edinburgh: Scottish Executive.

Aubrey, C. (2007) *Leading and Managing Early Years Settings.* London: Sage.

Audit Commission (1994) *Seen but not Heard: Coordinating Community Health and Social Services for Children in Need.* London: HMSO.

Audit Commission (1996) *Misspent Youth: Young People and Crime.* London: HMSO.

Audit Commission (2004) *Youth Justice 2004: A review of the reformed youth justice system.* London: HMSO.

Ayotte, W. and Williamson, L. (2001) *Separated Children in the UK: An Overview of the Current Situation.* London: Save the Children.

Balls, E. (2007) Disabled children must stay at the top of the agenda, *Community Care,* 6.12.2007: 23.

Ball, S.J. (2007) "Going further?" Tony Blair and New Labour education policies', in K. Clarke, T. Maltby and P. Kennett (eds), *Social Policy Review 19: Analysis and Debate in Social Policy.* Bristol: Policy Press.

Barclay, P.M. (1982) *Social Workers: Their Role and Tasks.* London: Bedford Square Press.

Barnardo's (2008) *Like Any Other Child.* Barkingside: Barnardo's.

Barnes, C. and Mercer, G. (2003) *Disability.* Cambridge: Polity Press.

Bauman, Z. (2003) *Wasted Lives, Modernity and its Outcasts.* Cambridge: Polity Press.

Bean, P. and Melville, J. (1990) *Lost Children of the Empire.* London: Unwin Hyman.

Bell, M. and Shaw, I. (2008) *Integrated Children's System Evaluation: Summary of Key Finding.* Research Brief DCSF-RBX 02-08. London: DCSF.

Bellamy, C., Perri, 6 and Raab, C. (2005) Joined-up government and privacy in the United Kingdom: managing tensions between data protection and social policy. Part II, *Public Administration*, 83(2): 393–415.

Belsky, J., Barnes, J. and Melhuish, E. (2007) *The National Evaluation of Sure Start.* Bristol: Policy Press.

Belsky, J., Melhuish, E., Barnes, J., Leyland, A.H. and Romaniuk, H. (2006) Effects of Sure Start local programmes on children and families: early findings from a quasi-experimental, cross sectional study, *British Medical Journal*, 332: 1476–8.

Beresford, P. (2007) *Shaping Our Lives: The Changing Roles and Tasks of Social Work, from Service Users' Perspectives: A Literature Informed Discussion Paper.* London: Shaping Our Lives National User Network/GSCC.

Beveridge, W.H. (1944) *Full Employment in a Free Society.* London: Allen and Unwin.

Biehal, N., Clayden, J., Stein, M. and Wade, J. (1992) *Prepared for Living? A survey of young people leaving the care of three local authorities.* London: National Children's Bureau.

Blair, T. (1993) Why crime is a Socialist issue, *New Statesman*, 29(12): 27–8.

Blair, T. (1998) *The Third Way: New Politics for the New Century.* Fabian Pamphlet 588. London: The Fabian Society.

Blair, T. (1999) 'Beveridge Revisited: Welfare State for the 21st Century', in R. Walker (ed.), *Ending Child Poverty: Popular Welfare for the 21st Century.* Bristol: Policy Press.

Blair, T. (2001) Foreword in Social Exclusion Unit, *Preventing Social Exclusion.* London: Stationery Office.

Blair, T. (2006) BBC News Interview, 30 August, available from www.bbc.co.uk (accessed 6 September 2006).

Blewett, J., Lewis, J. and Tunstill, J. (2007) *The Changing Roles and Tasks of Social Work: A literature informed discussion paper.* General Social Care Council.

Border and Immigration Agency (2008a) *Better Outcomes: The way forward, improving the care of unaccompanied asylum seeking children.* London: Home Office.

Border and Immigration Agency (2008b) *Code of Practice for Keeping Children Safe from Harm.* London: Home Office.

Bottoms, A. (1974) 'On the decriminalisation of the English juvenile court', in R. Hood (ed.), *Crime, Criminology and Public Policy.* London: Heinemann.

Bottoms, A. (1995) 'The Philosophy and Politics of Punishment and Sentencing', in M.V. Clarkson and R. Morgan (eds), *The Politics of Sentencing Reform.* Oxford: Oxford University Press.

Bottoms, A. and Dignan, J. (2004) 'Youth Justice in Great Britain', in M. Tonry and A. Doob (eds), *Youth Crime and Youth Justice: Comparative and Cross-National Perspectives.* London: University of Chicago Press.

Bottoms, A. and Kemp, V. (2007) 'The Relationship between Youth Justice and Child Welfare in England and Wales', in M. Hill, A. Lockyer and F. Stone (eds), *Youth Justice and Child Protection.* London: Jessica Kingsley.

Bottoms, A., Brown, P., McWilliams, B., McWilliams, W. and Nellis, M. (1990) *Intermediate Treatment and Juvenile Justice: Key Findings and Implications from a National Survey of Intermediate Treatment Policy and Practice.* London: HMSO.

Brewer, M., Goodman, A., Myck, M., Shaw, J. and Shephard, A. (2004) *Poverty and Inequality in Britain.* London: Institute for Fiscal Studies.

Brewer, M., Sibieta, L. and Wren-Lewis, L. (2008) *Racing Away? Income Inequality and the Evolution of High Incomes*. London: Institute of Fiscal Studies.

Burney, E. (2005) *Making People Behave: Anti-Social Behaviour, Politics and Policy*. Cullompton: Willan.

Butler, I. and Drakeford, M. (2005) *Scandal, Social Policy and Social Welfare*. 2nd edn. Bristol: Policy Press.

Byrne, D. (2005) *Social Exclusion*. 2nd edn. Buckingham: Open University Press.

Cabinet Office (1999) *Modernizing Government*. London: Stationery Office.

Cabinet Office, Social Exclusion Task Force (2007a) *Reaching Out: Progress on Social Exclusion*. London: Cabinet Office.

Cabinet Office, Social Exclusion Task Force (2007b) *Reaching Out: Think Family: Analysis and Themes from the Families at Risk Review*. London: Cabinet Office.

Cabinet Office, Social Exclusion Task Force (2008) *Think Family: Improving the Life Chances of Families at Risk*. London: Cabinet Office.

Carpenter, J., Brown, S. and Griffin, M. (2007) Prevention in Integrated Children's Services: The Impact of Sure Start on Referrals to Social Services and Child Protection Registrations, *Child Abuse Review*, 18(1): 17–31.

Cemlyn, S. and Briskman, L. (2003) Asylum, children's rights and social work, *Child and Family Social Work*, 8(3): 163–78.

Chief Secretary to the Treasury (2003) *Every Child Matters* (Cm5860). London: Stationery Office.

Children and Young People's Unit (CYPU) (2002) *Local Preventative Strategy: Interim Guidance for Local Authorities and Other Local Agencies (Statutory and Non-Statutory) Providing Services to Children*. www.cypu.gov.uk/corporate/services/preventative.cfm accessed 04/06/04.

Children's Workforce Development Council (2008) *The State of the Children's Social Care Workforce: A statistical overview of the workforce providing children's and families' social care in England*. London: CWDC.

Clarke, J. (1980) 'Social Democrat Delinquents and Fabian Families: A Background to the 1969 Children and Young Persons Act', in The National Deviancy Conference (eds), *Permissiveness and Control: The Fate of the Sixties Legislation*. London: Macmillan.

Clarke, J., Gewitz, S. and McLaughlin, E. (eds) (2000) *New Managerialism: New Welfare*. London: Sage.

Clarke, J. and Glendinning, C. (2002) 'Partnership and the Remaking of Welfare Governance', in C. Glendinning, M. Powell and K. Rummer (eds), *Partnerships, New Labour and the Governance of Welfare*. Bristol: Policy Press.

Clarke, J., Smith, N. and Vidler, E. (2006) The Indeterminacy of Choice: Political, Policy and Organisation Implications, *Social Policy and Society*, 5(3): 327–36.

Cleaver, H., Unel, I. and Aldgate, A. (1999) *Children's Needs – Parenting Capacity: The Impact of Parental Mental Illness, Problem Alcohol and Drug Use, and Domestic Violence on Children's Development*. London, The Stationery Office.

Cleaver, H., Walker, S., Scott, J., Cleaver, D., Rose, W., Ward, H. and Pithouse, A. (2008) *Integrated Children's System: Enhancing Social Work and Inter-Agency Practice*. Research Brief DCSF-RBX 01-08. London: DCSF.

Clouston, A. (unpublished) How has NPQICL affected participants with a social work background, and what have they gained? Corby: Pen Green.

Commission for Social Care Inspection (2006) *The State of Social Care in England 2005–6*. London: CSCI.

Commission for Social Care Inspection (2007) *Growing Up Matters: Better transition planning for young people with complex needs.* London: CSCI.

Commission on Families and the Wellbeing of Children (2005) *Families and the State: Two-way Support and Responsibilities – An Inquiry into the Relationship between the State and the Family in the Upbringing of Children.* Bristol: Policy Press.

Cooper, J. (1983) *The Creation of the British Personal Social Services 1962–74.* London: Heinemann.

Corby, B. (1990) Making Use of Child Protection Statistics, *Children & Society*, 4(4): 304–14.

Corby, B., Doig, A. and Roberts, V. (1998) Inquiries into Child Abuse, *Journal of Social Welfare and Family Law*, 20(4): 377–95.

Corby, B., Doig, A. and Roberts, V. (2001) *Public Inquiries into Abuse of Children in Residential Care.* London: Jessica Kingsley.

Crawford, A. and Newburn, T. (2003) *Youth Offending and Restorative Justice.* Cullompton: Willan.

Cree, V. and Davis, A. (2007) *Social Work: Voices from the Inside.* London: Routledge.

Crimmens, D. and Pitts, J. (2000) *Positive Residential Practice: Learning the lessons of the 1990s.* Lyme Regis: Russell House Press.

Cunningham, S. and Tomlinson, J. (2005) 'Starve Them Out': Does every child really matter? A commentary on Section 9 of the Asylum and Immigration (Treatment of Claimants, etc.) Act, 2004, *Critical Social Policy*, 25(2): 263–75.

Curtis, P. and Ward, L. (2007) Fitter, happier and better educated: the hope for 2020, *The Guardian*, 12 December, 6–7.

Curtis Report (1946) *Report of the Care of Children Committee.* Cmd6922. London: HMSO.

CWDC (2008) *The State of the Children's Social Care Workforce: A Statistical Overview of the Workforce Providing Children's and Families' Social Care in England.* London: Children's Workforce Development Council.

Dennis, J. (2007) 'The legal and policy frameworks that govern social work with unaccompanied asylum seeking and refugee children in England', in R. Kohli (ed.), *Working with Unaccompanied Asylum Seeking Children: Issues for Policy and Practice.* Basingstoke: Palgrave.

Department for Children, Schools and Families (2007a) *Children and Young Persons Bill Policy Paper, Disabled Children and Young People.* London: Stationery Office.

Department for Children, Schools and Families (2007b) *The Children's Plan: Building Brighter Futures.* London: Stationery Office.

Department for Children, Schools and Families (2007c) *ContactPoint – Policy Statement, June 2007*, http://www.everychildmatters.gov.uk/ContactPoint (accessed 18/07/07).

Department for Children, Schools and Families (2007d) *Staying Safe: A Consultation Document.* London: Stationery Office.

Department for Children, Schools and Families (2007e) *Children's Social Services, Local Authority Circular 2210070011, Unaccompanied Asylum Seeking Children – Leaving Care Costs, 2007–08 Guidance.* London: Stationery Office.

Department for Children, Schools and Families (2008a) *The Sure Start Journey: A Summary of the Evidence.* London: DCSF.

Department for Children, Schools and Families (2008b) *Youth Taskforce Action Plan: Give Respect, Get Respect – Youth Matters.* London: DCSF.

Department for Children, Schools and Families (2008c) *Care Matters: Time to Deliver for Children in Care*. London: DCSF.

Department for Children, Schools and Families (2008d) *Building Brighter Futures: Next Steps for the Children's Workforce*. London: Stationery Office.

Department for Education and Skills (2004a) *Every Child Matters: Change for Children*. London: DfES.

Department for Education and Skills (2004b) *Every Child Matters: Next Steps*. London: DfES.

Department for Education and Skills (2004c) *Every Child Matters: Change for Children in Social Care*. London: DfES.

Department for Education and Skills (2005a) *Children in Need in England: Preliminary Results of a Survey of Activity and Expenditure as Reported by Local Authority Social Services' Children and Family Teams for a Survey Week in February 2005*. DfES, SFR 52/2005.

Department for Education and Skills (2005b) *Higher Standards, Better Schools for All: More Choice for Parents and Pupils*. Cmd. 6677. London: Stationery Office.

Department for Education and Skills (2005c) *Youth Matters: Next Steps. Something to Do, Somewhere to Go, Someone to Talk to*. London: DfES.

Department for Education and Skills (2006a) *Care Matters: Transforming the Lives of Children and Young People in Care*. London: DfES.

Department for Education and Skills (2006b) *Children's Workforce Strategy: Building a World-class Workforce for Children, Young People and Families: The Government's Response to the Consultation*. London: DfES.

Department for Education and Skills (2006c) *The Lead Professional: Managers' Guide. Integrated Working to Improve Outcomes for Children and Young People*. London: DfES.

Department for Education and Skills (2006d) *The Lead Professional: Practitioners' Guide. Integrated Working to Improve Outcomes for Children and Young People*. London: DfES.

Department for Education and Skills (2006e) *The Common Assessment Framework for Children and Young People: Practitioners' Guide. Integrated Working to Improve Outcomes for Children and Young People*. London: DfES.

Department for Education and Skills (2006f) *Common Assessment Framework for Children and Young People: Managers' Guide. Integrated Working to Improve the Outcomes for Children and Young People*. London: DfES.

Department for Education and Skills (2007a) *Aiming High for Disabled Children: Better Support for Families*. London: DfES.

Department for Education and Skills (2007b) *Care Matters: Time for Change*. London: DfES.

Department for Education and Skills (2007c) *Governance Guidance for Sure Start Children's Centres and Extended Schools*. London: DfES.

Department for Education and Skills (2007d) *National Standards for Leaders of Sure Start Children's Centres*. London: DfES.

Department of Health (1988) *Protecting Children: A Guide for Social Workers Undertaking a Comprehensive Assessment in Cases of Child Protection*. London: HMSO.

Department of Health (1994) *Children Act Report 1993*. London: HMSO.

Department of Health (1995a) *Child Protection: Messages from Research*. London: HMSO.

Department of Health (1995b) *Looking After Children: Good Parenting Good Outcomes Training Guide*. London: HMSO.

Department of Health (1998a) *Modernising Social Services: Promoting Independence, Improving Protection, Raising Standards*. (Cm4169). London: Stationery Office.

Department of Health (1998b) *The Quality Protects Programme: Transforming Children's Services*. LDC(98): 28.

Department of Health (2000a) *Assessing Children in Need and their Families: Practice Guidance*. London: Stationery Office.

Department of Health (2000b) *Learning the Lessons*. London: Stationery Office.

Department of Health (2000c) *Studies which Inform the Development of the Framework for the Assessment of Children in Need and their Families*. London: Stationery Office.

Department of Health (2000d) *The Prime Minister's Review of Adoption*. London: Stationery Office.

Department of Health (2001) *The Children Act Now: Messages from Research*. London: Stationery Office.

Department of Health (2002) *Safeguarding Children: A Joint Inspectors' Report on Arrangements to Safeguard Children*. London: Department of Health.

Department of Health (2003) *About the Integrated Children's System*. www.children. doh.gov.uk/integratedchildrensystem (accessed 04/06/04).

Department of Health (2004) *National Service Framework for Children, Young People and Maternity Services*. London: Department of Health.

Department of Health and Cleaver, H. (2000) *Assessment Recording Forms*. London: Stationery Office.

Department of Health, Home Office and Department of Education and Employment (1999) *Working Together to Safeguard Children: A Guide to Inter-agency Working to Safeguard and Promote the Welfare of Children*. London: Stationery Office.

Department of Health, Department of Education and Employment and Home Office (2000a) *Framework for the Assessment of Children in Need and their Families*. London: Stationery Office.

Department of Health, Cox, A. and Bentovim, A. (2000b) *The Family Assessment Pack of Questionnaires and Scales*. London: Stationery Office.

Department of Health, Department for Education and Skills, Home Office, Department for Culture, Media and Sports, Office of the Deputy Prime Minister and the Lord Chancellor's Office (2003) *What to Do if You're Worried a Child is Being Abused*. London: Department of Health.

Devo, J. (2007) Deaths Spark Media Storm, *Professional Social Work*, September: 5.

DHSS (1974) *Non-Accidental Injury to Children*. LASSL(74)(13).

DHSS (1976a) *Non-Accidental Injury to Children: Area Review Committees*. LASSL(76)(2).

DHSS (1976b) *Non-Accidental Injury to Children: The Police and Case Conferences*. LASSL(76)(26).

DHSS (1978) *Child Abuse: The Register System*. LA/C396/23D.

DHSS (1980) *Child Abuse: Central Register Systems*. LASSL(80)4, HN(80).

DHSS (1982) *Child Abuse: A Study of Inquiry Reports 1973–1981*. London: HMSO.

DHSS (1985) *Review of Child Care Law: Report to Ministers of an Interdepartmental Working Party.* London: HMSO.

DHSS (1988, re-issued 1999) *Working Together: A Guide to Inter-agency Co-operation for the Protection of Children from Abuse.* London: HMSO.

Dixon, J and Wade, J. (2007) 'Leaving Care'? Transition planning and support for Unaccompanied Young People', in R. Kohli and F. Mitchell (eds), *Working with Unaccompanied Asylum Seeking Children: Issues for Policy and Practice.* Basingstoke: Palgrave.

Dobrowolsky, A. and Jenson, J. (2005) 'Social investment perspectives and practices: A decade in British politics', in M. Powell, L. Bauld and K. Clarke (eds), *Social Policy Review 17: Analysis and Debate in Social Policy.* Bristol: Policy Press.

Donzelot, J. (1980) *The Policing of Families.* London: Hutchinson.

Driver, S. and Martell, L. (1997) New Labour's Communitarianisms, *Critical Social Policy,* 17(3): 27–46.

Dryfoos, J.G. (1990) *Adolescents at Risk: Prevalence and Prevention.* Oxford: Oxford University Press.

Eisenstadt, N. (2007) Foreword in J. Belsky, J. Barnes and E. Melhuish (eds), *The National Evaluation of Sure Start – does area-based early intervention work?* Bristol: Policy Press.

Ennew, J. (1986) *The Sexual Exploitation of Children.* Cambridge: Polity Press.

Etzioni, A. (1969) *The Semi-professions and their Organization: Teachers, Nurses and Social Workers.* New York: Free Press.

Etzioni, A. (1993) *The Spirit of Community: Rights, Responsibilities and the Communitarian Agenda.* New York: Simon and Schuster.

Etzioni, A. (1997) *The New Golden Rule: Community and Morality in a Democratic Society.* New York: Harper Collins.

European Commissioner for Human Rights (2005) *Report by Mr Alvaro Gil-Robles, Commissioner for Human Rights on his Visit to the United Kingdom 4–12 November 2004.* Strasbourg: Council of Europe.

Fairclough, N. (2000) *New Labour, New Language?* London: Routledge.

Farrington, D. (1996) *Understanding and Preventing Youth Crime.* York: Joseph Rowntree Foundation.

Farrington, D. (2000) Explaining and Preventing Crime: The Globalisation of Knowledge, *Criminology,* 38(1): 1–24.

Fawcett, B., Featherstone, B. and Goddard, J. (2004) *Contemporary Child Care Policy and Practice.* Basingstoke: Palgrave/Macmillan.

Ferguson, H. (2004) *Protecting Children in Time.* Basingstoke: Palgrave.

Fildes, V. (1988) *Wet Nursing.* Oxford: Blackwell.

Finch, J. and Groves, D. (eds) (1983) *A Labour of Love.* London: Routledge and Kegan Paul.

France, A. and Utting, D. (2005) The Paradigm of Risk and Protection-focussed Prevention and its Impact on Services for Children and Families, *Children & Society,* 19(2): 77–90.

Franklin, A. and Sloper, P. (forthcoming) Supporting the Participation of Disabled Children and Young People in Decision-making, *Children and Society.*

Franklin, B. (ed.), (1986) *The Rights of Children.* Oxford: Basil Blackwell.

Franklin, B. (ed.) (1995) *A Comparative Handbook of Children's Rights*. London: Routledge.

Franklin, B. (2003) 'The Hand of History: New Labour, News Management and Governance', in A. Chadwick and R. Heffernan (eds), *The New Labour Reader*. Oxford: Polity Press.

Franklin, B. and Parton, N. (eds) (1989) *Social Work, the Media and Public Relations*. London: Routledge.

Franklin, B. and Parton, N. (2001) 'Press-ganged! Media Reporting of Social Work and Child Abuse', in M. May, R. Payne and E. Brunsdon (eds), *Understanding Social Problems: Issues in Social Policy*. Oxford: Blackwell.

Franklin, B. and Petley, J. (1996) 'Killing the Age of Innocence: Newspaper Reporting of the Death of James Bulger', in J. Pilcher and S. Wagg (eds), *Thatcher's Children? Politics, Childhood and Society in the 1980's and 1990's*. London: Falmer Press.

Freeman, M.D.A. (1983) *The Rights and Wrongs of Children*. London: Francis Pinker.

Freeman, R. (1992) 'The Idea of Prevention: A Critical Review', in S. Scott, G. Williams, S. Platt and H. Thomas (eds), *Private Risk and Public Dangers*. Aldershot: Avebury.

Freeman, R. (1999) Recursive Politics: Prevention, Modernity and Social Systems, *Children & Society*, 13(4): 232–41.

Frost, N. (1992) 'Implementing the Children Act 1989 in a Hostile Climate', in P. Carter, T., Jeffs and M.K. Smith (eds), *Changing Social Work and Welfare*. Buckingham: Open University Press.

Frost, N. (2003) A problematic relationship? Evidence and practice in the workplace, *Social Work and Social Sciences Review*, 10(1): 38–50.

Frost, N. (2005) *Partnership, professionalism and joined-up thinking*. Dartington: Research in Practice.

Frost, N. and Robinson, M. (2007) Joining Up Children's Services: Safeguarding Children in Multi-disciplinary Teams, *Child Abuse Review*, 16: 184–99.

Frost, N. and Stein, M. (1989) *The Politics of Child Welfare: Inequality, Power and Change*. London: Harvester Wheatsheaf.

Frost, N., Mills, S. and Stein, M. (1999) *Understanding Residential Care*. Aldershot: Ashgate.

Gardner, J., von Hirsch, A., Smith, A., Morgan, R., Ashworth, A. and Wasik, M. (1998) Clause 1 – The Hybrid Law from Hell?, *Criminal Justice Matters*, 31 (Spring): 25–7.

Garrett, P.M. (2008) Social Work Practices: silences and elisions in the plan to 'transform' the lives of children 'looked-after' in England, *Child and Family Social Work*, 13(3): 311–18.

Geach, H. and Szwed, E. (eds) (1983) *Providing Civil Justice for Children*. London: Arnold.

Gelsthorpe, L. (2002) 'Recent Changes in Youth Justice Policy in England and Wales', in I. Weijers and A. Duff (eds), *Punishing Juveniles: Principle and Critique*. Oxford: Hart Publishing.

General Social Care Council (2008) *Social Work at its Best: A Statement of Social Work Roles and Tasks for the 21st Century*. London, GSCC.

Giddens, A. (1994) *Beyond Left and Right: The Future of Radical Politics*. Cambridge: Polity Press.

Giddens, A. (1998) *The Third Way: The Renewal of Social Democracy*. Cambridge: Polity Press.

Giddens, A. (2000) *The Third Way and its Critics*. Cambridge: Polity Press.

Giller, H. and Morris, A. (1981) *Care and Discretion: Social Work Decisions with Delinquents*. London: Burnett Books.

Gillies, V. (2008) Perspectives on Parenting Responsibility: Contextualising Values and Practices, *Journal of Law and Society*, 35(1): 95–112.

Glass, N. (1999) Sure Start: The development of an early intervention programme for young children in the United Kingdom, *Children and Society*, 13(4): 257–74.

Glass, N. (2005) Some mistake surely?, *The Guardian*, 5th January.

Glendinning, C., Powell, M. and Rummery, K. (eds) (2002) *Partnerships, New Labour and the Governance of Welfare*. Bristol: Polity Press.

Goldblatt, P. and Lewis, C. (eds) (1998) *Reducing Offending. Home Office Research Study No 187*. London: HMSO.

Golding, P. (1986) *Excluding the Poor*. London: CPAG.

Goldson, B. (2000) 'Children in need' or 'young offenders'? Hardening ideology, organizational change and new challenges for social work with children in trouble, *Child and Family Social Work*, 5(3): 255–65.

Goldson, B. and Muncie, J. (2006) Rethinking Youth Justice: Comparative Analysis, International Human Rights and Research Evidence, *Youth Justice*, 6(2): 91–106.

Goodwin, R.E. (1996) Inclusion and Exclusion, *European Journal of Sociology*, 37(2): 343-71.

Gray, J. (2002) 'National Policy on the Assessment of Children in Need and their Families', in H. Ward and W. Rose (eds), *Approaches to Needs Assessment in Children's Services*. London: Jessica Kingsley.

Gulland, A. (2008) Better off at the frontline, *Community Care*, 23rd July.

Hagell, A. and Newburn, T. (1994) *Persistent Young Offenders*. London: Policy Studies Institute.

Haines, K. and Drakeford, M. (1998) *Young People and Youth Justice*. Basingstoke: Macmillan.

Hall, P. (1976) *Reforming the Welfare*. London: Heinemann.

Hawker, D. (2006) 'Joined up Working – the Development of Childhood Services', in G. Pugh and B. Duffy (eds), *Contemporary Issues in Early Years*. London: Sage.

Hek, R. (2005) *The Experiences and Needs of Refugee and Asylum Seeking Children in the UK: A literature review*. Birmingham: University of Birmingham.

Hek, R. (2007) 'Using Foster Placements for the Care and Resettlement of Unaccompanied Children', in R. Kohli and F. Mitchell (eds), *Working with Unaccompanied Asylum Seeking Children: Issues for policy and practice*. Basingstoke: Palgrave.

Held, D. and McGrew, A. (2002) *Globalization/Anti-Globalization*. Cambridge: Polity Press.

Hill, M. (2000) 'What are Local Authority Social Services?' in M. Hill (ed.), *Local Authority Social Services: An Introduction*. Oxford: Blackwell.

Hilton, Z. and Mills, C. (2007) Ask the Children, *Criminal Justice*, 16: 16–18.

HM Government (2006a) *Reaching Out: An Action Plan on Social Exclusion*. London: Cabinet Office.

HM Government (2006b) *Working Together to Safeguard Children: A Guide to Inter-Agency Working to Safeguard and Promote the Welfare of Children*. London: Stationery Office.

HM Government (2008) *Youth Action Plan 2008*. London, Stationery Office.

HM Treasury (2002a) *2002 Spending Review: Opportunity and Security for All, Investing in an Enterprising Society: New Public Spending Plans 2003–2006*. London: Stationery Office.

HM Treasury (2002b) *Report of the Inter-departmental Childcare Review*. London: Stationery Office.

HM Treasury and Department for Education and Skills (2005) *Support for Parents: The Best Start for Children*. London: Stationery Office.

HM Treasury and Department for Education and Skills (2007a) *Policy Review of Children and Young People: A Discussion Document*. London: Stationery Office.

HM Treasury and Department for Education and Skills (2007b) *Aiming High for Children: Supporting Families*. London: Stationery Office.

HM Treasury, Department for Education and Skills, Department for Work and Pensions and Department of Trade and Industry (2004) *Choice for Parents, the Best Start for Children: A Ten Year Strategy for Childcare*. London: HM Treasury.

Hodge, M. (2005) A reply to Norman Glass, *The Guardian*, 8th January.

Home Office (1965) *The Child, the Family and the Young Offender*. London: HMSO.

Home Office (1968) *Children in Trouble*. London: HMSO.

Home Office (1997) *No More Excuses: A New Approach to Tackling Youth Crime in England and Wales*. Cm.3809. London: HMSO.

Home Office (1998) *Supporting Families*. London: HMSO.

Home Office (1999) *Guide to the Final Warning Scheme: Guides to the Crime and Disorder Act 1998*. Circular 9/1999. London: Home Office.

Home Office (2003) *Youth Justice – The Next Steps*. London: Home Office.

Home Office (2005) *Controlling our Borders*. London: Stationery Office.

Home Office, Department of Health, Department of Education and Science and the Welsh Office (1991) *Working Together under the Children Act 1989: A Guide to Arrangements for Inter-Agency Co-operation for the Protection of Children from Abuse*. London: HMSO.

Horton, S. and Farnham, D. (1999) *Public Management in Britain*. Basingstoke: Palgrave/Macmillan.

House of Commons Children, Schools and Families Committee (2008) *The Department for Children, Schools and Families and the Children's Plan: Second Report of Session 2007-08. Report, together with formal minutes, oral and written evidence*. London: Stationery Office.

House of Commons Education and Skills Committee (2005) *Every Child Matters: Ninth Report of Session 2004–05*. HC40-1. London: Stationery Office.

House of Commons Home Affairs Committee (2008) *A Surveillance Society? Fifth Report of Session 2007–08. Volume I, Report together with formal minutes; Volume II, Oral and Written Evidence*. London: The Stationery Office.

Howe, D. (1992) Child Abuse and the Bureaucratization of Social Work, *Sociological Review*, 40(3): 491–508.

Howe, D. (1996) 'Surface and depth in social work practice', in N. Parton (ed.), *Social Theory, Social Change and Social Work*. London: Routledge.

Hoyle, C. and Rose, D. (2001) Labour, Law and Order, *Political Quarterly*, 72(1): 76–85.

Hudson, B. (2005a) Partnership Working and the Children's Services Agenda: Is it Feasible?, *Journal of Integrated Care*, 13(2): 7–17.

Hudson, B. (2005b) User Outcomes and Children's Services Reform: Ambiguity and Conflict in the Policy Implementation Process, *Social Policy and Society*, 5(2): 227–36.

Hudson, B. (2005c) 'Not a Cigarette Paper Between Us': Integrated Inspection of Children's Services in England, *Social Policy and Administration*, 139(5): 513–27.

Hudson, J. (2002) Digitising the Structures of Government: The UK's information age government agenda, *Policy and Politics*, 30(4): 515–31.

Hudson, J. (2003) E-galitarianism? The Information Society and New Labour's repositioning of welfare, *Critical Social Policy*, 23(2): 268–90.

Hughes, B. (2007) Joining up Children's and Adult Services, Speech, 13.6.2007. www.dfes.gov.uk/speeches

Ife, J. (1997) *Rethinking Social Work: Towards Critical Practice*. Melbourne: Longman.

Immigration and Nationality Directorate of the Home Office and Association of Directors of Social Services (nd) *Age assessment: Joint working protocol*.

Information Commissioner's Office (2005) *Information Commissioner's Memorandum to the Education and Skills Committee in respect of the Committee's enquiry into Every Child Matters (2005)*. http://www.ico.gov.uk/upload/documents/library/corporatenotices/memo-to-the-education-and-skills.select-committee-every-child-matters:pdf (accessed 21/02/05).

Information Policy Unit Social Care (2003) *Defining the Electronic Social Care Record: December 2003* (final version 23/01/04). London: Department of Health. Available online at www.doh.gsi.gov.uk (accessed 10 January 2006).

Jackson, S. and Kilroe, S. (eds) (1996) *Looking After Children: Good Parenting, Good Outcome Reader*. London: HMSO.

Jeffery, L. (2001) 'New Labour, New Initiatives: Sure Start and the Children's Fund', in N. Frost, A. Lloyd and L. Jeffery (eds), *The RHP Companion to Family Support*. Lyme Regis: Russell House.

Jenks, C. (1996, republished 2006) *Childhood*. London: Routledge.

Jones, C. (2001) Voices from the Front Line: State Social Work and New Labour, *British Journal of Social Work*, 31(4): 547–62.

Jordan, B. (1996) *A Theory of Poverty and Social Exclusion*. Cambridge: Polity Press.

Jordan, B. (1999) 'Bulger, "Back to Basics" and the Rediscovery of Community', in B. Franklin (ed.), *Social Policy, the Media and Misrepresentation*. London: Routledge.

Jordan, B. (2001) Tough Love: Social Work, Social Exclusion and the Third Way, *British Journal of Social Work*, 31(4): 527–46.

Jordan, B. (2005) New Labour: Choice and Values, *Critical Social Policy*, 25(4): 427–46.

Jordan, B. (2006a) *Social Policy for the Twenty-First Century*. Cambridge: Polity Press.

Jordan, B. (2006b) Public Services and the Service Economy: Individualism and the Choice Agenda, *Journal of Social Policy*, 35(1): 143–162.

Jordan, B. with Jordan, C. (2000) *Social Work and the Third Way. Tough Love as Social Policy*. London: Sage.

Kahan, B. and Levy, A. (1991) *The Pindown Experience and the Protection of children*. Stoke: Staffordshire County Council.

Kearney, M. (2007) 'Friends and family care of unaccompanied children', in R. Kohli and F. Mitchell (eds), *Working with Unaccompanied Asylum Seeking Children: Issues for Policy and Practice*. Basingstoke: Palgrave.

Kirkpatrick, T. (2006) Taking Stock of the New Managerialism in English Social Services. *Social Work and Society*, 4(1): 14–24. http://www.socwork.net/2006/1/series/professionalism/kirkpatrick (accessed 25/04/07).

Kohli, R. and Mitchell, F. (eds) (2007) *Working with Unaccompanied Asylum Seeking Children: Issues for Policy and Practice*. Basingstoke: Palgrave.

Kruger, D. (1997) Access Denied, *Demos Collection*, 12: 20–1.

Labour Party (1996) *Tackling Youth Crime: Reforming Youth Justice*. London: Labour Party.

Laming Report (2003) *The Victoria Climbié Inquiry: Report of an Inquiry by Lord Laming* (Cm5730). London: Stationery Office.

Lasch, C. (1977) *Haven in a Heartless World*. New York: Basic Books.

Levitas, R. (ed.), (1986) *The Ideology of the New Right*. Cambridge: Polity Press.

Levitas, R. (1996) The Concept of Social Exclusion and the New Durkheimian Hegemony, *Critical Social Policy*, 16(1): 5–20.

Levitas, R. (2005) *The Inclusive Society? Social Exclusion and New Labour*. 2nd edn. Basingstoke: Palgrave/Macmillan.

Lewis, J. (2001) *The End of Marriage? Individualism and Intimate Relations*. Cheltenham: Edward Elgar.

Lister, R. (1990) *The Exclusive Society: Citizenship and the Poor*. London: CPAG.

London Borough of Brent (1985) *A Child in Trust: Report of the Panel of Inquiry Investigating the Circumstances Surrounding the Death of Jasmine Beckford*. London: London Borough of Brent.

London Borough of Greenwich (1987) *A Child in Mind: Protection in a Responsible Society; Report of the Commission of Inquiry into the Circumstances Surrounding the Death of Kimberley Carlile*. London: London Borough of Greenwich.

London Borough of Lambeth (1987) *Whose Child? The Report of the Panel Appointed to Inquire into the Death of Tyra Henry*. London: London Borough of Lambeth.

Longford Committee (1964) *Crime: A Challenge to us All*. London: Labour Party.

Luckock, B. (2008) Adoption Support and the Negotiation of Ambivalence in Family Policy and Children's Services, *Journal of Law and Society*, 35(1): 3–27.

Luckock, B. and Hart, A. (2005) Adoptive family life and adoption support: policy ambivalence and the development of effective services, *Child and Family Social Work*, 10.

McAnulla, S. (2007) New Labour, Old Epistemology? Reflections on Political Science, New Institutionalism and the Blair Government, *Parliamentary Affairs*, 60(2): 313–31.

McDonald, C. (2006) Institutional Transformation. The Impact of Performance Measurement on Professional Practice in Social Work, *Social Work and Society*, 4(1): 25–37. http://www.socwork.net/2006/1/series/professionalism/Mcdonald (accessed 25/04/07).

McDonald, R. (2006) Creating a Patient-led NHS: Empowering 'consumers' or shrinking the state?, in L. Bauld, K. Clarke and T. Maltby (eds), *Social Policy Review 18: Analysis and debate in social policy*. Bristol: Policy Press.

Marriott, S. (2001) *Living in Limbo*. Birmingham: Save the Children.

Martin, S. (2005) Speeches and Addresses: Evaluation, Inspection and the Improvement Agenda: Contrasting Fortunes in an Era of Evidence-Based Policy-Making, *Evaluation*, 11: 496–504.

Meadows, P. (2007) 'The methodologies for the evaluation of complex interventions: an ongoing debate', in J. Belsky, J. Barnes and E. Melhuish (eds), *The National Evaluation of Sure Start – Does Area-based Early Intervention Work?* Bristol: Policy Press.

Melhuish, E. and Hall, D. (2007) 'The policy background to Sure Start', in J. Belsky, J. Barnes and E. Melhuish (eds), *The National Evaluation of Sure Start – Does Area-based Early Intervention Work?* Bristol: Policy Press.

Millar, J. and Ridge, T. (2002) 'Parents, Children, Families and New Labour: Developing Family Policy', in M. Powell (ed.), *Evaluating New Labour's Welfare Reforms*. Bristol: Policy Press.

Mills, S. and Frost, N. (2007) 'Growing Up in Substitute Care', in J. Coleman and A. Hagell (eds), *Adolescence, Risk and Resilience: Against the Odds*. Chichester: Wiley.

Mitchell, F. (2003) The Social Services response to unaccompanied children in England, *Child and Family Social Work*, 8(3): 179–89.

Mitchell, F. (2006) 'Assessment Practice with Unaccompanied Children: Exploring Exceptions to the Problem', in R. Morgan (ed.), *About Social Workers: A Children's View Report*. London: CSCI.

Morgan, R. (2007) One of the truly remarkable changes from Old to New Labour is that incarcerating more young people is viewed as an achievement, *Professional Social Work*, March: 16–17.

Morgan, R. and Newburn, T. (2007) 'Youth Justice', in M. Maguire, R. Morgan and R. Reiner (eds), *The Oxford Handbook of Criminology*. 4th edn. Oxford: Oxford University Press.

Morris, A., Giller, H., Szwed, E. and Geach, H. (1980) *Justice for Children*. London: Macmillan.

Morris, J. (1999) *Hurtling into a Void: Transition to Adulthood for Young Disabled People with 'Complex Health and Support Needs'*. Brighton: Pavilion.

Morris, J. (2003) *The Social Model of Disability, Care Knowledge Briefing No.10*. www.careknowledge.com

Morris, T. (2001) 'Crime and Penal Policy', in A. Seldon (ed.), *The Blair Effect*. London: Little Brown.

Mrazek, P.J. and Haggerty, R.J. (eds) (1994) *Reducing Risks for Mental Disorders: Frontiers for Preventive Intervention Research*. Washington, DC: Institute of Medicine/National Academy Press.

Muncie, J. (2004) *Youth and Crime*. London: Sage.

Munro, E. (2004a) The Impact of Audit on Social Work Practice, *British Journal of Social Work*, 34(8): 1079–95.

Munro, E. (2004b) State regulation of parenting, *Political Quarterly*, 75(2): 180–5.

Munro, E. and Parton, N. (2007) How far is England in the process of introducing a mandatory reporting system?, *Child Abuse Review*, 16(1): 5–16.

Murray, C. (1990) *The Emerging British Underclass*. London: IEA.

Murray, C. (1994) *The Underclass: The Crisis Deepens*. London: IEA.

Nandy, L. (2005) The Impact of Government Policy on Asylum-seeking and Refugee Children, *Children and Society*, 19: 410–13.

National Statistics (2007) http://www.statistics.gov.uk/CCI/nugget.asp

Nelson, S. (1987) *Incest: Fact and Myth*. Edinburgh: Stamullion.

Newburn, T., Crawford, A., Earle, R., Goldie, S., Hale, C., Masters, G., Netten, A., Saunders, R., Hallam, A., Sharpe, K. and Uglow, S. (2002) *The Introduction of Referral Orders into the Youth Justice System: Final Report*. Home Office Research Study 242. London: Home Office.

Newman, J. (2001) *Modernising Governance: New Labour, Policy and Society*. London: Sage.

NSPCC/University of Sheffield (2000) *The Child's World: Assessing Children in Need. Training and Development Pack*. London: NSPCC.

O'Hara, M. (2008) A 'compromise' candidate?, *Society Guardian*, 23 January, p. 7.

Olds, D., Henderson, C.R., Cole, R., Eckerode, J., Kitzman, H., Luckey, D., Pettit, L., Sidora, H., Morris, P. and Powers, J. (1998) Long-term effects of nurse home visitation on children's criminal and antisocial behaviour, *Journal of American Medical Association*, 280: 1238–44.

Oliver. M. (1983) *Social Work with Disabled People*. London: MacMillan.

Ormerod, P. (2005) The Impact of Sure Start, *Political Quarterly*, 76(4): 565–7.

Orton, M. and Rowlinson, K. (2007) A problem of riches: towards a new social policy research agenda on the distribution of economic resources, *Journal of Social Policy*, 36(1): 59–77.

Packman, J. (1981) *The Child's Generation,* 2nd edn. Oxford: Basil Blackwell and Martin Robertson.

Packman, J. (1993) From prevention to partnership: child welfare services across three decades, *Children & Society*, 7(2): 183–95.

Page, R. and Clarke, G. (eds) (1977) *Who Cares?* London: National Children's Bureau.

Parker, R., Ward, H., Jackson, S., Aldgate, J. and Wedge, P. (eds) (1991) *Looking After Children: Assessing Outcomes in Child Care. The Report of an Independent Working Party Established by the Department of Health*. London: HMSO.

Parton, N. (1985) *The Politics of Child Abuse*. Basingstoke: Macmillan.

Parton, N. (1991) *Governing the Family: Child Care, Child Protection and the State*. Basingstoke: Macmillan.

Parton, N. (ed.) (1997) *Child Protection and Family Support: Tensions, Contradictions and Possibilities*. London: Routledge.

Parton, N. (2004) From Maria Colwell to Victoria Climbié: reflections on public inquiries into child abuse a generation apart, *Child Abuse Review*, 13(2): 80–94.

Parton, N. (2006a) *Safeguarding Childhood: Early Intervention and Surveillance in a Late Modern Society*. Basingstoke: Palgrave/Macmillan.

Parton, N. (2006b) 'Every Child Matters': The shift to prevention whilst strengthening protection in children's services in England, *Children and Youth Services Review*, 28(8): 976–92.

Parton, N. (2008a) The 'Change for Children' Programme in England: Towards the 'Preventive-Surveillance State', *Journal of Law and Society*, 35(1): 166–87.

Parton, N. (2008b) Changes in the form of knowledge in social work: From the 'Social' to the 'Informational'?, *British Journal of Social Work*, 38(2): 253–69.

Parton, N. and O'Byrne, P. (2000) *Constructive Social Work: Towards a New Practice*. Basingstoke: MacMillan.

Parton, N. and Thomas, T. (1983) 'Child abuse and citizenship', in B. Jordan and N. Parton (eds), *The Political Dimensions of Social Work*. Oxford: Basil Blackwell.

Pascall, G. (1986) *Social Policy: A Feminist Analysis.* London: Tavistock.

Payne, M. (2005) *Modern Social Work Theory.* London: Routledge.

Penna, S. (2005) The Children Act 2004: Child Protection and Social Surveillance, *Journal of Social Welfare and Family Law*, 27(2): 143–57.

Perri 6, Raab, C. and Bellamy, C. (2005) 'Joined-up government and privacy in the United Kingdom: managing tensions between data protection and Social Policy, Part I, *Public Administration*, 83(1): 111–13.

Philp, M. (1979) Notes on the form of knowledge in social work, *Sociological Review*, 27(1): 83–111.

Philp, A.F. and Timms, N. (1962) *The Problem of the Problem Family.* London: Family Service Units.

Pitts, J. (2001) *The New Politics of Youth Crime: Discipline or Solidarity?* Lyme Regis: Russell House.

Pitts, J. (2003) 'Youth Justice in England and Wales', in R. Matthews and J. Young (eds), *The New Politics of Crime and Punishment.* Cullompton: Willan.

Platt, D. (2007) *The Status of Social Care – A Review, 2007.* London: Department of Health.

Power, M. (1997) *The Audit Society: Rituals of Verification.* Oxford: Oxford University Press.

Pugh, G. and Parton, N. (eds) (2003) New labour and its outcomes for Children, *Children & Society Special Issue*, 17(3), June.

Respect Task Force (2006) *Respect Action Plan.* London: Home Office.

Rhodes, R. (1997) *Understanding Governance.* Buckingham: Open University Press.

Robinson, M., Anning, A. and Frost, N. (2005) When is a teacher not a teacher? Knowledge creation and the professional identity of teachers in multi-agency settings, *Studies in Continuing Education*, 27(2): 175–91.

Rodger, J. (2006) Antisocial families and withholding welfare support, *Critical Social Policy*, 26(1): 101–20.

Rush, F. (1980) *The Best Kept Secret: Sexual Abuse of Children.* New York: McGraw-Hill.

Rutherford, A. (1992) *Growing Out of Crime: The New Era.* Winchester: Waterside Press.

Rutter, M. (1990) 'Psychosocial Resilience and Protective Mechanisms', in J. Rolf, A.S. Masten, D. Cichetti, K.H. Nuechterlein and S. Weintraub (eds), *Risk and Protective Factors in the Development of Psychopathology.* Cambridge: Cambridge University Press.

Rutter, M. (2006) Is Sure Start an effective preventive intervention?, *Child and Adolescent Mental Health,* 11(3): 135–41.

Rutter, M. (2007) 'Sure Start Local Programmes: an outsider's perspective', in J. Belsky, J. Barnes and E. Melhuish (eds), *The National Evaluation of Sure Start – Does Area-based Early Intervention Work?* Bristol: Policy Press.

Rutter, M. and Giller, H. (1983) *Juvenile Delinquency: Trends and Perspectives.* Harmondsworth: Penguin.

Schweinhart, L., Barnes, H. and Weikhart, D. (eds) (1993) *Significant Benefits: The High/Scope Perry Pre-School Study Through age 27.* Ypsilanti: High/Scope Press.

SCIE (2007a) Supporting disabled parents and parents with additional support needs, *Knowledge Review,* 11. scie.org.uk

SCIE (2007b) Necessary stuff: social care needs of children with complex health needs and their families, *Knowledge Review*, 18, scie.org.uk

SCIE (2007c) The social care needs of refugees and asylum seekers. www.scie.org.uk

SCIE (2007d) Children with complex health and social care needs, *Community Care*, 8 November: 24–25.

Scruton, P. (ed.) (1997) *Childhood in Crisis*. London: UCL Press.

Seacroft Sure Start (2006) *Making a Brew*. Leeds: Seacroft Sure Start.

Seager, A. (2008) Ministers risk missing key Labour target, *The Guardian*, 11 June: 6.

Secretary of State for Social Services (1974) *Report of the Inquiry into the Care and Supervision Provided in Relation to Maria Colwell*. London: HMSO.

Secretary of State for Social Services (1988) *Report of the Inquiry into Child Abuse in Cleveland*. Cm413. London: HMSO.

Seebohm, F. (1968) *Report of the Committee on Local Authority and Allied Social Services*. Cmnd 3703. London: HMSO.

Sefton, T. and Sutherland, H. (2005) 'Poverty and Inequality under New Labour', in J. Hills and K. Stewart (eds), *A More Equal Society? New Labour, Poverty, Inequality and Exclusion*. Bristol: Policy Press.

Shaw, I. and Clayden, J. (forthcoming) Technology and Professional Practice: Reflections on the Integrated Children's System. *Policy and Politics*.

Sinclair, R., Hearn, B. and Pugh, G. (1997) *Preventive Work with Families: the role of mainstream families*. London: National Children's Bureau.

Skinner, C. (2003) 'New Labour and Family Policy', in M. Bell and K. Wilson (eds), *The Practitioners' Guide to Working with Families*. Basingstoke: Palgrave/Macmillan.

Smith, C. (2001) Trust and confidence: possibilities for social work in high modernity, *British Journal of Social Work*, 31(2): 287–305.

Smith, D. (1999) 'Social Work with Young People in Trouble: Memory and Prospect', in B. Goldson (ed.), *Youth Justice: Contemporary Policy and Practice*. Aldershot: Ashgate.

Smith, D. (2003) 'New Labour and Youth Justice', in G. Pugh and N. Parton (eds), New Labour Policy and its Outcomes for Children, *Children & Society Special Issue*, 17(3): 226–35.

Smith, D.R. and Home Office (1993) *Safe from Harm: a Code of Practice for safeguarding the Welfare of Children in Voluntary Organisations in England and Wales*. London: Home Office.

Smith, R. (2007) *Youth Justice: Ideas, Policy, Practice*. 2nd edn. Cullompton: Willan.

Social Exclusion Unit (2001) *Preventing Social Exclusion*. London: Stationery Office.

Social Services Committee (1984) *Children in Care (HC360)* (Short Report). London: HMSO.

Squires, P. (2006) New Labour and the politics of antisocial behaviour, *Critical Social Policy*, 26(1): 144-68.

Stanley, K (2001) *Cold Comfort: Young Separated Refugees in England*. London: SCF.

Stein, M. (2004) *What Works for Young People Leaving Care?* Barkingside: Barnardo's.

Stein, M. (2006) Wrong turn, *The Guardian*, 6th December

Stein, M. and Carey, K. (1986) *Leaving Care*. Oxford: Blackwell.

Stevenson, O. (2005) 'Genericism and Specialization'. The story since 1970, *British Journal of Social Work*, 35(5): 569–86.

Stevenson, O. and Parsloe, P. (1978) *Social Services Teams: the Practitioners' View*. London: DHSS.

Sure Start Unit (1998) *Guide for Sure Start Trailblazers*. London: Department for Education and Skills.

Sure Start Unit (2000) *Service Delivery Agreement*. London: Department for Education and Skills.

Sure Start Unit (2003) *Guidance on Children's Centres*. London: Sure Start Unit.

Sure Start Unit (2005) *A Sure Start Children's Centre for Every Community. Phase two Planning Guidance (2006–08)*. London: Sure Start Unit.

Surveillance Studies Network (2006) *A Report on the Surveillance Society. A Report for the Information Commissioner*. London: Office of the Information Commissioner.

Tarleton, B., Ward, L., and Howarth, J. (2006) *Finding the Right Support? A Review of Issues and Positive Practice in Supporting Parents with Learning Difficulties and their children*. London: Baring Foundation.

Taylor, A. (2007) So many contradictions, *Community Care*, 6.12.2007: 18–19.

Taylor, L., Lacey, R. and Bracken, D. (1980) *In Whose Best Interests?* London: Cobden Trust/Mind.

Thorpe, D., Smith, D., Green, C. and Paley, J. (1980) *Out of Care: The Community Support for Juvenile Offenders*. London: Allen and Unwin.

Tilbury, C. (2004) The influence of performance measurement on child welfare, *British Journal of Social Work*, 34(2): 225–41.

Tilbury, C. (2005) Counting family support, *Child and Family Social Work*, 10(2): 149-57.

Topliss, E. (1979) *Provision for the Disabled*. London: Blackwell and Robertson.

Townsend, P. (1970) *The Fifth Social Service: A Critical Analysis of the Seebohm Proposals*. London: The Fabian Society.

Townsend, P. (1971) *Poverty in the United Kingdom*. Harmondsworth: Penguin.

Tunstill, J. and Allnock, D. (2007) *Understanding the Contribution of Sure Start Local Programmes to the Task of Safeguarding Children's Welfare*. Sure Start Report 026. London: National Evaluation of Sure Start Team, Birkbeck College.

UNICEF (2007) *Child Poverty in Perspective: An Overview of Child Well-being in Rich Countries*. Innocenti Report Card 7. Florence: United Nations Children's Fund Innocenti Research Centre.

Utting, D. (1995) *Family and Parenthood: Supporting Families, Preventing Breakdown*. York: Joseph Rowntree Foundation.

Utting, D. (ed.) (1998) *Children's Services: Now and in the Future*. London: National Children's Bureau.

Utting, D., Bright, J. and Henricson, C. (1993) *Crime and Family: Improving Child-rearing and Preventing Delinquency*. London: Family Policy Studies Centre.

Utting, Sir W. (1991) *Children in the Public Care*. London: HMSO.

Utting, Sir W. (1997) *People Like Us: The Report of the Review of the Safeguards for Children Living Away from Home*. London: HMSO.

Veit-Wilson, J. (1998) *Setting Adequate Standards*. Bristol: Policy Press.

Wade, J., Mitchell, F. and Baylis, G. (2005) *Unaccompanied Asylum Seeking Children: The Response of Social Work Services*. London: BAAF.

Walker, A. and Walker, C. (1997) *Britain Divided: The Growth of Social Exclusion in the 1980s and 1990s*. London: CPAG.

Walker, S. and Scott, J. in collaboration with members of the ICS multi-disciplinary research team led by Professor Hedy Cleaver at Royal Holloway, University of London (2004) *Implementing the Integrated Children's System – A Phased Approach.* Briefing Paper 6. London: DfES.

Ward, H. (ed.) (1998) Assessing outcomes in child care: an international perspective, *Children & Society Special Issue*, 12(3), June.

Ward, L. and Tarleton, B. (2007) Sinking and Swimming? Supporting parents with learning disabilities and their children, *Learning Disability Review*, 12(2): 22–32.

Wardhaugh, J. and Wilding, P. (1993) Towards an explanation of the corruption of care, *Critical Social Policy*, 37: 4–31.

Waterhouse, R. (2000) *Lost in Care: Summary of Report.* London: Stationery Office.

Watson, D., Abbott, D. and Townsley, R. (2007). 'Listen to me, too!' Lessons from involving children with complex healthcare needs in research about multi-agency services, *Child Care Health and Development*, 33(1): 90–5.

Webb, S. (2001) Some considerations on the validity of evidence-based practice in social work, *British Journal of Social Work*, 31(1): 57–79.

Welshman, J. (2006) From the cycle of deprivation to social exclusion: five continuities, *The Political Quarterly*, 77(4): 475–84.

Welshman, J. (2007) *From Transmitted Deprivation to Social Exclusion: Policy, Poverty, and Parenting.* Bristol: Policy Press.

Wilkinson, R.G. (1996) *Unhealthy Societies: The Afflictions of Inequality.* London: Routledge.

Wilkinson, R.G. (2005) *The Impact of Inequality: How to Make Sick Societies Healthier.* London: Routledge.

Williams, F. (1989) *Social Policy: A Critical Introduction.* Cambridge: Polity Press.

Williams, F. (2005) 'New Labour's Family Policy', in M. Powell, L. Bauld and K. Clarke (eds), *Social Policy Review 17: Analysis and Debate in Social Policy, 2005.* Bristol: Policy Press.

Williams, S. (2006) *Evaluation of National Professional Qualification for Integrated Centre Leadership (NPQICL) Rollout Programme, Final Evaluation Report.* Henley: Henley Management College.

Wintour, P. and Curtis, P. (2008) 'I will close up to 270 failing schools to improve standards' says minister, *The Guardian*, 10 June: 3.

Zander, M. (1975) 'What happens to Young Offenders in Care', *New Society*, 24 July: 185–7.

Index

Research Methods Books from SAGE

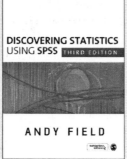
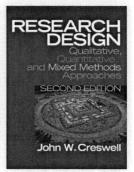

The Qualitative Research Kit

Edited by Uwe Flick

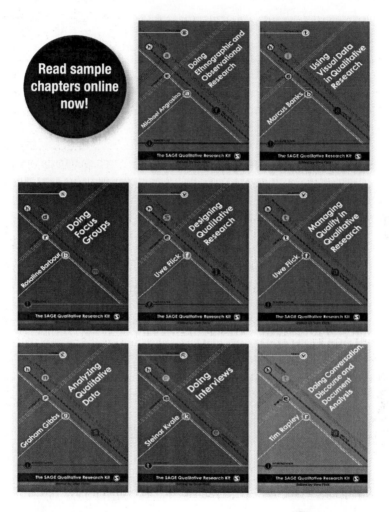

Read sample chapters online now!

Doing Ethnographic and Observational Research — Michael Angrosino

Using Visual Data in Qualitative Research — Marcus Banks

Doing Focus Groups — Rosaline Barbour

Designing Qualitative Research — Uwe Flick

Managing Quality in Qualitative Research — Uwe Flick

Analyzing Qualitative Data — Graham Gibbs

Doing Interviews — Steinar Kvale

Doing Conversation, Discourse and Document Analysis — Tim Rapley

www.sagepub.co.uk

Supporting researchers for more than forty years

Research methods have always been at the core of SAGE's publishing. Sara Miller McCune founded SAGE in 1965 and soon after, she published SAGE's first methods book, Public Policy Evaluation. A few years later, she launched the Quantitative Applications in the Social Sciences series – affectionately known as the "little green books".

Always at the forefront of developing and supporting new approaches in methods, SAGE published early groundbreaking texts and journals in the fields of qualitative methods and evaluation.

Today, more than forty years and two million little green books later, SAGE continues to push the boundaries with a growing list of more than 1,200 research methods books, journals, and reference works across the social, behavioral, and health sciences.

From qualitative, quantitative, mixed methods to evaluation, SAGE is the essential resource for academics and practitioners looking for the latest methods by leading scholars.

www.sagepublications.com